MEDICINE TRAILS

A Life in Many Worlds

MEDICINE TRAILS

A Life in Many Worlds

Mavis McCovey and John F. Salter

Foreword by Freeman House

Heyday Books, Berkeley, California

The publishers are grateful to the BayTree Fund, to Marion R. Weber and the Flow Fund Circle, and to contributors to Heyday's California Indian Publishing Program for the support that made this book possible.

© 2009 by Mavis McCovey and John F. Salter

Library of Congress Cataloging-in-Publication Data

McCovey, Mavis, 1933-
  Medicine trails : a life in many worlds / Mavis McCovey and John F. Salter.
     p. cm.
  Includes bibliographical references.
  ISBN 978-1-59714-117-8 (pbk. : alk. paper)
  1. McCovey, Mavis, 1933- 2. Karok women--California--Biography. 3. Indian women healers--California--Biography. 4. Indian women shamans--California--Biography. 5. Karok Indians--Religion. 6. Karok Indians--History. 7. Karok Indians--Social life and customs. I. Salter, John Frederick. II. Title.
  E99.K25M33 2009
  305.897'570794--dc22
  [B]
                                             2009002888

Book design: Lorraine Rath
Cover photo by Allie Hostler

Printing and Binding: Thomson-Shore, Dexter, MI

Orders, inquiries, and correspondence should be addressed to:
    Heyday Books
    P. O. Box 9145, Berkeley, CA 94709
    (510) 549-3564, Fax (510) 549-1889
    www.heydaybooks.com

green press
INITIATIVE

Heyday Books is committed to preserving ancient forests and natural resources. We elected to print this title on 30% post consumer recycled paper, processed chlorine free. As a result, for this printing, we have saved:

13 Trees (40' tall and 6-8" diameter)
4,589 Gallons of Wastewater
9 million BTU's of Total Energy
535 Pounds of Solid Waste
1,015 Pounds of Greenhouse Gases

Heyday Books made this paper choice because our printer, Thomson-Shore, Inc., is a member of Green Press Initiative, a nonprofit program dedicated to supporting authors, publishers, and suppliers in their efforts to reduce their use of fiber obtained from endangered forests.

For more information, visit www.greenpressinitiative.org

Environmental impact estimates were made using the Environmental Defense Paper Calculator. For more information visit: www.papercalculator.org.

10 9 8 7 6 5 4 3 2 1

The authors would like to honor and acknowledge Frederick Ferris, Bessie Tripp, Orville Allen Jr., and Duane Allen.

Our thanks go to Spring W. Salter for a valuable critical reading of the manuscript.

This book is dedicated to Alberta Ferris Canclini, who convinced me to write a book rather than a fairy tale on my life.
—*Mavis McCovey*

CONTENTS

Foreword by Freeman House • ix
Introduction • xiii

Section One:
Ancestors and Childhood, 1832–1950 • 1

*On Full-Bloods and Mixed-Bloods • The Medicine Women • The
Other Side • Being Sealed • Ceremonies • Keeping the Peace •
Family History: Vid-ik-it's Story • Alvirius Ferris and Vid-ik-it •
Ferris Family Background • Marriage Traditions • The Red Cap
Wars • Slaves in Indian Country • Klamath River Country in
the late 1800s • All Different People • Gold on the Klamath • The
Impact of Diseases • Manners, Morality, and Religion • Grand-
mother Nancy Evans Ferris • Stories from My Grandfather Ferris
• Aunt Caroline's Childhood • Aunt Caroline's Gifts • The Ferris
Children in Orleans • The Ferris Family in San Francisco • Back
to Orleans • My Mother, Beatrice Ferris • My Father, William
Shirley Smither • My Father's Family • My Early Childhood • My
Parents' Deaths • Growing Up in Orleans • The War Years •
Sherman Indian School • My Grandfather's Death*

Section Two:
Marriage and Children, the Happy Years, 1950–1965 • 133

*Darrell McCovey's Story • World War II Service • The Bright
Lights of Klamath • Married Life in Yurok Country • "The White
Man Set Me Free" • The McCovey Family • Stories about Sadie
• Traditions of Family • Raising the Children • Back Trouble •
Downriver Indian Devils*

Section Three:
The Medicine Returns, 1965–2005 • 185

*The White Deerskin and Jump Dances • Moving Back to Orleans •
Aunt Caroline's Last Years • Getting Tribal Recognition • Working as a Community Health Representative • Herbicide Spraying • Police Brutality • Psychic Abilities • UFOs • Long Gone Is Shot • Picking Up Power • The Fatawanun • The Fatawanun's Woman • A Psychological Medicine Woman • Mothers' Sounds and Cradle Baskets • Heart Disease • Becoming a Nurse • Carol's Death • Indian Country Nurse • In Sickness and Health • A Shifting Population • Daypay's Murder • On Being a Medicine Woman • Prayer • Upriver Indian Devils • Upsancutta • Vision of a Murder • Medicine Stories • The Fire • Medicine Woman for the Brush Dance • A Change for the Better • White Deerskin Dance, 2002 • Beavi's Illness*

Epilogue: Darrell's Death • 313
Notes • 319
Map of Karuk and Yurok Places • 336
Mavis and Darrell McCovey Family Tree • 338

FOREWORD

Freeman House

"I have often wondered in what way forgotten history
abides, and what the consequences are of its being forgotten or
brought to mind again....Walt Whitman was right when he
celebrated the epic and melancholy beauty created in a place by all
the transient multitudes and generations that pass through it."
—*Marilynne Robinson, Amherst College Commencement, 2007*

WHEN I RAN ACROSS MS. ROBINSON'S TRIBUTE to forgotten
histories, I forgot for a moment that she was speaking of the Under-
ground Railroad, and mused about my conviction that a great part
of American history is hidden, forgotten, or purposely denied. And
about what epic and melancholy beauty we might realize if we fully
knew all the "multitudes and generations" that have preceded us.

Almost all of the generations of people who have passed through
northwest California—where I live—have been Indian generations,
and of those, there is every likelihood that the vast majority of them
were of Karuk ancestry. As a people, they've seen a lot. The earli-
est archaeological findings place them on their home ground some
eighty-five hundred years ago. Given the spotty nature of archaeological research, it's likely they've been here quite a bit longer.

Mavis McCovey's people probably witnessed the tail end of the
last ice age and for the next few thousand years lived in a place much
warmer and drier than it is now. There is every indication that as a
life place it was quite different than the lush country we experience

today. The people responded to it as necessary, living in small mobile groups and moving when that is what the landscape required of them, and then gradually settled along rivers that had become rich in salmon when the climate turned more cool and moist. Such stability gave rise to a robust and enduring ceremonial culture. It was a life change as significant as that brought on by the invasion of Euro-Americans. Their resilience in the face of both events is one of the truly remarkable things about the Karuk people. The Karuk are survivors.

When the first ethnographers began to explore northwest California a few decades either side of the turn of the twentieth century, they assumed that they were documenting dying cultures; they called what they were doing "salvage anthropology." They were arriving at the nadir of the aftershock of the gold rush, the flood of Euro-American invasion and development that took place between 1850 to 1870. Diseases to which native populations had no immunity, as well as displacement and outright murder, had decimated them. Survivors had been scattered to corruptly managed reservations. It's hardly surprising that the ethnographers of the time drew the conclusions that they drew of a depressed and moribund culture: it is more difficult to explain why those attitudes have survived in our schools in the face of resurgent Indian cultures. (The 2000 census of Humboldt County, where Mavis McCovey lives, showed that 11 percent of the population identifies itself as Native American. Within the last generation, northwest California has gained a reputation as a hotbed of cultural revival among tribal peoples.)

Over the years, a handful of contemporary ethnographers have attempted to demonstrate that native culture lives on among current generations—Keith Basso, Thomas Buckley, and Kat Anderson spring to mind—but their observations have been slow to enter the public mind. John Salter is a member in good standing of this group, and he has produced a book that is readily accessible to anyone that reads. After spending hundreds of hours in Mavis's kitchen with a tape recorder and many additional hours editing the results into narrative form, Salter has chosen to remove his own voice and allow Ms. McCovey's voice to carry her story.

It was a wise decision. Mavis McCovey's talk is so accessible, matter-of-fact, and full of good humor that non-Indian readers forget for extended periods of time that they are wandering in a culture that is quite different than their own. This is a book that might do a great deal to relieve the misconceptions laid down by salvage anthropologists more than a century ago. As a medicine woman, Mavis McCovey makes no exotic claims about her powers, but describes those functions as seamlessly integrated in Karuk culture. More importantly, she describes a living contemporary culture, enriching the melancholy beauty of our shared world.

INTRODUCTION

MAVIS MCCOVEY, BORN IN 1933, is a medicine woman of the Karuk Tribe of California, located in far northwestern California. This book is the result of some seventy-five hours of taped conversations between Mavis and myself from 2004 to 2008. Mavis's life story is filled with events which are characteristic of Native American life in the twentieth century, informed with good sense, tragedy, and the will to keep going. It also recounts the extraordinary thread of her life as a trained medicine woman relying on visions and repeated trips to what she calls "the other side." The many worlds referred to in the title are the Indian and white cultural worlds, and ordinary reality and the alternative reality of the medicine woman's life. Mavis's story goes beyond a simple account of her life, leaving the reader feeling uplifted when she talks about her beliefs and her traditional sense of what makes up a good life. Her story also has unusual historical and generational depth as a result of her having been raised by her grandfather and an aunt, herself a trained Indian doctor, both of whom passed on to Mavis a closely recalled history of her family and of the Karuk tribe.

Mavis first told me of her longstanding intent to write her autobiography following her retirement in the early 1990s. At the time I was working as tribal anthropologist for the Karuk Tribe of California and had gotten to know Mavis through a series of interviews I did with her on environmental and political issues, and through her work as a nurse in the tribal clinic. Unfortunately her health, which had not been good for years, began to fail, and in 1998 her house burned. The fire destroyed her grandfather's journals, family letters, and four thousand photographs she had intended to use in her writing.

Around 2002 I was interviewing Mavis for a tribal white paper concerning the effect of a series of dams on the Karuk tribe's health and well-being, particularly in regard to the dams' effect on the salmon, which remain the major nutritional and cultural resource of the Karuk. In the course of this discussion we agreed to collaborate on the book and to get it done.

Mavis told me that she had agreed to work with me because Bessie Tripp had trusted me enough to tell me the story of her life, and when Mavis asked her grandson Cogie what he thought about working with me, he told her that I was a pretty smart fellow for a white man. I have worked with the Karuk intermittently since 1968, beginning with my master's thesis on a commune in the area and going on to a doctoral dissertation on the social ecology of the various groups living in this region.

Mavis's voice is that of a remarkably strong woman making her way through difficult circumstances, and not only cross-cultural but cross-reality events and considerations. In the discussions that make up this book, Mavis is herself carrying on the Karuk oral tradition combining elements of literature, history, religion, and philosophy of life. Her deep humanity, devotion to family, sense of reality, sense of humor, and sense of responsibility to her spiritual training, culture, and people make this a book of interest to feminists and students of history, culture, and Native American studies, as well as the greatest audience of readers—those who will simply be drawn into a compelling story. There has been solid support in the tribal community for our collaboration on this autobiography and for the past three years, whenever I have been in the town of Orleans working with Mavis, I have been hailed with a supportive "Working on your book?" Mavis tells me that when Karuk friends refer to us as "Mavis and her white man," she corrects them by adding "Mavis and her high-quality educated white man."

In Orleans, this writing is compared to a real account of what was fictionalized in the Carlos Castaneda series and to *Black Elk Speaks* as a clear statement of tribal values and life. Young Karuk repeatedly tell me that they are waiting to read this book, which they are confident will open their eyes to important aspects of local history and their own culture. Names have been changed throughout the text to obscure the identity of individuals and families who would not want details of their lives revealed. A family tree is included to make it easier for the reader to follow the thread of the six generations of Mavis's family that are the subject of her story.

As you read, visualize yourself sitting at Mavis's kitchen table, engaged in the long conversation that makes up this book. There will be the smell of coffee, and in the background you may hear Mavis's daughter Beavi talking to her children, and the sound of forty-year-old reruns of *The Andy Griffith Show* on television. An old friend of Mavis's arrives and I am introduced as Dr. Salter. She starts to hitch up her sweatshirt, pointing to the general area of her liver and telling me she has had pain there. Mavis quickly tells her I am a different kind of doctor and she pulls down her sweatshirt. Mavis's husband, Darrell, asks if anyone knows where his cigarettes are, and an endless stream of visitors and relatives arrive in the daily swirl of life. Because of the busyness of Mavis's home, on a good day of sitting together for five or six hours we might end up with three hours of recorded material. I would then transcribe our discussion, combining sentences, dealing with repetitions, and generally turning Mavis's spoken speech into an appropriate form for the written word. The next step was for Mavis to critically read over what I had written, and I would modify the text accordingly.

Mavis felt it was important to follow her grandfather's wish that she make available to subsequent generations the truth of Indian life and what took place when the gold rush brought a flood of Europeans to the Klamath River country to clash with, intermarry with, and change forever the indigenous culture. Mavis's account of her life and times also lays out the unending struggle of the Karuk to maintain their identity as Native Americans in the nineteenth, twentieth, and now twenty-first centuries as she recounts the history of six generations of her family caught up in these historic changes.

Mavis has also involved herself in this writing because she wanted to preserve a sense of those elements of Karuk history and culture which are threatened by the passage of time. Her life story goes deeply into the nature of her training, as a child, to be a medicine woman, beginning when she was three years old. This training is discussed with a remarkable detachment and objectivity and an educated skepticism which finally concludes that although such cultural and spiritual practices as seeing the future through visions, changing the future through prayer, and appearing in a spirit form to people in need may not make sense, this is what she has been trained to do in the service of her people and she accepts her place in this alternative cultural reality.

ONE

Ancestors and Childhood
1832–1950

I NEVER GOT TO LEAVE THIS RIVER COUNTRY. When I got married I moved to Yurok country, and then I moved back home to Karuk country, so I moved from one closed society to another and then back again. The Yurok society was closer to its origins than we were up here; there were more full-blooded Indians still living in that area. By the time I married Darrell, in the early 1950s, there were not many full-blooded Karuk left. The Yurok were less disturbed and had fewer white influences on their reservation. Those Yurok not living on the reservation but living in towns, like Klamath, lived just like the Karuk did in Orleans.

Even though Yurok society of that time was more traditional, the Karuk still had men and women who had power, and they still dominated our part of society, the Indian part, up through the Second World War. The medicine women were always part of my life, so I just thought that was the way things were. I didn't realize that some of them were reading my mind and controlling me before I even had a chance to think to do something. They knew what you were about to do before you knew. They understood human nature.

On Full-Bloods and Mixed-Bloods

Here I am, seventy years old, living this life all this time in the Klamath River country and still, I really don't know how a white person lives—because all the people I'm friends with are mixed-bloods. My parents were mixed-bloods and my grandparents were mixed-bloods. I've known full-bloods, because my husband's family has full-bloods that lived the Indian life, so I have heard about the Indian life from the people that lived it, but I never heard about the white man's life from a white man that lived it. My grandfather did, but I never have.

My grandparents on my father's side were half-breeds from the East Coast. They had a mixed cultural perspective and really didn't know what white people thought either. With most of the people I grew up around, the woman in the family was Indian, so the children were raised by someone not really familiar with the white culture and did not pick up the white culture, because they were not raised by a white person. Children learned their morals and their culture from their mother because she was home with them. You didn't get that from your dad. He worked and didn't stop to teach you those things. He wasn't with you all the time. So the child's values and culture were usually passed on through their mother, white or Indian.

I don't know quite how to define how I was raised. If I was a full-blood Indian I might say I was raised like a white person, but I really don't know how white people are raised. My husband's younger brother, nicknamed Shoe Shine, would always laugh and say, "I think I might be doing this like a white person might," but he was never quite sure about how they did it, so it was a joke when he said that. His nickname was Shoe Shine because he was this tiny dark Indian kid who played with shoes as his toy cars and trucks, and he reminded his family of a shoe shine boy. That's kind of how I think I was raised, like a white person might be raised, because I was raised by my grandpa and his daughter, my aunt Caroline, who were both half-breed Indians. There weren't many full-blood Indians left around Orleans by the time I was born, in 1933.

The Medicine Women

Sometime in 1933, after I was conceived but before my birth, a Karuk medicine woman named Daisy Jones had a vision that the next priest's, or Fatawanun's, woman would be the unborn grandchild of my grandmother Nancy Ferris and could be recognized by her light-colored hair and eyes. The Fatawanun that this girl would be trained to serve would be the priest for the White Deerskin Dance at the old medicine village of Tishaniik, a few miles downriver from the town of Orleans, which is where I was born and have lived for most of my life. When I was born, Daisy Jones, my grandmother Nancy, and other medicine women agreed that I was that child. The Fatawanun that I was to serve would not be born until I was eleven or twelve years old. The Fatawanun's woman is always older than the Fatawanun she serves so that she will have a certain dominance over him and the Fatawanun will not be sexually attracted or drawn to her during all the time that they stay together during the ceremonies when she feeds and takes care of him.

Georgia Henry was another medicine woman, and she didn't want someone who looked white to be a medicine woman. She was vehemently against it and said that I was a bastard because my parents had only been married in the white man's way and had never been married in the Indian way. My grandmother was also a women's doctor, and when she heard that Georgia Henry had called me a bastard she got really angry and said that she was never going to talk to Georgia again. But then Georgia got to thinking about it. Georgia was a spiritual medicine woman like me; she was the Fatawanun's woman and she was one of the people who would have to help train me. My grandma was an Indian doctor for women and children and she had more power than I have or Georgia Henry had, a different kind of power. Doctors like my grandmother carried a lot of respect and influence in our society and also had more direct hands-on training, using herbs and other forms of treatment for her patients.

So Georgia got to thinking about my grandmother's power and decided that she had better start making amends for her hasty words. She made me a great big clothesbasket with two little handles for carrying it. She also made a little Indian baby hat for me to wear to my first White Deerskin Dance, and she commenced to give these little gifts to my mother and grandmother, to make amends for saying those things about me. She agreed with Daisy that she would help train me. She didn't do much training that I remember, but she did accept that duty. Daisy did most of my training and gave me her Indian name, O-ya-nee, which means red willow. That was a great honor because I can't see anything like as well as she could.[1] I don't think you have the help to gain our medicine power in this world today that was around at the beginning of the last century, but a lot of people can still come together, like at a dance, and pull in the power, the spiritual energies.

I became aware of these medicine women when I was about three and a half years old. Georgia Henry and Jennie Blue, who was the daughter of Sandy Bar Bob, a powerful medicine man, came to our house and asked me about my dreams: "What do you dream? What do you see?" I told them that I dreamed repeatedly of being on a road with a red sweater on and being absolutely alone. When I told them about this dream, they said that they knew and that they were going to help me. They said they were going to help me out, but they never went into any details. In my mind as a child, they just knew. They didn't tell you and you didn't ask. They knew all about it. and the feeling of distress from this dream I had been having was gone. At the time I first had this vision of being alone, my parents were still alive and I didn't know what it meant, but by the time I was six years old, after my parents had died, I knew that it meant that I was alone because I had no parents or brothers and sisters. I was truly alone. I had an aunt and a grandfather, but there were ways in which I was literally alone.

My parents died when I was six years old and I was raised by my grandfather and my aunt Caroline. My grandfather died when I was sixteen, so he was only around for ten years after my parents died, but my aunt stayed with me until I was in my forties. I always thought of Aunt Caroline as my aunt because I remembered my mother, and although Aunt Caroline took care of me, she stayed my aunt in my mind. She didn't want to be called "mother" when I wasn't her child.

Daisy Jones and the other medicine women made me focus on whatever I had dreamed. When they asked me about my dreams I would go into a little trance. That is my first memory of going into trance, and that was the beginning of my training. When you're being trained they tell you things, and if you're not quite sure what it means, you don't ask them anything and they don't tell you any more. They just tell you what you need to know. I don't know whether they did things before that first visit to me, but after that visit it got so I would focus on my dreams. And when I got older, when they weren't around, places would talk to me and tell me things, and I would report that to the medicine women who were training me.

I would be someplace and all at once something would start talking to me. There are special high-country places, like Doctor Rock and Chimney Rock, that are known to everyone as being medicine places, places where medicine people go to get their powerful gifts. Then there are other places that don't look special or distinct. For instance, there is a place here on this property. And I have learned that these places are the crossroads where the spirit world can come into this world and we can go into the spirit world. These are the places that talked to me, but as a child I didn't know that there were these special places. They just looked like any ordinary place to me and I had no way of anticipating that this was a place that would talk to me, or a place where I would hear voices. Down the hill from here there was a place that talked, so evidently there was a crossroads there, a spiritual place. When the places talk to you, you have gone into a spirit space. The experience was just like someone was talking to me. It was like being talked to by the medicine women. The voices just told me little things.

When I was very young I began to get messages from places about things that were going to happen—sometimes just minor things that would happen in people's lives that they wouldn't expect, things that at my age I should not know anything about. Sometimes what I was saying didn't make sense to me. It was like I was talking about Einstein's theory of relativity and had no idea of what it was. I was talking about things that were beyond my comprehension.

When I was about ten years old I got into big trouble because of something I said. I was coming from my great-uncle Harry's and walking the back trail by the Ruben place, and somebody, someone, something, a voice, told me that one of my cousins was going to have "man trouble." I didn't know what man trouble was, it wasn't a phrase I was familiar with. Well, I told my cousin Laverne, who evidently knew what it was, because she was more worldly than I was, and she told someone else and it went all through the school. I got called on it and since I didn't know who told me, I was accused of telling lies.

Grandpa came over to the school and I don't know what he said to them, but he got across to them to ask me what it is, man trouble, and I didn't know. I didn't have the slightest idea. He said, "Well then, someone must have told her, because it isn't something that she knows. She doesn't know what she's talking about. Someone had to tell her and she didn't make it up, because she doesn't know what she's talking about." So I got off that time but people were kind of mad at me for a long time.

Mamie Allen and the medicine women knew what had happened, but they didn't say. They knew what I was, but they didn't tell. They knew what I knew, but they understood that it was something that had not yet happened but was going to happen with my cousin and a man. Grandpa knew it was something that was going to happen, but he got me out of it by showing them that I didn't know what I was talking about. About three years later, when my cousin was seventeen, she got pregnant and that caused a big family ruckus. By then I knew what I had been talking about, I just didn't know what it meant at the time. By the time I was thirteen or fourteen years old I had more of an idea of what man trouble meant. Remember, you're talking about a child who was totally unsophisticated, no television, no nothing. Sometimes [laughing] the voices say the damnedest things.

That taught me one thing, like they told me: "Don't say anything to anyone. Don't say anything. You will only get yourself in trouble." My grandmother, Daisy, and the other women kept cautioning me not to say anything about my training because white people would kill you if they knew you did these things. "They'll kill you for this. Even if you know that it's going to happen and you see it in your mind, don't tell the person. Don't tell them unless you are told you have to tell them. Don't say anything unless that voice tells you to tell them." When I am told that I have to tell people something that I've learned, I hate to do it to them, because it's usually something you don't want to hear. It's like death and taxes.

Now, if I think about this just using my intellectual capacities, I know that it is insane. But the medicine women worked really, really hard when I was a child and convinced me that that's the way it actually was. They catch you before you are seven years old, between the ages of three and seven, and begin training you. When it comes right down to it, you are indoctrinated in that way of thinking and that's the way you come to believe. They picked me as a medicine woman the same way that, years later, I picked a local man's son as a medicine man because I saw him coming to that certain family. I just knew that he was the next one. Even though the father had five sons, I knew which one would be the medicine man. Actually, I see that he should be an Indian doctor rather than a medicine man. But he hasn't done so. Whether he chooses to do that or not is not a judgment for or against him. The choice is his. I ran away from mine for half a lifetime because I'd rather be happy than be a medicine woman. This man says that he's happy because he is having children and married and working, busy. Things may change in later life, or not.

The training was very subtle...they would put my mind in a bubble. When I was young they liked me to do mindless, repetitive things, like pick up acorns, which are one of our main foods. You can't pick up acorns without using part of your mind, or you would pick up nuts with wormholes in them. You have to look at the nuts. But it was just the same activity over and over, like picking sticks for basket material. First you'd pick the sticks and then you had to sort them. I wasn't a basket maker, but I had to sort the fine sticks. I think they wanted me to do these things to calm myself. I was an antsy child. I remember walking down the street with my mother, turning handsprings instead of walking. [Laughing] I remember her saying, "Oh, my daughter. I don't know what I'm going to do." So this emphasis on repetitive, calming things may have had something to do with my personality.

Nothing was ever overt in their training of me. They would just make a light impression on you about something. There was no push. It was like you were making a clay pot and gently molding it, so that there was no pressure, no obvious pressure to do something. They were just gently molding me and impressing little things on me. It is altogether different than training to become a nurse, which I did when I was in my fifties. Nurses' training is a really strong and forceful process. Training to be a medicine woman was very subtle. Sometimes one of them would sort of point with her chin toward a situation where people were doing something, interacting with one another in a way they thought would be instructive to me as a spiritual medicine woman.

I was born with these medicine powers, but there are other people who want to have them and can go through this spiritual training. Through training I developed the powers I was born with and learned how to do these things.

I also had to speak in a certain tone of voice, a certain pitch, and I could not speak in a loud voice. They'd tell me to hit that pitch and then stay on it. Besides the medicine women, my grandfather and my aunt would tell me when I started to use sharp-pitched sounds in my conversation. And they didn't like you whistling. In later life my husband, Darrell, told me that if you whistle in the house you're calling in the devil, according to the Yurok. At any rate, that's what he heard when he was a child.

When you look at a vision, it is like looking at shadows and hints, and it takes years and years to learn to interpret what you are really seeing. A lot of my training and all my youth was mostly devoted to understanding the gift of seeing and visions. In the old days we didn't call them visions. What was said was that you could see. After years of training some of the older women were so good at seeing, they could sit down with a person and tell you your whole life history and what would happen to you in the future. Not in the sense of telling you about your day-to-day living, but an overall view of your life with some incidents in it that were specific.

In my experience, the visions come in dreams. This isn't like a dream where you go to sleep and have dreams that come in fragments. Visions are usually a clearer picture, and you remember the dream clearly, like my dream of being on the road and my feeling of being desperately alone, with no one around, and the trees around me and the gray dirt of the road and the green grass on the side of the road are like a picture in my mind which stays there. I first had that vision when I was three and a half years old, and now I am seventy-four years old, and I can still see that distinct picture. So the visions stay with you.

Sometimes you have a nightmare and you think, "Now, is this a vision or not?" because it stays in your mind, but then when you try to examine it, it's like trying to examine fog or something. It just drifts away from you the closer you try to look at it, but in the dream vision you can put it up and look at everything that happened, every word and every scene. My vision when I was three and a half years old was a premonition of my parents being killed in a wreck when I was six. When the old ladies asked me about this vision at the time it first took place, they knew it was a premonition of my parents' death. This was the first vision I remember having, and the first one I remember being questioned about. They may have questioned me earlier about other visions that I don't remember because I was so young.

As a person becomes deeper in their understanding of visions, you can know something that you never saw anything about, but the thought comes into your mind and sometimes it comes out of your mouth and you don't mean it to—it kind of surprises you and you just say it. What you're saying is absolutely so, but you never saw anything other than a vision to inform you of it. That speaking out is also a part of the seeing. After some time of working with having visions, I no longer had to see a vision. In some cases the knowledge would just come into my mind and I could speak that content. What I said at that time was a fact. It wasn't something that I thought up, dreamed up, or had done.

I always had this feeling that the medicine part of my life is a separate thing from my life. I draw the analogy that when a Christian person gets a call to preach and is made a priest or preacher, he is expected to be on that plane of being a priest all the time. He is just a priest and he can't be simply human. But with the Indian people, you are human and at times you are a spiritual person, but you are not expected to be that spiritual person every day. I don't know about other medicine people's visions, because you don't ask and they don't tell you. They only tell you what you need to know personally, yourself, for your training. They may have other gifts, but if you don't need to have these other gifts it doesn't matter and they don't train you in them.

The training had more to do with believing than it did with "You take nine drops of this fluid here and add these herbs…" The training had more to do with getting your mind set in this certain way, understanding the world from this other perspective. They worked on that harder than they ever worked at the other level of training. It was always "What did you dream and what did you see?"

More than likely, when they asked me about my dreams they already knew my parents were going to die. They never told me that, but my assumption is that they knew, because they had that kind of knowledge. They knew my whole damn life when I was three and a half years old, but they didn't know that there would be no Fatawanun born for me. That was something they did not know, so at the time that they were training me, the parents of that Fatawanun were alive. I figure the father of this Fatawanun probably died in World War II, because the boy would have been eleven or twelve years younger than I was, so I was being trained to serve a Fatawanun who was not yet born.

They thought it was more than likely his father was killed in World War II. That would have been the right time frame. They also thought the father could have been killed in a car accident or anything else, but since there was a big war they figured that was probably the cause. That's logical. I don't care how far out we sound, the medicine people are logical.

By 1945 and the end of the war I was around twelve years old, and they knew there was no Fatawanun for me. They only told me what I needed to know, which was that he had not been born. If you want to know something from a medicine person, they would only tell you what you needed to know. You could ask large questions about being a medicine person. They would not tell you, because you had no need to know everything. So with his not being born, that was all I needed to know and was all I was ever told. So mostly, with the Indians, if you don't ask the right question they will give you a facetious answer. You have to ask a precise question to get a real answer. You have to know what you want to know. If you are an Indian and a medicine person, you had better have a very precise question if you are going to get an answer from another medicine person.

After my parents died, the medicine women's help became more intense and I could see more things. I think their deaths made me older and matured me. Before their deaths my mother took care of me and I was a baby. She babied me and I had simplistic little visions. Then the realities of life hit when they died, and I realized the seriousness of life, that you could be here one day and the next day you could be gone forever. I realized then that life wasn't simple. Before my parents died, life for me was just kind of little likes and dislikes.

The medicine women told me not to ask anyone anything. They told me to go to Elk Valley and the valley would talk to me and tell me what I needed to do. "The Creator will tell you." Elk Valley has a little creek running through it. It's open, with cedar trees, and I would say it's flat for about a half-mile and then goes up on a bench, and the whole valley is about three miles long and about a quarter-mile wide. It has spectacular rock structures, like Chimney Rock, which sticks up like a great big chimney. It also has the Little Doctor Rock, which looks like the real Doctor Rock, which looks kind of like a big clamshell.

I was probably six or seven years old the first time they took me to Elk Valley, and I was too young to stay all night, because I didn't belong there. There's a subtle difference between going to Elk Valley to visit and going there to make medicine for a ceremony. If I'm just going to go up the trail and do a few little prayers and soothe my soul, not doing anything except for myself, I can stop at the first camp, where the creek crosses the trail, and I can stay there and the valley doesn't talk to me. It doesn't do anything and I just stay there. I'm just visiting. I don't go up to Chimney Rock, because I'm just there to bless myself, just like you would go up to an altar and pray in a church. I'm praying for my soul, to soothe myself. My aunt used to go up the hill in the morning and bathe and stay there until late afternoon and come down. If you are praying for someone in your family, it is still praying for yourself, because it is a personal thing. You don't stay all night when you are on the mountain for personal reasons, because you might pick up too much power. Like when I went out there and made medicine for the Brush Dance and the voice told me to go home, it was because I had everything I needed to have for the dance to go. My directions were never to stay in the valley all night unless I was getting ready to be the medicine woman for a dance.

I had to work like everyone else when I was young. Everyone had to work, and medicine people have to work just as hard as everyone else. You didn't have to go out and kill or gut a deer, but you had to work. You had to pick up acorns, make baskets, carry water, cut kindling, and carry wood. You had to do all these things that everyone else had to do. Bringing in the eggs and packing in kindling were things I had to do, chores that were set out for me, but if anything upset me, the medicine women who were taking care of my spiritual growth figured out a way that I could do things so that I would not become upset.

I didn't like packing kindling because the wood poked my arms and hurt me. I think it's because my head was injured in a wreck when I was five years old and the nerves in my arms were sensitive. So when I was six or seven years old and would have to pack wood, my arms would hurt really badly. I would whine around about it and I didn't want to do it and I felt mean about it because it hurt. Auntie Caroline complained to Daisy that I was being mean about packing wood and that it was upsetting me. So Daisy whips out a little basket for me that was about two feet long with a handle, and I could put the kindling in it and pack the basket and it didn't prickle my arms and upset me. She did this so that I would feel good and I wouldn't feel mean about packing kindling.

It's like the women who trained me put my mind in a bubble. They do something to you. You know how children fight with each other? They didn't allow me to fight, and I didn't play until after they sealed me. I had no greed. When people did things to me I didn't get mad. I would get angry when somebody did something to someone else, but if they did something to me, I was passive. I wasn't allowed that emotion and I didn't have it. I didn't have greed and I didn't want anything because I had everything I needed.

Once, when I was a little girl, I dropped the little tin bucket that we packed the eggs in and broke the eggs that I had gathered from the henhouse. Grandpa got after me for breaking the eggs and told me I should be more careful. My mentor Daisy made me two egg baskets, all woven and rounded, small around the top and big at the bottom. One basket was small and one was big and I would choose which basket to carry, depending on how many eggs there were that day. She made me the baskets so that I could pack the eggs and they wouldn't break if I stumbled. She did that so I wouldn't get upset, because as the Fatawanun's woman, I was supposed to make the world—this little world that we live in, here on the Klamath River—a happy place. Everything has to be good and happy when we are renewing the world with the Pikiawish ceremony.

I don't care what happened to me, they'd make it okay. Daisy Jones and my aunt Caroline protected me in this spiritual way and there may have been other medicine women looking out for me too, more than likely there were. In the Karuk society women never trained men. Men trained men and, before the present times, men never trained women. I had these women training me. No Fatawanun came in and said anything to me. The women trained me in what I needed to do and the men trained the men in what they needed to do.

In the old days medicine people ran the society. The headman ran the village and kept peace amongst the people. They weren't medicine people, but they had a personality that was not easily upset. They could come from a medicine family, but mostly there were headman families and there were medicine families. My grandfather was a headman, that's the kind of people he came from. Headmen could get angry, but they didn't fight with people or argue very much and they would keep people from bickering and keep everything in balance. You know, when you live in a closed society there is a lot of bickering, especially when those men had more than one wife. The men and women lived in separate houses [laughing] but they had more than one wife, so they could bicker.

Headmen were not trained, like medicine people. They were chosen regardless of their status. A headman could come from a poor family but be chosen for his personality as a nice calm person who got along with other people, was affable and could manipulate people really well. Each headman chose his successor based on his personality. Since a village was for the most part one big extended family, the headman was the head of that family.

This was true of all the villages except for Katamin. Katamin was the open village and any family could go there. The more problems a person had living in other villages, like if they argued a lot, or they hollered a lot and made too much noise, they would send you out of the village and then you would live in the open village. For the Karuk this was Katamin, the center of the Karuk world. You can't kick someone out of Katamin, you can't lock them out of Katamin. Katamin is where you go when you are having problems. These days if a person uses too much dope and they go to Katamin, it means that they are there for the Creator to heal them.

No medicine people came out of the open village of Katamin. Across the river, the village of Ishi Pish had the medicine people, up the river had medicine people, but the open village did not have medicine people. A person went to Katamin for healing. It was also [laughing] where most of the fish were.

The same principle carried over to the Yurok. Kenek was the center of their world. Anyone who was Yurok could come and stay at Kenek because that was their place for the malcontents and those who couldn't get along well with other people. The open villages were like safety valves that let the pressure off for other villages. Then they didn't have to be thrown out into the world to starve or wander. They were sent to a place where they would be healed. That was our belief.

The Other Side

When I was a child, something would come at night and take me away. The child who gets picked up and taken to the other reality does not see anyone, but the brother or sister in the same bedroom who sees it happen will say that they saw an old woman or an old man pick up and take the child. Those who get picked up refer to it as a spirit or power. Since I was an only child, I had no brothers or sisters to say they had seen something take me away. One medicine man always called it the old man. Another would say it's not an old man. I think it shows itself as an old man so it doesn't scare you.

The feeling was like nothing you can imagine. I have no description of it. The closest adjective I can come to is "awesome." I had no feeling of humanity being involved, but the sensation was awesome. I have no idea whether it took my body or just my spirit, and I've asked other medicine people, and [laughing] they have no idea either. One of them had a little brother who slept in the room with him when he was picked up as a child. The little brother saw the figure who came for him as being an old man, but he would tell his little brother that it wasn't a man, it was a power. That was his description, a power. It was not human; it was a power. The only thing the little brother knew was that he was frightened by the old man who looked at him. It never gave me any sense of familiarity, nothing was familiar about it. That's why I can't describe it other than to say it was awesome. The other child called it a power. It gave us no illusion that it was human. It threw up an illusion for the little brother so it would not scare him, but it scared him anyway. It didn't care if it scared me and the other child it was taking away, but it didn't scare us anyway [laughing], because we never saw anything.

I think being picked up was part of the training. I think it was teaching us the trails. We would come back with no sense of having learned anything. You would just know that you had been gone and came back, and whatever it was that was involved was not human.

You might be gone for a half-hour, fifteen or twenty minutes. I would go up that medicine trail…if you take me out there right now and try to take a walk up that trail, the only thing I can do is take you to the crossroads where the trail begins. It's called the crossroads because it's where the powers can step into this world.

Later, when I was older, when I came back from the other side I knew things that I had not known before. That went on for years. I have found that when you come back from being out into the other reality, you kind of have a malaise about you and you're not quite your normal self. Sometimes it takes a few days to get back to being yourself. You're kind of…hazy and not very clear. When I was a girl, and later as a young woman, I didn't know what I was doing when I went into a trance, but after I was in my forties I realized I was changing into a spirit shape. When I was young and came out of trance I would be disoriented and kind of daydream afterward, so that the teachers would complain about my daydreaming, but the trances are very disorienting. For example, I might be gone from here for five hours but it only feels like I was gone for about fifteen minutes. My body is actually gone during this period. You won't come out and find my body lying in the field or [laughing] flapping around in the wind.

When I was younger, this force would come and pick me up and take me away. I call it a force because I don't know what else to call it. I never knew where I was taken, I just remember coming back—feeling the presence of the spirits and coming back. When the power picks you up it usually comes at night, probably because you won't be missed at night. I do not know where it took me; I just remember coming back. When you come back you are in an altered state of mind, and I was hell for knocking the lamp over, getting back in bed.

Grandpa didn't like me going outside in the middle of the night, so he fixed it by moving all the latches on the doors to where I couldn't reach them. Then I couldn't get out. I didn't realize that I was getting up and going outside. The first thing I knew was getting back into bed and knocking the lamp over because I was disoriented. He probably knew exactly what was taking me outside, but he never said anything at all except that he didn't like me getting up and wandering around at night. And he never said anything about it, because if Grandpa said something, that's what we did. I don't know how many lamps I broke because of when I'd come back in a sleepwalking state and I'd knock the lamp table over.

The other gifted people that I have known all talked of the same force. Some of them see it as an old man, some would see it as a light. I didn't see it, really; I felt it as a presence. I don't know what the difference is. I was going outside to get picked up. Then after Grandpa locked the door, the power came inside and picked me up from where I was. Before that I would go outside.

As a part of the training, Daisy told me to just talk to the Creator like I'm talking to another person, just tell him what you're responding to, whatever you're dreaming about, whatever visions you see. If you're having problems, just ask him what it means. Whatever is bothering you, or whatever you think, you just talk to the Creator about it. Ask him, "What do you want me to do with this?" And then the Creator tells you what to do. The spirits don't answer my prayers like the Creator does. The spirits come to you with messages, whether you want them to or not.[2]

There are two kinds of prayers. Ceremonial leaders pray structured prayers during the ceremonies. These are the ritual prayers where certain words are said each time, and there are personal prayers, where the person just raises up their hands and talks to the Creator about what is on their mind. The medicine is saying prayers and having prayerful thoughts.

Being Sealed

When I got to be about twelve years old and the Fatawanun I was being trained to serve had not been born, there was no reason to continue to train me to be the Fatawanun's woman. This training is very specific. I was being trained to help a specific individual at a specific place. They had no idea who he was or what family he was to be born into, but they knew that he had not been born. If he had been born they would have seen the baby and recognized him as the Fatawanun, like they recognized me as being the Fatawanun's woman. He wasn't there. He never came.

A medicine woman only served one Fatawanun, and when he died or stopped being Fatawanun, then she would quit and someone else would become the Fatawanun's woman. You still had the power and you were still gifted and you still had all these things that you had been trained to do, but you didn't work actively at it as you did when you had been the Fatawanun's woman. Even though I was trained to be the Fatawanun's woman, I had no experience in directly working in that capacity, because the Fatawanun I was trained to serve was never born.

There was no special ceremony to seal me off. The medicine women would have just prayed, and some would have smoked their pipes and others would have fanned smoke on themselves, and they would have talked to the Creator and said that since the Fatawanun had not been born, then Mavis could go on with her own life and she no longer has to do this. That part of my life was over and behind me. To seal me off they went to a power site near here and prayed and sang and burned herbs in a fire. To make medicine you pick certain plants and put them in a basket, then build a fire and put your plants in the fire and talk to God and tell him what you're talking about and why, and dance and sing. You face the four winds and pray and talk to God and tell him what your problem is. That's making medicine.

They told me that I wouldn't have to do what I was supposed to have done if the Fatawanun had been born. That part of my life was over and behind me. Now I would have a happy life of my own.

They sealed me from the eight years or so of training to be the Fatawanun's woman, but they didn't take away my power. They left my power with me because there was no reason to take it away. Evidently I met their approval and was as good a person as they had expected me to be, had wanted me to be. Being an only child, I was terribly spoiled, but that never seemed to bother them.

After they sealed me, I began to feel anger. If somebody did something to me, pushed me, I would push them back.

After I was sealed I could get married and have children and I could have a happy personal life. I wouldn't have to serve all the time. Before I was sealed, my life was going to be one of always having to serve people and I would never have a life of my own until I was finished with that, whenever the boy, ten or eleven years younger than I was, had stopped being a Fatawanun.

After I was sealed they prayed and made medicine because Daisy Jones could see that because of my physical problems, my children weren't going to live if they did not make medicine and pray for me. So then they made all kinds of medicine. I had seventeen dolls and they made seventeen baskets, one for every doll, so that there would be no empty baskets and no doll without a basket. This was making medicine for my children to live. She told me that she thought most of them would make it to adulthood and have children of their own, that they would have some life and would live long enough to have children of their own. But she said she couldn't stop all of the bad things that would happen and that I was going to have to lose some of them. It was true.

My mother was still alive when I got the dolls. We had been living in Eureka, where my mother was running a boardinghouse and working for the WPA, and I was mostly home alone. She worked for the WPA at a little manufacturing shop in Eureka where she sewed clothes for people who were out of work and had children but didn't have any clothes for them or food for them. If she sewed fast enough she could make me a few things while she was at it. Like if she made two pair of pants for the WPA, [laughing] she could make one for me. She had to work four hours a day for the WPA, but she didn't make enough to live in Eureka, so she ran a little boardinghouse to pay for rent.

One day I had been home after school, playing on a little sun porch in the backyard. I had taken my dolls out in the backyard and was playing on the back steps with them in the sunshine. When it started to get dark my mother told me to bring the dolls in, but I didn't want to bring them in. I was tired and I didn't want to. My mother told me that it was going to rain and that the dolls would get ruined. If they got ruined she would give them to the firehouse for the firemen to fix up for poor children—not that we weren't poor, but for really poor children. We [laughing] had a roof over our heads. I didn't bring in the dolls and she had told me the consequences: she would give the dolls away if they got rained on. So all my dolls got ruined and my mother gave them to the firehouse. Then at Christmastime we came to Orleans from Eureka, and Grandma and Grandpa were here, and everybody, including the church, gave me dolls. I got seventeen dolls that Christmas because my mother gave my dolls away and everybody thought she was being mean. I did not get another doll from my mother—she gave me books that year [laughing]. My aunt Caroline gave me a handmade layette with the doll she gave me, and my aunt Hazel crocheted little blankets and sweaters for the dolls that she gave me. So I had all these dolls, and then Daisy had a vision, later, when I was getting sealed, around eleven years old. My parents were long gone and Daisy asked my aunt Caroline how many dolls I had. I had given some away, but I still had seventeen dolls. I had developed diabetes when I was nine years old from pancreatitis, which I got from being poisoned from a whooping cough shot. Daisy saw that diabetes was going to cause me to lose a lot of my children, and she could see me not having children, that my children were going to die. So she made the little baby doll baskets for every single doll I owned so there would be no empty baskets, so there would be no doll without a baby basket and no bed without a baby in it. This was to make positive medicine for my children to live.

Daisy told me that when I had children, the ones that lived would grow to be adults. I took that to mean they would live to be grown. I didn't realize that she was saying that all of my children who lived would have a child before they died. So what happened was that I had Carol, who died at thirty-six with one son. I had Daypay, who died at sixteen, and he had one son. Beavi had four children, and Long Gone had three children, and they both lost a child. Even though Daisy saw when I was eleven years old that I was going to have trouble having children, my diabetes wasn't diagnosed until I was twenty-three years old and had had two miscarriages. Because of the diabetes I threatened to miscarry with all of my children.

The medicine women told me that even though I had been sealed, if I was ever asked to do a ceremony, like a Brush Dance, I was to do it because I could, I had that power, and that I should not listen to anything anyone says or what complaints they have, because the Creator will tell me what I have to do. I have the power to pick up this medicine, bring it down and get it out to the child being treated at a Brush Dance, and to bless the people who are at the dance. I can do that. It isn't exactly what I was born to do or trained to do, but it is something I can just do because the training carries over to that, even though it is not my specialty. [See Section 3 for details of the Brush Dance.]

Ceremonies

The Pikiawish ceremony is to put the world in balance and make things right that have gone wrong over the past year. This is our world renewal ceremony when the fish and the people are prayed for. The White Deerskin Dance takes place every other year during Pikiawish, and on those years you just get an extra blessing. The White Deerskin Dance takes about ten days overall, but the dance only takes up about five of those days. The medicine man serves as long as he wants to or until he can find someone else dedicated enough to carry out those responsibilities. The medicine man chooses the Fatawanun and prays with the man he has chosen and this Fatawa-nun fasts for two or three days and then starts going on all the various medicine trails. There are fifty-seven miles of medicine trails around Orleans, which was the old village of Panamniik. He brings the power down to the river and prays for the fish, then goes to the sweathouse, where he spends a night and a day. Then there is a dance and the next day he goes out on another trail and prays for the fish again and there is another dance at the sweathouse. The next day he goes out on another set of trails. One of the Fatawanun told me that it's really dangerous coming down, because you're not really clear-minded, and you are running along the trail like you are half dreaming, and you will catch yourself because you almost stepped off a bluff. The trail may have been there at one time, but it caved off and now you have to go around and pick your way down and find the trail again. It takes a lot of strength to be a Fatawanun, because [laughing] they don't travel that trail the way I do. They have to do it in this world, and it's a lot harder. Like my aunt Caroline said, when she went out to Doctor Rock to pick up her doctor medicine and she and the woman with her were going along the trail, she said she could feel the trail moving under her feet, and she was going a lot faster than she could walk. She was quite certain she was not in her ordinary form. She knew that she could not get there that fast physically, herself. She had been fasting for three days by then.

The Jump Dance is to place the importance of your family over the importance of yourself, placing your family between yourself and the Creator. To begin the Jump Dance, the medicine boy catches the first fish and gives it to the medicine woman. She cooks the fish and leaves it for the medicine man. He doesn't need the medicine woman to be there to serve him, she just cooks the fish and leaves. The boy is already gone. He just gave her the fish to cook. After the fish is cooked she puts it on a big round basket tray with ferns on it and walks away. Then the medicine man comes down and eats as much of the fish as he can, then he digs a hole and buries what is left. Then he crosses the river in a boat and goes to Amikiarum and walks up the hill to a rock that has hieroglyphics of fish and bones all over it. The rock has a crack in it about a foot wide and the medicine man sings and dances and prays for the fish on this rock. When he finishes at dawn he puts his torch out in the crack in the rock and you can see the carbon there from where it's been done for centuries. When that is done he crosses the river again and the medicine man begins fasting and praying, and goes to Elk Valley with the medicine woman and the medicine girl. They stay in seclusion until the dance starts. The medicine man doesn't eat from the time he ate the fish until the dance is over ten days later. The medicine man and the medicine woman fast for ten days, the others only fast for three days.

All of the medicine people have, not a personal relationship, but an amicable relationship with each other. The medicine woman doesn't tell the medicine man what he is supposed to do and he doesn't tell the medicine woman what she is supposed to do. He assumes you know what you're doing and why you're doing it. My main job as the Fatawanun's woman is to make the world a happy place—this world right here on the Klamath River—that people have peace and are happy with each other. So when people have problems and anxieties and are fighting with each other and leaving each other or just having any kind of vehement problems, my job and my training, outside of the World Renewal [Pikiawish] training, is to make people content with what they have or what their life is, or what the circumstance of their life is, so you give them another outlook on their life.

Keeping the Peace

A person might be looking at life from a certain negative direction and be in the pits, but after talking with me, then they know they are freer than they had been thinking they were, and can get jobs and do things to get on with their lives. I accomplish this by giving them another mindset, just talking and telling them things. I remember a couple that always fought. All their life together they argued constantly, for about twenty years. Then the woman found somebody else and the husband asked me if it was true, because he had heard that his woman was seeing another man.

I told him that I had heard the same thing, but I had never seen it, so I couldn't tell him positively that she is going around with someone else, because I just heard gossip and sometimes gossip is wrong. And I told him that if she is seeing someone else, you don't know, it might be the best thing that ever happened to you. You may find a more contented life and be happier without her. Now you just think it's terrible because you love this person and you don't want to lose her, but it might be a good thing. He kind of didn't like hearing that. It was giving him a little bit too bitter a taste, but after he found out that it was so, when he left her he found another woman to live with that he didn't argue with all the time. He came back to see me and told me that he kind of got mad with me the time I told him that it might be a good thing and he might be happier.

"Now when I look back at it, it was a good thing. One of the better things that happened to me was that she left me, because I became happier for the rest of my life. I don't regret having the children with her, but I'm happier now than I was then." So that's how you change people's minds.

After I was sealed, I wasn't quite as obedient as I had been when those old ladies were controlling my mind. I think they were controlling my mind. I'm not sure, but I feel like there was a big difference in my reactions because they let up a little bit and weren't totally controlling my mind any longer. Anyway, when I would do something that Auntie didn't approve of, I remember her looking at me and I would have a feeling of what she thought about what I had done, her disappointment. I felt that she was telling me what was right and what was wrong, and I think now that she wasn't talking to me, she was using telepathy, but I did not realize this until close to the end of her life. She just looked at me, and what she thought, I felt. I knew what she thought, because she was telling me mentally. She didn't move her mouth. I just remember her eyes.

There are probably some young people being trained now. I haven't trained any. I haven't been called to train any. I think people are into drugs too damned much anyway to train. We had enough problems before contact and now we have more. We have their kind of problems and our kind of problems.

Grandpa told us all these moral stories about not lying. "Don't tell a lie, because no village will want you. Your family won't want you. No one will want you around if you lie or steal. If you steal no one wants you around." Then one of my older cousins said, "Mavis always lies."

Grandpa told them, "Mavis doesn't lie. It just hasn't happened yet." You know, I was playing with children all the time and sometimes something would come to me and it would just slip out and I would say something, and it has happened with me all my life. Like I was riding along one time about ten years ago and a man had drowned and gotten lost in the river. We saw someone digging around down at the end of the gravel bar by the river and my husband, Darrell, said, "There's poor Tule, still looking for his brother."

I said, "He's not there. He's at Fort Bragg." So in other words, the river had washed him out into the ocean and he came back in at Fort Bragg, down the coast. If the river is real high the body will come out of the ocean up in Oregon, if it's not too high it will come out down around Fort Bragg. Sometimes things like that will just pop out of my mouth and I'd never mean to say it. It wasn't me, it was that other thing talking. So when I was little, I thought I was crazy because these voices would talk to me and tell me things that other people didn't seem to know, or weren't aware of. I was convinced I was insane. The other thing I always wonder is, is any of it real or is this some twisted working of a mind, an imagination? But too many things come true that first came to me in this alternative reality, so…

One of the things the medicine women taught me was to always speak in a certain tone of voice. Whenever I started to talk in an excited, loud, high-pitched voice, they would indicate that I should take it down to a certain pitch. So I learned to speak in that voice when I was a child and that has always been my voice. Years later, when I was working as a nurse, I read an article that said psychologists had determined that the voice that calmed patients and gave them confidence in their therapist was in G flat. I wondered about that and got a tuning fork in that key and saw that that was close to the tone I had been trained to speak in. It was no surprise to me.

Family History: Vid-ik-it's Story

My great-grandmother Vid-ik-it was a Karuk Indian born in 1832. She came from the village of Chimakinee, near what is now the town of Orleans, and was the daughter of Po-ka-noc-tish-karuk. He came from further north, up the Klamath River at the village of I-ees-i-rum. I only know the names of two of his children, his son I-ees Steve and his daughter Vid-ik-it, but he may have had other children by his other wives, who wouldn't have the prestige that his first family had.

At marriage a woman left her country and went to live with her husband's family if she married into another tribe. The daughters of medicine women and headmen learned the basics of four or five languages, and other customs and other ways of being of other tribes near them so they could get along if they married into that tribe. When you got to the other country, you stayed with your mother-in-law and she taught you all their customs and all the things you had to do, because if you made a mistake in their customs, the family you had married into had to pay other people for your mistake if you were in that upper class. If you were in that class you were expected to have unimpeachable manners and not to do or say anything that was against their customs.

Vid-ik-it was taken north for her marriage by her uncle and a couple of young men who were related to her. She was being sold as a bride and since she came from a headman's family, more than likely she would be sold out of the country, to the Tolowa, Yurok, or Modoc or to one of the other tribes in the area. This was a way to make alliances and keep trading active between the tribes of this region. Later in her life, Vid-ik-it thought she was about fourteen years old that year but she may have been a little younger. Her uncle could speak some English at this time, just before the gold rush, around 1846 or 1847, but she could not.

She was taken north into what is now Oregon. She had never been there before and once she went home, she never went back. Oregon had been settled before this part of California and there were farmers and farmland there at this time. She had to be somewhere around Medford, but she was never certain, nobody told her. It was none of her business who she was getting married to. That's the way it was. Up north she was captured by soldiers and her uncle and the young men were run off. The soldiers raped her repeatedly and she didn't think she was going to live through it, but she did and an itinerant pot-and-pan salesman named Stone happened to be up in this country where she was being held captive.

After learning of what had happened to Vid-ik-it, Stone talked the soldiers out of keeping her. He told them that they would start an Indian war if they did not turn her loose to him. If she had men guarding her and escorting her from one place to another, then she would have to be of the wealthier families and the family would fight to get her back. After this she got through to him where she came from and he brought her back down to the Klamath River and her home country. It took them four or five or six months, and I don't think he went out of his pot-and-pan route to get here. Stone did not know the route they had taken to bring her to Oregon and ended up bringing her back down the Salmon River to get her home to the Klamath River. Her son Frederick Ferris, my grandfather, told me that Stone had given pots and pans as gifts to her family and everybody in her village to pay for the insult to Vid-ik-it of being raped and not having a father for her baby. Stone claimed the baby as his own. It wasn't his, but because he knew it would cause problems for Vid-ik-it with the village if the baby did not have a father and the mother had not been paid for, he gave the baby his name. The baby was Caroline Stone, my great-aunt. I was raised by her niece Caroline Ferris.

When Vid-ik-it went into labor she was staying up at the village of I-ees-i-rum, about twenty miles upriver from here, probably with her father or one of her stepmothers, because as a headman her father would have had as many as five or six wives. Vid-ik-it wanted to give birth downriver at her family's birthing house in the village of Chimakinee, so she started walking and made it more than halfway before she had to stop to give birth at McCash'es village, where she had distant relatives. She used the birthing house in that village and then came on down the river after a week or two and went to live with her sister, who was married to a medicine man over at the village of Tishaniik, at Camp Creek.

Alvirius Ferris and Vid-ik-it

Vid-ik-it lived in that village for a while and then went to work, because she wasn't going to get married and there was no one to really support her. Her sister took care of the baby—my great-aunt Caroline—for her while she worked. In the mid-1850s, when Caroline was probably around three years old, Vid-ik-it went to work for a white miner named Alvirius Ferris who had a mining claim below where Orleans is now. Working for Ferris, she earned enough to feed herself, her sister, and her baby. Alvirius did not care for his first name and always went by A. Ferris or Mr. Ferris. He claimed river bar on both sides of the river as his mining claims and mined the gravel bar below the Karuk village of Panamniik, where the town of Orleans is located now. Later Ferris built a sawmill to supply timber for his mine, but at this time he just had the mining claims and had other miners working for him.

After Vid-ik-it had worked for him for some time, A. Ferris made arrangements with Vid-ik-it's brother-in-law, Peter Thom, to marry her. Her brother-in-law was the medicine man of the village she had been living in and was the man who had been looking out for her. The surviving dominant male of the family—father, uncle, or brother—negotiated marriages.

A. Ferris married her in the Indian way and paid three bags of gold dust and five mules for her, which was a really, really high bride price. This high bride price redeemed her in the eyes of the tribe because it proved that she was still valuable. In return, A. Ferris got Vid-ik-it and the use of about a hundred acres along the river as a mining claim. Then, when the preacher came around, he married them in the white man's way before she had Harry, her first son. By 1860 she was married to A. Ferris in both the white man's and Indian ways. They stayed together until she died, around 1884. Then he stayed with his grandchildren and children until he died, in 1920. He never moved from the Klamath River country once he got here.

Ferris Family Background

My great-grandfather A. Ferris was a farmer and a working man. He was six feet tall and weighed one hundred and eighty pounds. He looked like a worker, with centuries of hardworking farmer ancestors behind him, and he was a literate man who kept a daily journal for something like forty years. The Ferrises were country landowners in England as far back as the 1600s. They came here because of this vast new country and lived first in upper New York State, then in

Michigan, and finally came to California. There were six Ferris brothers. One stayed in Michigan and inherited the farm, like English people do; the oldest son inherits everything and the rest inherit nothing. So the brother that stayed inherited the little forty-acre ranch in Michigan and the other five Ferris brothers came west to California with the gold rush, via the Isthmus of Panama. Four of them married Indian women and ended up farming. The brothers probably did the same thing A. Ferris had done and negotiated marriages and land because they were more interested in land than in gold. One brother went to Utah and became a Mormon and was the only one to marry a white woman. The one brother who did not farm was killed in Los Angeles.

Around 1939 Grandpa went back to Michigan and looked over the family ranch. He said there was a little four-foot-high stone wall around it where they had cleared all the rocks from the fields and made a fence about a foot or two feet wide around the forty acres. I know Great-grandpa A. Ferris had a sister, because he said that the men would work in the fields all day long from before daylight, and every day around noon their sister would come out with a jug of milk and some bread and cheese. Grandpa said his father was very close-mouthed about his family. He would tell you little things like that and then nothing. He just didn't talk much. He said that supper in Michigan was a twelve-inch pie with meat, potatoes, carrots, and onions in it. The parents, the girl, and all six boys would cut nine slices out of the pie and that, with milk, would be supper. That's all they had. So when the boys heard about the gold rush they decided to come west.

Their ancestors had been colonists. They came to the New World before the revolution. Samuel Ulysses Ferris was in upper New York State by 1732, so they came across to New England sometime prior to that. Even after the Ferrises had been in this country for one hundred and fifty years, Alvirius Ferris still spoke English without the western inflection. His speech had a crisper sound to it and was grammatically correct, according to his son Frederick Ferris, who was my grandfather. They would say, "may I," not "can I." When Darrell would ask me if I could get him a cup of coffee, I would always joke, "I can, the question is, will I?"

I could be a Daughter of the American Revolution, but I don't think they used to let Indians do that. Maybe they do now. They accepted my daughter Beavi in the 1970s because she just gave them the name of her ancestor Samuel Ulysses Ferris, who married Anna Newhall in New York State in 1732. They looked it up and found him and gave her a partial scholarship to UCLA. She wrote a five-hundred-word essay and got a $500-a-year award from them.

A. Ferris used to say to his son, my grandfather Frederick Ferris, "I was a chuckle-headed fool. I walked over a thousand miles of bottomland and made a farm in Orleans, California." He was looking for gold, so he came to the Klamath River, but he ended up farming because he made more money selling food to miners than he did from mining. In those days farmers didn't pump water out of the river like they do today. They settled down and farmed along the creeks where there was water available for the farm.

Marriage Traditions

In the romantic story the woman marries a wonderful man, but that's not the way it happened in this story. For his part, Ferris was after the land and Vid-ik-it was a means of making this happen. For Vid-ik-it, A. Ferris gave her stature in her tribe by buying her at a high price. I think Vid-ik-it married A. Ferris because of her early experiences and she felt like he could protect her and her child, but from what I know about the life they had together, I don't think there was any big "love match," like they say: the Indian princess marries the wonderful man. I don't think so. Of course he loved the children that they had together. Most people love their children. It wouldn't matter if they were half-breeds or not, they're your children.

Indian marriage was just the opposite of the English dowry system. Among the Karuk, the women had a value and the men paid according to their value. And there was a loose class system. It's like they told me, it did not matter whether you were rich or poor, you could always dance and take part in the ceremonial dances. You don't have to have fancy clothes to dance; you could dance in your work clothes. If you were a girl and did not have a dress for the ceremonies, usually some rich person would loan you one. You could dance whether you were rich or poor, because even if you're poor now, you may become rich and move up into that higher class later in your life. Or the rich may become poor—like a fire could come and burn everything out and then you'd have nothing and would have to start over.

A person could be rich with regalia and regalia could be lost, but if you come from a family of headmen or medicine people, you don't lose that birthright. If your father was a headman and got old and wasn't rich anymore, you were still a headman's son or daughter and you still had that higher value on you. You still had that raising and that quality to you that you don't lose, no matter what happens. The only time you lost status was if you married below your class. Then you married for a pretty face. That's what I did [laughing]. Darrell and I actually married for romantic love like you find in the storybooks.

The male relatives of a woman negotiated a marriage price for her with the suitor's family. If they didn't like the man's family, or if they thought his family wasn't high enough quality, and was not their equal, or if a man was known for being mean to his women and they didn't like that, then they wouldn't care what price was offered, they would not agree on a marriage. They usually wouldn't sell their daughters to a man who would not treat them properly. Sometimes they did and sometimes they didn't, depending on the people and the situation.

But class wasn't the only consideration in marriage. A woman could be really poor and some man would take a fancy to her, fall in love with her, and even though she's poor his people would let them marry. They'd just agree that their children could marry. Like one of my grandmothers' friends' brother married a woman who sang a love song during the Brush Dance. The song told how she was a poor woman and she loved a man who came from a family of headmen. After she sang about her love for this man of a higher class, his family let them marry. They never had any children, but they married and stayed together their whole lives. So the high-class family would relent every once in a while, but mostly people married within their class.

Indian people on the river talked to and were friends, some-times close friends, with people from across the class lines. You were closely related to the families that lived in houses that faced toward your family's house and not so closely related to those families who lived in houses that faced away from your house. Most houses faced semi toward the river. That way it's easier to go bathe and to be able to look at the river and watch people and the fish come and go.

A. Ferris made the white people around here call his wife Mrs. Ferris. Behind her back they called her Wildcat. With some of her experiences in life, I imagine if she wasn't a fighter she wouldn't have lived. The whites always made up their own names for Indian people, and they called Vid-ik-it Mary as well as Wildcat. She gave birth to her son Harry and then she lost two daughters to whoop-ing cough and the childhood diseases that came with the miners. Vid-ik-it had probably caught these illnesses herself and survived, since most of the native people caught them.

When Grandpa was about ten or eleven years old, around 1880, A. Ferris built Vid-ik-it a two-story house that stood until the 1964 flood. This house was painted white and had a downstairs living room with two bedrooms upstairs and one bedroom downstairs. There was a great big kitchen, a dining area, and a storeroom. The girls stayed downstairs and the boys stayed in the bunkhouse and didn't move into the house. Vid-ik-it didn't like the house because it was too big. The rooms were too big and the ceiling was too high. It was so big that it scared her, so she moved into the store-room, sort of a root cellar at the end of the house off the kitchen, and lived there. You had to go outside to go into it. She wouldn't sleep in the bedroom because she wouldn't stay in the house at night. During the day she came into the house and cooked and worked in the kitchen. At night, or any time she wanted to rest or do something on her own, she went into her little storeroom. She never did stay in the big house like she was supposed to.

Even though Vid-ik-it would not live in the fancy house A. Ferris had built for her, it still disgruntled the white people around Orleans that an Indian woman had such a house to live in, on top of him making them call her Mrs. Ferris in front of him. They still called her Wildcat behind his back, because she was known to be ornery. She had good reason to be ornery. She didn't trust white people and she didn't like them. I guess half the time she didn't like her husband either, but she kept him in his place. And she made all her children get educated in the white man's way, even though she wasn't white. I guess she figured it was a white man's world and you might as well learn how to live in it, push your children into it, but she kept her own religion.

The Red Cap Wars

Grandma Nancy [the wife of Vid-i-kit's son Frederick Ferris] knew that she was born in August of 1873 but didn't know what day of August—they did know that she was born on a day the fish were running—and they chose August 15 for her birthday. When she was fourteen years old, Grandma and her brother Horace Evans Jr.—he was called Irish Evans because that is how his mother pronounced Horace—were picked up by the Army and taken to Fort Gaston, in Hoopa, where they were imprisoned with Georgia Henry and Daisy Jones and other Karuk medicine people. The Army charged them with inciting to riot, even though they were still just children in their teens. I was looking through the Bureau of Indian Affairs records for my children's Yurok heritage and ran across the story of my grandmother being in Fort Gaston when she was in her early teens. She wasn't yet a grown woman when they threw her in prison.

Because they were medicine people, they were telling what they saw and what they knew from their visions. When my grandpa told me about this, he said that they were medicine people and they were arrested because of what they knew, because they had the knowledge of medicine people.

The medicine people acted as the conscience of the tribe, the spiritual conscience of the tribe. They would tell people the way things are going and the way they should be, ideally. They wouldn't put you in a stockade because you didn't live up to the ideal [laughing]. They would tell people what they felt was the right thing to do, and the right way to be. They had a lot of influence, but what they said wasn't the law. The whites said the medicine people were instigating uprisings, but they were only trying to help people deal with the change of the world they lived in, and that ran counter to what the Europeans wanted. They could see things and they could see ahead and see where things were leading. They would have visions about what was going to happen. They would see all the sickness and the death, all the obstacles that were coming up. They were trying to get people to conform more to the old ways and not give in, not give up.

They were told they were being imprisoned for working against the government. Being medicine people, they spoke out on what they thought was detrimental to the people and told them that what was happening with the government wasn't right. They were just trying to help the people in their plight, commiserating with them and praying for them. Native people believed what they said because they were medicine people. They were really imprisoned for being too powerful in Karuk society.

I would find it very hard right now if somebody came and said, "Today you're going to think like an Arab. The Arabs have taken over and you're not going to be a Christian anymore. They will kill you if you are that way. You have to believe this way." I think all the Europeans that are over here would have a hard time with that one too. People get disheartened, everything is different. There is nothing to fall back on that is stable and true to your way of being before, and now your way of being is absolutely, totally turned around. So they threw them in prison and they killed some of them.

We knew that they were going to get rid of the Indians, and we already knew they were coming, and the Spaniards had been here for a couple of hundred years before, as far north as San Francisco and Santa Rosa. I don't care how isolated we look, the tribal people did move around and trade all the way out to the East Coast, and the East Coast traded all the way back to here. We knew which trail to take, and we are talking about people who could run forty miles a day at a dead trot. I am quite certain that they knew about white people being back on the East Coast. The Navajo knew about them, the Hopis knew about them—and they were down there in the desert and they had word of what was happening in Florida and Alabama. It was like a rumor. So for a long time they had had knowledge that these new people were changing things across the country. The native people were having to change and were having a hard time. As primitive as our mode of getting around was, a headman or a spiritual leader would think nothing of sending a runner as far as Portland, Oregon, to pick up something for him. So the headmen, the spiritual people, and the traders had inklings.

We didn't have real wars here, because when food was scarce, it was scarce for everybody. We didn't starve to death even though we got hungry. The early springtime was called a second winter. When the dogwoods bloomed, my mother-in-law would say it was the second winter, because the fish hadn't started running yet, and the deer were having their young, and you didn't kill the deer at that time, so it was a hungry time. The acorns that had been stored in the fall were getting low and it was a hungry time. You didn't eat as much but you didn't starve. No one was lying down and starving to death. I imagine that if the people next door were your relatives, you could go over and sit there and they would invite you to eat, because you never, ever, did not feed whoever came to see you. It was their way of proving that God would take care of you.

I think the fort was probably founded in the 1880s, because there was an Indian village at Kepel. They first wanted to build Fort Gaston in that area, about twenty-five or thirty miles inland from the ocean. The government raised hell with the Yurok. They wanted to get rid of the village at Kepel, so they killed every single person who lived in that village. I know a woman who is around ninety years old now whose mother was a little girl living in the village at Kepel, where her grandfather came from, and on this particular day they were visiting her mother's people in a village downriver. Everyone in the village was killed except her grandmother, her mother, and her grandfather. Her grandfather was a young man and he ran and dove into the river. He swam underwater until he reached the place where there was some willows growing and he could come up and just stick his nose out and breathe, but he wouldn't raise his head out of the water. They shot at the water when he was swimming, but then he disappeared and they walked along the bank looking for him. They never found him and he waited until dark and swam downriver a ways, got out and walked to the next village. So of that entire village, only four people survived. The same thing happened to my old friend Bessie Tripp's grandfather in the 1850s or 1860s. He had to jump in the Klamath River and swim underwater to avoid being shot by miners, and then hide out in the mountains for five years.

After the government had thrown Grandma Nancy and her brother into prison, it made them Hupa Indians. They were in prison in Fort Gaston for a couple of years and then they were designated as Hoopa Valley Indians by the government and assigned a quarter-acre of land in Hoopa with a couple of cows and some pigs. Some of the Hupa Indians killed cattle for them to eat, but other Hupa people didn't want them there and poisoned the animals the government had allotted them, so they left and came back upriver to the renegade camp downriver from Orleans, out someplace on Red Cap Creek. [This camp should not be confused with the village called Red Cap.] People were living in the camp who had run away from the prison, or they were hiding out there because they knew they were going to be taken to prison if the Army captured them. This was the hiding place that had been discovered by a Karuk medicine man named Rape-chien (like many Karuk names, this had no meaning as words but was chosen as a name because the sound was pleasant). He had had a vision of the coming invasion.[3]

The Karuk stayed in the renegade camp for another year, and Grandma Nancy had a baby boy while they were there. When Grandpa Ferris married Grandma, he gave the boy his name although he was not the father.

When the soldiers would come looking for the medicine people, of course none of the Indians knew anything about them. They never saw them. They didn't know where they were, and they obviously were not in their own camp. I don't know if the renegade camp was ever found by the Army.

When I was young, it was no longer there as a camp, so there would be no reason for me to go there. I knew about where it had been and kind of how it sat so that it was hard for the soldiers to find, but by the time I came along, the uprising was over and it had nothing to do with my training. They only tell you things you need to know. They didn't talk very much about the renegade camp—just little hints and stories, but not exactly where it was. We knew it was up on the north fork of Red Cap Creek someplace, but they didn't take you there. Being in that camp was better than being in Hoopa, but it wasn't quite like being at home.[4]

My grandmother's uncle Sandy Bar Bob was the main religious leader for the whole tribe, all the villages. He was the Siv-thom and he supported the renegade camp as much as he could. After that time there have been people who have some power, but they don't have as much power as the earlier medicine people had.

After the full-blood women were gone, there was no one there to step up in their place and answer certain questions. I can't go back and ask something. In the earlier days there would have been someone alive by the time I was thirty who had been trained and may have the answer to questions I had, and because there were different kinds of medicine women, they could answer different kinds of questions. Like Josephine Peters, who works with healing herbs and spiritual things, and I work only with spiritual things. I make the world a happy place, so evidently I work on the spirit. It's just another name for Indian psychologist [laughing].

Because the government thought Sandy Bar Bob and his people were supporting the Red Cap renegade camp, they moved the whole village of Red Cap, along with Sandy Bar Bob, up to Sandy Bar, closer to what is now Orleans but then was the village of Panamniik. Panamniik was the largest Karuk village and was at the center of our cultural area. The government couldn't prove that either he or Red Cap Tom, the old captain, were in the renegade camp, because no one ever gave them up, but they supported the renegades and had sympathy with them. The government never caught them supporting the renegades, but logically, Red Cap Tom and Sandy Bar Bob had to know what was going on, since they were tribal leaders.

The pack trains used to come over Mill Creek or up over Big Hill from Hoopa, and when they got over this way they would come down kind of where the road is now. Sandy Bar Bob attacked the pack train because the renegade camp was low on food. They didn't wear masks, because they would put on war paint and take off their clothes down to loincloths, and then one thin brown body, one Indian, looks just about like another. The lead mule fell off the trail and pulled the other mules with it down the hill, and there was flour down the bluff and down the canyon clear to Red Cap Creek. They didn't get any food and it became a big joke among the Indians how Sandy Bar Bob was trying to rescue these renegade Indians, but the mule fell off the trail and they didn't get anything. I don't think the people up at the renegade camp thought it was very funny, because they were still hungry.

Their leader was called Red Cap Tom because he had a red stocking cap that he pulled down over his ears, and he absolutely loved it. He wore it all the time. This reminds me of the story of Bessie Tripp's grandfather, who had a pair of red underwear that he loved and he wore them for clothes. When it was cold, he'd get all dressed up and put on his red underwear and go down to dip for salmon and steelhead at Ike's Falls. He wore this pair of red under-wear outside like clothes, and he thought they were just great. He liked the color and the warmth. If you had been walking around in a loincloth all your life, I imagine when you got older and went down there to dip where it's cold and windy all the time, a pair of long underwear would be pretty great. He was called New Paas, because that's how he referred to his new pants as his "new paas," because he couldn't pronounce "pants" clearly.

The government finally quit looking for the renegades and the Indians around here finally got back into their society and didn't get dragged back to Fort Gaston every time they slipped away from there.

The Karuk were like Mormons. A man would have as many

wives as he could afford. Sandy Bar Bob had a whole village full of wives—he had about twelve wives. They say he only lived with one of his wives. He had a bunch of children and one got killed working in the woods, building a bridge. The rest of them died of tuberculosis. His adopted son was the only one to live a long life, but most of the children lived to have children. Sandy Bar Bob claimed the children of all of his wives, whether they were his children or not. If it was his wife, it was his child.

Slaves in Indian Country

Then there are the slaves. They didn't have slaves like white people. Slaves were people who for some reason had gotten into bad circumstances, or they were really poor to begin with, or maybe their parents died or were killed by the white man, one never knows. But they wanted to get married and they wanted to have their family and start their life, but they didn't have any money to buy a wife. So if a man liked a woman and her family was agreeable and arrived at a bride price, the couple would sell themselves to a wealthy family and work for them for a period of years.

The period of slavery or indenture was whatever they negotiated. Everything was done by negotiation, so whatever the headman, the rich person, and the person who was negotiating to be a slave worked out was their agreement. Usually it was a few years, a year or two anyway. Then the person who bought you would pay the bride price to her family and you worked it off. Any children born during the time of servitude belonged to the rich man. Being a slave meant that you lived at the elder's village, and maybe he wanted help building another house for his new wife or his children. Or you would have to make nets for him, or you would have to fish for him; if he was older and couldn't fish like he did before, then you would have to go dipping for fish for him and tend to the fish you caught—whatever was needed, nothing special. Nothing that weighed on you. There was no stigma associated with being a slave like there was in this society, because it was a bargain that you had made. It was like you had taken a loan from someone and you were paying it back and the only way you had to pay it back was to work it off. It would be like being a sharecropper, but we called them slaves. No one was ever beaten or tortured, anyway. The worst thing we could do to someone was send them to Katamin to live. [Laughing] I guess that's sort of like sending them to paradise, because that's a sacred area with good fishing.

The slave owner may or may not claim the children of his slaves, it's up to him. If he wants to, he can keep that child born during the time of the parents' indenture. That's his child, or he can let them have their child. It depends; if he has enough children of his own, then he won't do that. But if he didn't have any children he could keep the slaves' child as his own and raise him as a rich child. As soon as the couple has worked for him for the agreed-to time, then they can go out and make their own life, build their own house and be in their own place.

That was one way of getting the money to advance in your own life. They sold themselves as slaves, but they weren't slaves like white people had slaves. Slaves were not captured and taken against their will. This went on up to close to 1920, when there were still people who did that in the villages. There were still Indian villages on the rivers in the teens and there were partial villages as late as the twenties.

Klamath River Country in the Late 1800s

My grandfather Frederick Ferris was born to Vid-ik-it and A. Ferris in October 1868, very late in the year for an Indian child to be born, because most Indian children were born in the late spring, when the weather was good and they would have time to grow strong before winter came.

My grandfather went to school in the summertime because the river was too high to go across in the winter and there was no bridge. He would have to work in the fields until it got dark when he came home from school. He and his older brother had to feed the horses and do all the chores. A. Ferris insisted that the Indian children in Orleans be allowed to go to school, full-bloods too if they wanted to, even though most of the full-bloods wouldn't let their children go to school. They didn't want them to be white, and I can see why. All the half-breed children in Orleans went to school, especially those that had a white father in their home. There weren't very many white women around in the early days following the gold rush.

In traditional Karuk society, men lived in one house and women and children in another, and men only came into the women's house to eat. The women had their own world. They lived in that world and the men didn't enter into it. The men had their own lives and were never there, so they weren't around the younger children and did not have much say over them. The mother and grandmother were there, taking care of the children. The children belonged to the man's family, and they were brought up by their mother and by their father's mother. The father's mother had a lot of say about how the children were raised. That was tradition, but I was raised by my mother's family. My grandmother and grandfather on my father's side were raising my first cousin; her mother had divorced and her grandparents were raising her. My grandpa Ferris in Orleans had a five-bedroom house and my other grandparents had a one-bedroom house with my cousin sleeping in the living room, so it made sense for me to be raised in the larger house.

I saw this pattern of divisions between men and women in my family, with my grandfather being the head of the family and my Uncle Alvie working with him. These two men discussed what they were going to do with the farm, with the apples, walnuts, the price of products here and there, and how they would divvy up the money, and how much Alvie would get for hauling things out because of the extra cost of transporting the farm products to sell them. They made their decisions on how the sharing was going to go before they would even start in. They never raised a crop and then decided on the details afterwards, because that would cause arguments. Everything was talked over beforehand, and Aunt Caroline had no say in it. She worked in the field with them, but she had no say about how the money her work earned would be spent.

Grandpa said that when he was a boy, every single day at daylight he had to get up and go bathe in the creek with his mother and take part in her religious practices. Rain, shine, snow, or otherwise, it did not matter. She ran over to the creek and bathed. Vid-ik-it never bathed in the river, she always bathed in the creek, but the river is kind of dangerous down by where she lived, so maybe that was why she bathed in the creek. After she had bathed, she threw water over her back and prayed. She looked to the east and talked. From what my grandfather told me, she was saying the same prayer every time, the same ritual prayer every day to the east.

When Europeans came to the Klamath River country, the Karuk were living in houses made of boards split from cedar trees because cedar was the easiest straight-splitting wood that was available to us and it resisted rotting. This is the same reason some graves were covered by cedar boards. The boards were split away from the down tree using stone mauls and wedges made of elk antler. We also would trade with the Yurok for their redwood canoes, which could be quite large and were even used for travel and fishing on the ocean. In order to shape the down redwood log, the insides were slowly burned down and then chipped out using stone adzes.

When the men got to be old, fifty or so, they could move in and live with one of their wives, usually their first wife. The children would be gone by then and he would move in with his wife because it was cold to go from that house to the sweathouse, and it was cold to walk out in the rain to go to bed in the men's house, so they stayed in the women's house and slept there with them.

Traditionally women wanted to have children after April and before September, like the deer. They were really apprehensive when children were born in December, because pneumonia was common in children who got bad colds. Babies are weak and the houses were cold, 50 or 60 degrees.

To build a house we dug a circular hole in the ground about four feet deep and ten feet across. Sometimes the houses were five-sided and the roofs of course corresponded to the shape of the house. Vertical posts buried in the ground were used to hold up the roof, which was laid out with a peak so the water would run off when it rained. The boards on the roof were left loose so you could move them to let in light and let out smoke, and when it rained you could move the board back into place.

In the center of the house was a fire pit with a little ladder so you could climb down to it, and boards holding the dirt back so the pit would not collapse. All the way around the inside of the house was a shelf about three feet wide. This shelf was used for storage of bedding and other things, but no one ever slept there. The part of the shelf near the cooking area was used to store things used for cooking. They all slept lower down, around the fire. The floor was made up of packed and tamped clay about a foot deep which could be swept and kept clean, so it was like having a pottery floor. These houses looked very much like our current dance pits.

In the past decades the Brush Dance has become a social event as well as a healing ceremony for a sick child. Before the white man came they would just lift the roof off a house and make Brush Dance medicine for the sick baby down in the fire pit of the house itself. I guess it got to be a little too much trouble and they just decided they would build the dance pit, and then they would take the baby to the pit instead of having the people come to the house for the ceremony. If the child was sick enough, they would still go back to the old way and take the ceremony to the house.

Outside the house was a second wall made of horizontal boards and separated from the inner wall. This was a place that wood could be stored for times when it got cold and rainy and you couldn't get out to gather firewood. In the winter they had deer hides hanging down the inside and outside doorways to help keep the house warm. Grandpa said they would stuff these areas just chockablock full of wood, like a beaver dam, stuffed tight. They picked up wood everyplace, all the time, wood from out in the woods and driftwood from the river. If they found a hollow tree, they would bring wood in from way out in the woods and stuff it in these hollow trees that were closer to the village so that when there was a break in the weather they could go out and drag that wood in. Then the government started putting in these little twelve-by-sixteen frame post-and-beam houses with sleeping lofts up under the eaves and the living area down below. The houses were set up off the ground, so then they started stuffing their wood under the house rather than between the two walls.

Sadie, my mother-in-law, told me that when she was about seven or eight years old she was staying with her grandmother, who lived in a traditional Indian house. She was sweeping the floor and moaning and complaining about how she had to do more work than her sisters because she was the oldest. Her grandmother laughed at her and told her, "When you grow up you will have two doors to throw your dirt out of, instead of just one, so you will have to work twice as hard!" This was very confusing to her because she couldn't figure out how a house could have two doors, but she said she found out, because when she grew up she lived in a frame house with a kitchen door [laughing] and a living room door, and she could sweep dirt out both doors.

Grandpa said it was really a hard life when you went to bed way after eleven o'clock at night, if it was summer, and got up at four-thirty in the morning, when it first got light. After my grandfather came home from school he worked in the fields until it got dark. Then he ate, and after eating he studied and then went to bed.[5]

He and his brothers and sisters went to school every day, like white children did. Usually the children were taken out of school to work, but Vid-ik-it wouldn't let his father do that to him. She wanted Grandpa to go to school and learn to read and write and do things that he wouldn't learn if he had not been in school, so she made sure his father didn't take the children out of school to work. He could only work their boys after school. But here is the paradox: he'd work the boys after school, and in the summertime he'd work them till dark, and when it became dark my grandfather wanted to come to his mother's cabin to study, but his mother wouldn't let him light a lamp. She told her children, "If the Creator meant you to have light at night, he'd have given you light all the time, as long as you need it. So you can't light a lamp here, you've got to go over to your father's cabin if you want to use a lamp." She worked from daylight to dark, and when it got dark she went to bed. If her children wanted to study after dark, they had to go over to their father's house.

So my grandpa would have to go and stay at his father's house at night to study before he went to bed, because his father would have a lighted lamp. He said he hated to stay at his father's house because it smelled so bad. The whites always talked about how Indians stunk. Grandpa said Indians always smelled like smoke, because they lived in little smoky houses and they always smelled like smoke, they didn't smell like anything but smoke. But he said, my God, it would burn your nose to walk into his father's house, because it smelled like sweat and feet. He said his dad bathed once a week, whether he needed it or not [laughing], usually on Saturday night, and then he would go to church the next morning. Grandpa said he just hated having to go over to his father's house, but he had to if he wanted to study.

After he was twelve years old, he didn't have to bathe and make medicine with his mother every morning anymore, but by then he was used to bathing every day so he went off by himself and bathed at another place on the creek.

All Different People

The Indians at Forks of Salmon and about halfway between Forks of Salmon and Sawyers Bar spoke a Karuk dialect. Further on up the north fork of the Salmon River they spoke the Shasta language. On the south fork of the Salmon River they spoke the Karuk dialect up to around Negro Creek, but after the invasion the Karuk claimed territory as far up as Methodist Creek because they had moved up there very rapidly when the whites came, in order to get away from the miners. Grandpa said there were villages up the Salmon River, but the people who lived there weren't your relatives, so it seems like the people who lived on the Klamath have bloodlines that are tighter with one another and the people who lived up the Salmon River are like another section of the same people. When the Karuk gave the White Deerskin Dance, the people from Forks of Salmon danced back and forth across the river at different villages, coming down to Katamin to take part in the White Deerskin Dance, and they brought their power down the river to the dance.

From what I gather of European society, they came over here to Karuk country after crossing this three-thousand-mile stretch of land that is ten thousand miles long, and they still expected us Native Americans to be one society. Even in this little tiny area around here, we have three different tribes that have totally different languages, and totally different viewpoints at times. Even though Europeans came from an area where there were many cultures, for some reason they thought the people of this gigantic United States, Canada, and South America were just one culture, that we had no differences.

We had similar beliefs and laws and similar points in our cultures, but we don't have the same perspective on everything. Up here in northern California, where we are, there are many cultures and many countries. Right here on the Klamath River, there were three major tribes, and fifteen or twenty miles away from the river there were the Modoc, and the Hupa on the Trinity River, and the Wintun. They weren't that far from each other, but they are all different cultures and we are all different people.

Even though we all have different regulations and ceremonies, the Hupa, Yurok, and the Karuk share some ceremonies, and the Tolowa over at Smith River used the same religious site out in Elk Valley as the Karuk, the Yurok, and the Hupa. We all went there for certain spiritual medicine powers because of the power places in Elk Valley. So if there is that much variety just in northern California, how much variety is there in the whole of the Americas? Even in the same tribe, between Orleans and Happy Camp and the Forks of Salmon, there are differences.

Grandpa said that before the white man came, Shasta territory started at Clear Creek, where we began the White Deerskin Dance ceremonies coming into the center of Karuk territory.

My mother-in-law told me the Karuk had had a village at Stawin, down at the mouth of the Klamath. Because the village was deserted when she was a little girl, she had felt sorry for the people who had lived in that village but were all dead. She was saying *awok*, meaning "I'm sorry," when they were near to where that village had been, and when her mother asked her why, she explained that she thought this was one of the villages in which everybody had gotten sick of diseases that came with the white men and died. Then her mother told her that this village was the place of the Karuk, only she called them "people from the holes in the ground," because we lived in caves in the time that we hid from the white men. No one was staying in that village at that particular time, but if, for example, someone wanted to come there and make a boat, they could come down and stay for six months or a year, gather seaweed and shells and trade with the Yurok, build their boat, and then go home up the river.

The big rock in the river on the other side of where Bluff Creek runs into the Klamath River was the boundary between the two tribes, according to the treaty forced on the Hupa, Karuk, and Yurok around 1850. Like the Yurok said when they went to court, "Congress never ratified it, but we lived by it." We lived up to it. We weren't killing whites, we weren't fighting. We just settled down and let the white people be. They should have honored their treaty, because we did.

The last Yurok village was at the foot of the hill where Bluff Creek comes out now. There was a long flat there. Quite a ways south from that was the last Karuk village. This was a native vegetable village, because they traded these plants with the Yurok. There were big flats there that grew large amounts of the Indian potatoes, brodiaea, and wild onions that the Karuk gathered and traded.

About the only thing all the tribes around here agree on is that the dams are killing the fish and killing the river. That's about it for agreement [laughing]. It's hard to know how to address this issue of the dams killing the river because we all have different attitudes and different thoughts on it. In actuality you just feel like throwing in your hat, letting it all go, and quit arguing and fighting about it and just let them have their ugly way, but…we are stubborn people, so we'll just keep on arguing and hassling and bickering about it. And when the river dies, we'll say, "We told you so."

Before the treaty with the U.S. government after the invasion, the Yurok had territory that was east of the boundary rock in the middle of the river. Following the treaty, the rock became the boundary designated by the government and marked the easternmost land of the Yurok on the river. Before that, Yurok territory went upriver to Bluff Creek and up on the flats, where the big onion flats were. The Yurok had territory on the river that was west of the rock, and they had a village at the base of Shelton Butte. Over the years and with floods, Bluff Creek has changed course and washed away a flat that used to be a Yurok village. That was their farthest east village. This was a fish camp that no one lived in because it was in the shadow of Shelton Butte and the sun never shone there during the winter. As far as my grandpa knew, that was as far west on the river as the Karuk went to fish and to put in weirs to catch fish.

Grandpa told me the story of a Yurok village destroyed by a group of Chinese miners who wanted to get rid of the village so they could mine there. They put something in the Indians' food and poisoned everyone who was in the village that day, except for one little boy and his grandmother, who lived. The boy's uncle was one of a group of five or six men who were out hunting while this took place, but when they came back and found out what had happened they killed all the Chinese miners who were responsible and threw them in the river. I don't know how many miners were killed, but since it was a small village and six men had been out hunting, the miners probably poisoned around fifteen people.

The boy's grandmother had not felt well that day, so her grandson was home taking care of her. Since she was sick she didn't eat much, and that's why she lived. Since she wasn't feeling well she probably didn't take much food and didn't feed the little boy very much either. Nobody said anything, and it didn't get much attention from the government because it was just a few dead Indians and Chinese. The Indians didn't say anything because they had retaliated and killed the miners. The Indians up here in Orleans and at Weitchpec knew about it, but they didn't say much, and the surviving Indians from that village didn't say anything because they knew they had murdered people themselves and would get in trouble if they called attention to the miners having murdered their relatives.

The surviving Yurok boy later worked as a bell boy on the mule train from the Korbel logging camp, and my relatives knew him as the little boy who had survived from that village, but nobody talked about it. At the time of the poisoning, since he was with his grandmother, he must've been over the age of three and younger than twelve. If he had been twelve or older he would've been out with the men, hunting. If he was between three and eight years old he would have been at home with his grandmother.

Our Karuk boundary to the north was probably in the area of Negro Creek, because the Bennett family has been there for a long time. There are still Indian families with white names living up that way who have been there since miners first came to this country—the Bennetts, the Grants, the McNeils, and the Georges. The McBrooms came from further up the north fork of the Salmon River, toward Sawyers Bar.

The government made a decree and drew a line that determined where each tribe's territory ended and another tribe's territory began. Some of those who had been living up by the border ended up being called Shasta and others were called Karuk by the government. When the government agent went to Greenville, just outside of Quartz Valley, it didn't matter whether you were Karuk or not, he wrote you down as being Shasta. Anyone living in Sawyers Bar, he was made Shasta. Down the river from Sawyers Bar, it didn't matter who you said you were, he wrote you down as being Karuk. In some cases full brothers and sisters were written down as Karuk and Shasta based on where they lived and not who they were. Grandpa said that around here they named everybody Karuk, and when they got down to around the boundary rock in the middle of the Klamath River the other side of Bluff Creek, then everybody became Yurok.

My grandfather said that since it was a governmental decree that he was Karuk, he would accept that. But since his grandfather's name was Po-ka-noc-tish-karuk, I would swear that his grandfather was probably Shasta, and that's why he said he would accept the government's decree. He never elaborated on this, but I surmised that Grandpa was part Shasta. I told that to Bessie Tripp once and she said, "I'm part Shasta." I told her that I thought she was full-blooded Karuk and she said no, she was part Shasta, but by governmental decree she was a full-blooded Karuk.

So that's how we got to be Shasta and Karuk and Yurok. If there had been a Hupa over here he would have become Karuk! It didn't matter what language you spoke or who you said you were; you were made a member of the tribe based on where you were living at that time. But then, the Indians had done the same thing for generations anyway. Every time a woman married a man and moved into his territory, she became part of that tribe.

When my friends and I went away to Indian school, the papers classified all of us as Northern California Klamath River Indians. We weren't listed as Shasta, Karuk, and Yurok. Even the Indians from the Scotts Valley were still called Klamath River Indians.

The Orcutt family that had been living in Orleans ran upriver about thirty miles, as far as Methodist Creek on the south fork of the Salmon River, to get away from the miners. By 1900 Karuk were moving upriver into the Happy Camp area to get away from the mining and the fighting downriver, because there wasn't as much gold upriver so there were fewer miners. Some Karuk went all the way out to Quartz Valley; others, like the Davis family, just stayed on where they had always lived and took the pressure. They came from Ti Bar and they stayed at Ti Bar. They didn't give a damn what the miners did, they were going to stay where they had always lived.

By the 1890s, forty years after the white man's invasion, the government had moved our territory on the map out to Quartz Valley, but that was actually an invasion of Shasta territory. The Shasta were more migratory and we were more settled as aboriginal peoples. The Karuk may have been in Happy Camp in earlier centuries, but not recently. I don't know if it's true or not, but anthropologists tell us that we were connected to the Klamath tribe within the last ten thousand years. According to the early maps the Karuk had pockets of people around New River and Forks of Salmon, and they did speak a different dialect of the Karuk language and some of their customs were different.

In the 1920s Karuk people were moving to Happy Camp because there was work there. By the 1940s there was work in the woods, logging, and in the sawmills around the town of Happy Camp. That went on for about thirty years, until around 1970, when the timber economy started dropping off. At one time Happy Camp had a movie house, three or four bars, three restaurants, and three grocery stores. It was a going little town. Then after the timber economy failed, people had to move even further out from where they had originally lived, so they moved into Yreka and up to Medford, Oregon, to get work. People were able to get work logging in Oregon up into the 1980s. The logging economy didn't fail there until the late eighties, when the mills started shutting down, but for a long time logging remained a viable way to make a living in Oregon after it had pretty much been shut down when California started getting more stringent in its environmental regulations.

In the days before roads, we traveled by foot on trails. The trails were always a hundred yards or so away from the creeks, and when we walked we followed the creek, but not down in the gulch. We walked above the slide points up to the top of the ridge and then walked along the ridge. These days it's thirty miles by road to Methodist Creek, which is upriver from Forks of Salmon, but if you went by the trail from here to Methodist Creek you would just follow the creek to the ridge and then drop down to Forks of Salmon or take the next creek and drop down to Methodist Creek, so even though you were on foot in those days, it was not so far from place to place as it is now, by road. You can make it from Forks of Salmon to Orleans packing a body in one day.

When I was a girl, in 1941, it took five hours to drive to Eureka from Orleans. Cars on these roads only went about twenty miles an hour, and the headlights were so dim that you could barely see in front of you at night, so you went really slow in the dark. Now you can drive that same distance in two hours. And there weren't that many cars. There were long stretches of road that if you had to walk, you could pretty well figure walking most of the day without having a car pass to pick you up.

Gold on the Klamath

Grandpa said that mostly the white people's diseases killed us. They didn't murder us as much as they killed us with their diseases. When tuberculosis came, whole families were gone. Almost all of the Sandy Bar village went that way. That's one thing that makes me doubt that aliens have ever landed on Earth, because if people from a foreign land have something that toxic about them, then aliens from another planet would probably be toxic to us and us likewise to them. If you're going to land on another planet [laughing], you would have to be ultra-careful and be well screened.

It really got bad around here after the miners settled in, around 1852, and it stayed bad for a long time. There is a story on the river of a Karuk man who found a nugget that was about six inches long and shaped like one of those old-fashioned grandmother clocks. He thought it was pretty and cleaned it up and sat it on a shelf in his house so people could see it and admire how pretty it was. He was proud of it. Then his friend told him, "That's the kind of rocks those white people are digging for." He said, "That's the kind they are all crazy about. You'd better not have that rock here, or they'll come kill you for it." He told him, "They're crazy about little bitty ones and you got this great big one you can hardly lift. You better get rid of it." Well, he thought about how much he liked that rock and hid it under his bedding for a while. Then pretty soon he took it back out, petted his yellow rock and took it out in the hills away from where he found it, dug a hole, and buried it so that he wouldn't get killed over that rock.

When Grandpa was a boy, in the 1870s, the miners were trying to run the Indians out of this country and killing off those who stayed. The killings continued off and on clear into the 1920s, when they were still murdering Indians up the Salmon River, which is more remote than the Klamath River country. The Indians of my great-grandparents' generation, who had lived through things in the 1800s, were always very apprehensive that the white people would start slaughtering them again. By the 1930s things were changing, but older Indians still had those memories. They still remembered the killings. I guess it's just like the blacks when they were real careful about what they said and did in front of white people. They never said what they really thought in front of a white person. They would only say it in front of themselves, each other. That's how it was for the older Indians around here.

Following her custom, Vid-ik-it and A. Ferris lived in separate houses. There were little cabins set next to each other and she lived with her children in her cabin and A. Ferris lived in his own cabin. He made wine and sold it to the miners and she didn't like that. When she would get angry at him she wouldn't understand English. She would stay in her cabin and not talk to him. She would cook for him, but she wouldn't talk to him. Grandpa used to think that was mean because it really hurt his father's feelings, but drinking was against her beliefs, so that was what she did. She believed that drinking was the downfall of the American Indian and she impressed that on my grandfather and he never drank, ever, because of her strict beliefs about the effects of drinking.

When she wasn't mad at A. Ferris she could understand and speak English very well, and she knew other languages besides Karuk because she was a headman's daughter. According to tradition she was taught basics of other languages so that when she was sold and married into another nation she would know how to basically survive until she learned their language. Eventually she would have to learn the other language fluently.

After my grandfather started school, he and his brother had to be rowed across the river every morning to get to the school in Orleans. They went to school in the summertime because in the winter the river was too high to row across. They started school around April and finished in October when the river got too high again. He said that some years he couldn't start school in April if the river was too high. If there was low water, then school would start whenever the teacher got here.

Grandpa talked about going to school with Elsie Pearch and Bill Tripp, who later married Bessie Tripp. Elsie lived on the other side of the river, around Pearch Creek, and was ferried across the river by a Karuk man called Redneck. I don't know what his real name was, but white people called him Redneck. Redneck watched everybody's boats in the winter when the water rose. In those days everybody needed their boats, and when the water came up he would move the boats so they didn't wash away. He always charged a dollar, a silver dollar to ferry someone across the river. Not a paper dollar, a silver dollar. You had to have a silver dollar to pay Redneck with, to go across the river.

Redneck got a silver dollar as ferryman because the Indian men played a game of standing on the sandbar below the bridge and skipping their silver dollars down the river. Before the white man came they had played this game with flat rocks, and they learned that silver dollars were weighted just perfect to be the best skipping stones ever, and they bet on who could skip their silver dollar the farthest. They would throw the white man's money and bet trade goods or whatever they valued. Those white people wondered why the Indians wanted that silver dollar, just that one silver dollar. Whatever it was, the Indians wanted a dollar for it, and that was like a day's wages at that time. A dollar was a lot to pay to come across the river, but the Indians were the only ones who had boats.

One summer day when he was about five years old and his brother was about twelve, my grandfather was coming home from school, and this meant he had to walk by the village to take a boat across to get home. All the young people were out of the village, like they always were. The women had gone out to gather and the men were out hunting and doing the other things they always did, so they were all gone, leaving the grandparents home with the children, who were around eight years old and younger.

By the time they were eight-year-olds, boys and girls were expected to go out and gather like everyone else and help with the work that needed to be done. The older children left the village with their parents, or more often with their uncles and aunts, because parents are too demanding on their children. The aunts and uncles could teach them easier without making them feel that they should be better than they are, so usually the uncles and aunts had the children with them. They kind of supervised them, and the grandmother would take care of the little children, three and under, down to the age of toddlers, who were taken care of by their mothers. The aunts and uncles wouldn't get upset if the child didn't learn right away. Parents expect children to be smarter than they are, because it's their child I guess.

It was about three-thirty in the afternoon, because my grandfather had just gotten out of school and his brother was already waiting for him down at the boat landing below the dance grounds, just downriver from town. The village houses were located below where the road is now and spread out along the river. Grandpa started to walk down the trail to the river to come home and saw white people burning the houses of the village and pushing the people back into the houses, trying to burn them up too.

He stood there and looked and was afraid to go on, because he looked just like those little children that were running around that they were trying to burn up. He looked just like them except he was dressed in white man's clothes. He was a half-breed, but he had black hair and brown eyes and brown skin, so he was afraid to go by them, afraid that they might grab him and try to burn him too. He stood there and looked at them and they kept burning more houses. The burners kept moving downriver. People got away and were taking their children and running back up through the oak trees to where the tribe's housing project is now. There were big oak trees there in those days. The white men didn't pay any attention to him, so he felt like it was okay and went on down to the boat landing, where his brother was growling at him because he hadn't come right away. They went home and told their father what had happened, and he went to town.

My grandfather said he didn't know what his father said or did, but that he was mad and went over to town. The white men were trying to run the Indians off from that village because they had found gold on the river bar just below there. But since A. Ferris owned most of that river bar by agreement with the Indians, I don't know how they were going to get the gold anyway, since he had mined that river bar back in the 1850s, right after he got here. After that the vein went too deep to make it profitable to bring the gold out.

There's still a vein of gold running out this way someplace, but it's too deep to go after. It was getting to be about two hundred feet deep at that time. I don't know anything about mines, but my great-grandfather, my grandfather, and my father were miners and I used to be half-owner of the old Steiner mine when I was a child. The mine wasn't worth anything at that time because the price of gold was too low, at thirty-two dollars an ounce, to make it worth mining. We had a hard time just coming up with a hundred dollars to maintain the mining claim. The later owners made good money with it in the 1960s and 1970s, when the price of gold was up, but Grandpa had sold it for me and my grandmother long before that.

There were lots of Chinese around here at that time. My grandfather could carry on a basic conversation and count to one hundred in Chinese. Bill Tripp and my grandfather could speak Chinese because they learned it when they were little kids. They were the same age and in the same grade of school. They used to run across the road from the school in Orleans and watch the Chinese mining along the river. About that time the Chinese would stop to eat, and my grandfather said they made the lightest steamed soda biscuits you could ever eat. He said he guessed he and Bill Tripp looked hungry and the miners would feed them, and after they had finished eating they would gamble, and that's how they learned all the numbers and how to understand their particular dialect of Chinese.

Grandpa said Bill Tripp was the first Karuk Indian to become non-Indian, because he was a one-eighth-blood. At that time if you were under a quarter Indian blood, you were no longer counted as

Indian by the BIA, and Bill Tripp was the first eighth-blood born in the Karuk tribe. So if he had lived until 1970, he would have become Indian again, because that was the year [laughing] the government recognized the Karuks' one-eighth-bloods as Indian. Bill and Bessie Tripp's daughter Ramona was nine-sixteenths Indian. She was one-half from her mother and one-sixteenth from her father. So Bill Tripp did what most of the Indians did. When you get way down there like that in blood percentage, you marry back into the Indians. It takes a lot of marrying back into the Indians to get the percentage of Indian blood way back up again. My husband, Darrell, is only a quarter more Indian than I am, and my children are only one-eighth over half, or five-eighths. If they married a full-blood their children would only be three-quarters. It's hard to get back.

From the 1850s through the 1920s, Indians were murdered on the Salmon River with no repercussions. I don't know if white people were killing white people over gold, but the Indians always got blamed for any white people who were killed on the rivers. Grandpa said that most of the full-blood Indians were pretty well gone from Orleans to more remote places further up the river, like Forks of Salmon and Methodist Creek on the south fork of the Salmon River, and up to Sawyers Bar on the north fork, and further out into Quartz Valley by 1880. But there were a lot of half-breed Indians down here in Orleans, and if one white person got killed anyplace in our territory, they'd say that we killed them and then come down and pick out five Indians that they would hang on the hanging tree, right in the middle of town, where the elementary school is now.

At that time this was Klamath County, not Humboldt County the way it is now. Klamath County was kind of where the Karuk territory was and it went bankrupt in the 1880s. You can't run a county on just one commodity, even if it is gold. Klamath County was small and its only commodity was gold. Klamath County just took in the Klamath and Salmon Rivers and ran down to the Yurok Reservation around Bluff Creek. That's all there was to it.

Grandpa said that one of the reasons we never got our reservation was because there were 368 mines in this area at that time, some of which were owned by people and companies from other countries, like England. I think the Bondo Mine was English-owned. They got the capital for some of the larger mines from those countries, not the United States. We didn't get our reservation in part because there were too many interests competing for the gold. They weren't going to give the Indians control over that much money.

The white miners left when the mining went down, and since it was the Depression, the only people around here were the people who were born and raised here, and that was mostly the Indians. They figure there were three to five thousand Indians on the river when the white people first got here, and it was decimated during my grandfather's early lifetime, between 1880 and 1920, when it dropped to about eight hundred full-bloods. Now there are only five or six full-bloods and everyone else is mixed, because we are a small tribe. It doesn't take much to whittle down a tribe of three to five thousand with sickness. As soon as the white people came, they started dying.

The Impact of Diseases

My grandfather said that they never tell the story of what really happened when the two races came into contact. What really happened was that the white immune system was immune to some things, and the Indian immune system was immune to other things, and when the two races met each other, the pure-bloods of each race couldn't live through it. The Indians had a particularly virulent pneumonia, so many of the white children died of pneumonia. The Indians didn't have many other diseases, but they did have pneumonia, and they survived it because their ancestors had been living with this particular illness and had developed resistance to the virus and knew how to doctor it, and their children could live through the crisis and survive. But the white children didn't have the resistance and it would kill them. Even though we had ways of treating it, pneumonia was the main killer, and it still is. It was treated with sweating, heat, and various herbs, including mountain balm. They made a syrup of boiled-down mountain balm roots and other herbs, and it was bad! Very bitter. The heat was very important too. The treatment was similar to the Brush Dance, when you put a covering over the sick baby and hold the flame overhead and get them sweating.

Grandpa said people talk about smallpox killing Indians, but it wasn't smallpox here, it was measles that killed us. There are around twenty-five hundred Karuk people now, but at one time it dropped down to around eight hundred, mostly as a result of death from disease brought in by the white people. Even chicken pox was fatal sometimes, but measles was deadly. A lot of the full-bloods would just die of chicken pox or measles. You didn't have to have smallpox or diphtheria to kill you. He said diphtheria killed everybody from both races, and in one generation we became a community of half-bloods because of the diseases that killed each of the separate races.

Of course the European diseases weren't really serious to the white race, but they were terribly serious for the Indians: by the time my grandparents were married, Orleans had become mostly a town of half-bloods. There were a few full-blood Indians left and the full-blood whites who ran the stores and the school and the church. About the only white people around here who survived and whose children weren't part Indian were some of the Solstroms and the Delaneys. Some of the full-blooded Indians, like the Orcutts, survived but the diseases really cut down the Indian population, with all the children dying. Before the invasion of Europeans, the Indians in this little valley lived in a closed community. Here the whites came into a small, isolated community and stayed, so the disease patterns were clear to the people who lived here, unlike where whites just traveled through, infected the native people, and moved on.

The Karuk tribe had historians who kept track of everyone's lineage and of historical things for hundreds and thousands of years. They could repeat verbatim the history of the tribe. My grandfather said that we got into trouble when the historians started dying.

They died in his lifetime or just before. They knew who you were related to and how the birthing houses were interlinked, so that inbreeding started happening when the historians weren't around to tell us who was related to who. Before that there was no inbreeding, because everyone knew who their relatives were. People knew their lineages and they were born in certain birthing houses of people they were related to. You might be living in some other village but you came back to your relatives' birthing house when the time came. For instance when my grandfather's mother, Vid-ik-it, was coming from the village of I-ees-i-rum downriver to the village of Chimakinee to give birth to her first child, the historians knew who was related to who by which birthing house a person had been born in, because the birthing houses belonged to specific families. It was noted in my family's oral history that my great-aunt Caroline Stone was born in McCash'es birthing house and not at the Chimakinee birthing house, because her mother could not make it all the way to Chimakinee. The Indians from various tribes in this area were sealed off in the north by the Oregon mountains, and running south from there and along the coast and over this way, they were all very closely related to one another. A doctor who was testing Indians' blood in this area told me that there was one blood type throughout the area that was essentially indistinguishable.

Manners, Morality, and Religion

Our entire history and sense of ethics and morals was taught to us in little stories. For instance, they told a story about a man who stole. He would steal things. He would just take things. He would see something pretty and bright that somebody had and take it. Or if someone had a nice piece of leather, some prize shell, or something else that he wanted, he would take it and keep it. He would take things like that and pretty soon, of course, the people he stole from would get insulted, so they would tell his family that he stole and he owes them this, and then the family would have to pay them. They would have to pay them more than the value of the object stolen, because of the insult of taking it.

If the stealing continued the family would get tired of it and the person would get kicked out of the village and couldn't go to another village because they wouldn't have him, as a thief. The only village you could go to was the open village up at Katamin. That was the only village that would accept all people, because it is the village at the center of the Karuk world, a dance village where ceremonies take place and a spiritual center. The Creator was supposed to heal them from this behavior, so that was the only place they could go. You couldn't go back to your family village, because they wouldn't have you, they would run you off, so if you lie or steal you'd have no place to go, have no family and have no home. That's the price you paid for doing things like that. That's part of the ethical training and everyone got that one. Since villages were so close and tight, a village with a hundred people was like having a hundred brothers and sisters, because you know them that well, you know every little thing about them. You know things about them that they don't know about themselves, because you don't see yourself as clearly as other people see you.

A person could be fined for what was considered an insult, any put-down or snobbishness, thinking you're too good for people or not behaving correctly. If you were from headman people or medicine people, you would get a bigger fine because we were supposed to act in accordance with our training and the higher standards that go with higher status. They expected you to live up to these higher standards, because they know you were trained in how to act, how to talk and how to move, how to hold your head. A person could spot the good girls and women who came from these families because they were well trained. They would expect you to pay for even the slightest insult from one of these families. Even a slight infraction of rules or saying something out of turn or saying a mean phrase to someone would result in a higher fine.

One of my sister-in-laws down the river says she never liked being from a high-level family, because in the white man's world, during the Depression, people had a lot of children and there wasn't much money to go around, and she said people just looked for something that you had done wrong so they could call you on it and get something out of it. That was her experience. Sometimes they wanted baskets for payment and sometimes they took money. When Darrell's cousin was shot, the shooter had to pay the family ten baskets for shooting him.[6] The headman negotiated the fine and the medicine man was in on it, and they would go back and forth between the families and talk. The injured parties or the one who did it were not the ones who talked, the negotiators were usually your uncles or your brothers or brother-in-laws.

Grandpa said the missionaries came to this country and started telling the Indian people about Christianity and all the wonderful things God did for them. The Indian people told them about all the things the Creator had done for us and all the wonderful things he did for us all the time, and the Christians told us it was devil worship and that all the things that we said the Creator had done for us just couldn't be so. But they expected us to believe that Jesus walked on water and a virgin had a baby. That one the Indians didn't believe...physically impossible. Even if she was a virgin when she got pregnant, she sure wasn't a virgin after he was born. There was no way you could get them to believe that one. [Laughing] That was the part they couldn't buy.

I really believe that there is only one Creator, and I worship the God I was raised with and that talks to me, guides me. Grandpa said the Creator was all of nature; all nature was a manifestation of the Creator, that was just natural. Then there's the white man God, and I kept worrying about it and asking about it when I was doing my medicine woman thing. Maybe people have just gotten so far away from things that they can't hear the voices, and so now they say that God is a man up there. The answer isn't in on that yet, either, but I prefer to think there is divine guidance in the voices I hear.

The Presbyterian church took over Hoopa, and the Episcopal church took up here eventually, and up in Somes Bar were the holy rollers. Then the Indian Shaker church came along and everybody started becoming Indian Shakers around 1900. Before that the Ghost Dance religion got clear to the Klamath River country. They would throw you in prison if you were a Ghost Dancer, because it connected all the Indians and they all started believing in the Ghost Dance. If they danced, they believed that the ghosts of the past would come back and bring back people to fight for you. They figured that was their last-ditch stand, their last chance. The Ghost Dance was brought into this tribe, and from what I gathered it looked more like a Plains Indian dance, where they stamp their feet and chant. The songs did not have the rhythm or the language of river songs. The Ghost Dance was a religious movement to bring back all our dead ancestors to help us fight off the Europeans. It did pass through here but didn't have a long-standing effect.

Like Bessie said, the white man made it so we could talk to God. Before the whites arrived, the medicine man talked to God for you, even for medicine people like me. The Indian doctor talked to God. They had their own prayers, but when it came down to taking care of someone, the medicine man talked to God for them. For example, Dick Gray was a respected man downriver. I don't know if he was the medicine man or if he was just the headman of that village, but he got sick and Darrell's mother, Sadie, said everyone was trying to treat him but they couldn't help him. Down there in Yurok country it would be the women who were praying for him and trying to help him, and Dick Gray said he wanted the man doctor from Orleans, so he got old Peter to go down and treat him. (Peter Thom was the one who got the money for Vid-ik-it because he was the dominant male watching out for her.) In this case Dick Gray paid him with five dentalium shells, each four inches long.

Grandmother Nancy Evans Ferris

Grandpa might have had some idea about how a white person was raised, because he was raised by a white man, A. Ferris, but my aunt Caroline and my mother both were raised by half-breeds. Their grandmother, my great-grandmother, was Iptapue, a full-blooded Karuk Indian that both my mother and I favor. Grandma Nancy had a white father, Henry Evans, but he was never around, so she had no idea how a white man raised his children. Henry Evans came here from some fancy English college to study Indian languages. He was an egghead I guess, because he spoke nine different languages. Judging from his photographs he was slightly built, a handsome and aesthetic-looking man. He had a bunch of Indian children with Iptapue that he half raised but didn't really claim and kind of ignored. Like A. Ferris, once he came to the Klamath River he never moved away, and he is buried in Orleans. His children were raised just like Indians, since they were raised by their Indian mother. So my grandma didn't have an inkling of how a white man raised a family.

My grandmother Nancy Evans Ferris was born in 1873 and was a doctor for Indian women and children all her life. She looked more like a dark white person than an Indian. She had fine features, fine hair, and long thin fingers. She looked aristocratic like her father, Henry Evans, that kind of aesthetic look. She was tall and slender, about five feet, seven inches, with a flat, angular body, long arms, and little slim feet. (When Grandpa built a house for her he built the drainboard in the kitchen to where it was up to my chest, and I'm five feet, four inches tall.) Grandma Nancy delivered babies and stayed with the mothers for about two weeks, until they were up and around and the baby was doing well, then she would come home. Auntie Caroline said she would wake up in the morning and her mother would have left sometime during the night and be away delivering a baby. She said Grandma left the children all the time to do her doctoring. She said she guessed it would be called child abuse now.

Grandma would leave and the children would just fend for themselves. Sometimes their father was there, and sometimes he was working. They cooked for themselves and cleaned house, took care of the ranch and went to school. It was a different day and age. It wasn't as if it was just one or two children doing the work, there were five or six children of different ages and they all had to do something. Auntie and her older brother Abner always cooked. She said her sister Hazel always did as little as possible and tried to get out of things. From her talking, I think her other brother Trumer was like that too, because she never talked about what he did. Probably the oldest boy and the oldest girl were held responsible for getting the work done.

Grandma was the kind of Indian doctor who treated her patients with medicine from the herbs she picked. She worked with the medicine man, who prescribed the dosage, and then she made the medicine. She never prescribed the dosage. She knew which plants to use, but the medicine man said how much of the plant was to be given. She gathered medicine and dried it in little bunches hanging from the lower branches of the walnut tree in the back of the house. I guess it didn't dry too fast there because beneath the walnut tree it is always kind of damp, but that is just my guess, because no one ever told me.

One thing I learned right away was if they didn't tell you, you don't ask if you are a child. Even if you're an adult, you don't ask, and if you're an adult and you ask the wrong question, the medicine people will not answer you. You have to ask the right question, and you can't be a child and expect answers to your questions. They didn't answer children very much. They would explain a little bit, kind of just over the top of it. It's a matter of the need to know. There would be no need for me as a child to know how to do Grandma's medicine, because I wasn't going to be an Indian doctor.

Grandma always got paid in food and never got money, ever. Auntie Caroline said she remembered when she was a little kid getting up in the morning and going out to wash her hands and face at the water tank. When she walked across the porch there would be a deer hanging from the rafters, or a salmon, or something else left for payment. She said she never knew who left it, but her mother always knew who had paid. It didn't make any difference whether they paid or not, she still took care of them.

There were all kinds of medicine people with different practices, and they would not give advice to people practicing other kinds of medicine. The Fatawanun's woman was another type of medicine woman, and the women who trained me were this type of medicine women.

If someone with pain wants a medicine woman to help them, they have to let go of it. People will tense up and hang on to pain when they need to relax and let it go. As soon as I sense that they have done that, it is like I just pull it into myself. Then I have that pain and they don't. It doesn't matter if they're white or Indian or Asian, all they have to do is believe that I can help them. Because I have treated some white women who lived with Indian men and believed in that concept. I would carry that pain as long as they would have felt it. That gave them a little more strength to deal with the inflammation or whatever sickness or injury was responsible for their pain. After being treated they could relax and rest and heal better.

The ability to heal was one of the Indian doctor's powers, and I don't have that particular gift. Other medicine women could hold their hands above the affected part of the patient's body and the patient would feel something like electricity. Then the medicine woman would brush her hands together and rid herself of the pain before doing another treatment. They would treat a patient for maybe an hour that way and pray during the treatment in a language that sounds like Christians speaking in tongues. Some of the more powerful medicine women have a gift of seeing inside the body, and it was like they had looked inside you with x-ray vision. For instance, when Darrell's gall bladder burst, his grandmother Aussie came down to our house and prayed for him. She finished praying and said, "There are rocks all over inside his belly."

Her daughter laughed and said, "Mom, we know that, he has a gallbladder."

Aussie said, "No, really, he has rocks inside his belly."

Two weeks later, when he was operated on, they found that his gallbladder had burst and the gallstones were all through his abdomen. Before cutting him open, the doctors and the X-rays didn't know what was wrong with him, but his grandmother did.

Vid-ik-it died in the 1880s. Grandpa said that she had been sick awhile, because she didn't get up and do things like she used to. He said she quit going over and bathing by the creek about six months before she died. He didn't know what killed her, but they wouldn't let her be buried in the white-man cemetery in Orleans. A. Ferris tried to bury her there and they wouldn't let him, so she was buried at the Ferris homeplace.

About four years after Vid-ik-it's death, both Grandpa and my great-aunt Caroline got married. She got married rather late in life, probably around thirty, to Mr. Ullathorne, an Englishman who lived at Ullathorne Creek, and they had two boys. Grandpa finished going to school when he was sixteen years old. The teacher told him he had learned everything he could teach him. He had gotten up to calculus and trigonometry and the teacher couldn't teach him any further, so he went to work for his father on the land. Like most farm children, he just worked for his room and keep. He worked sixteen hours a day in the summertime, and in the winter he worked ten hours a day, daylight to dark. As a teenager, after he had finished school and after his mother had died, he went out to the Scotts Valley and worked, haying for his uncle. He was born in 1868, so by the middle 1880s Karuk people were already settled out there, were well established and owned farmland. When the whites came into an area the Karuk would move out ahead of them, first to get away from the killing, and then later to find work.

Stories from My Grandfather Ferris

Grandpa Ferris married my grandmother Nancy Evans in 1888, when he was twenty and she was sixteen years old. They had seven children before she passed away, in 1938. Around 1888 the Allotment Act came into effect and in 1890 Grandpa went over to Eureka to get an allotment. They told him, "You're not an Indian, you're a half-breed. You can't get an allotment."

So he came home and told his dad, A. Ferris, "I can't get an allotment because I'm a half-breed."

His father said, "Well then, I guess you'd better go to Eureka and get yourself a homestead." Now he was going for a 160-acre homestead instead of an allotment, and he had picked out a place over here that was north of the Ruben allotment. He made the three-day trip to Eureka, down to Martin's Ferry, across the river and up over the top of the mountain, stayed overnight on top of Bald Hills, traveled down to Orick, stayed there overnight, then went on down to Eureka.

The next day, when he went to the Humboldt Bay Area Bureau of Land Management office to sign up for a homestead, they told him, "We can't give you a homestead, Mr. Ferris. You're a half-breed. You have to be white to get a homestead, and you're an Indian." He told them that he had already been denied an allotment because the government said he was a half-breed white, but now they tell him they can't help him because he is a half-breed Indian. He traveled the three-day trip back to Orleans and told his father that now he couldn't get a homestead because he's an Indian.

His father said, "Well, we'll see about that. We're going to town again tomorrow." So he and Grandpa make the same old three-day trip, over the top of the hill on the stage. They went on horseback to Martin's Ferry, then went over the hill on the stage to Eureka, and then got the stage back to Orick. (Sometimes they rode horses; sometimes they took a boat part of the way. I think it depended on how much they were bringing back with them. If they were bringing a lot of supplies back up the river they would take the boat, otherwise they probably went by horse, but they didn't ride clear to Eureka by horse. They caught the stage at Martin's Ferry and left the horses with the stable there. Then, coming back, you picked up your horses and paid the stable for taking care of them.)

So they went clear down to Eureka to talk with the agent down there again. He told them the same thing, that my grandfather was an Indian and he couldn't have a homestead. Old man Ferris tells them, "Well, he went to get an allotment, and they wouldn't give him one because he's white, and his Indian mother is dead,"—a half-breed could get an allotment if his full-blood mother was still alive—"so I'm here with him now and you're telling me he can't get a homestead because he's an Indian? I'm telling you I'm a white man, and he's my son, and you'd better give him a homestead. His mother was an Indian, but he can't get an allotment because she's dead, but I'm alive and you'd better give him a homestead. I'm telling you he's gotta be something, and it's gotta be white now, because I'm white." And that's how Grandpa got his 160-acre homestead.

When Grandpa was about eight years old, around 1876, something else happened that shows you the mindset of whites toward Indians at that time. Some horses had gotten away during the night and Grandpa went out to find and catch them where they had strayed back uphill into some grassland and open fields. He found the horses and lassoed one of them. Then he looped the rope around his hand, something his father had warned him never to do because of the danger. He was walking the horse back to down below here when a coiled-up rattlesnake buzzed and the horse bolted. When it bolted, the rope wrapped around his thumb and pulled it off. Just pulled it off. Grandpa said he walked back down to the house and his dad came up and got the horse, because it was still dragging the rope. His dad tended the horse first, and his mother put a poultice on his hand and stopped it from bleeding.

The next morning they got up and went on that same long trip downriver. They rode horseback down to Martin's Ferry, took the stage up to the top of the hill, stayed overnight at Orick, and finally got to Arcata. At that time Mad River still ran into Humboldt Bay, but the Mad was up and Humboldt Bay was up and the tide was in, so they couldn't get to Eureka because the road was covered with water, so they had to see a doctor in Arcata. When they got to the doctor and tried to get him to see their boy's thumb and do what he could—this is four days after it was pulled off—the doctor said no, he couldn't do it, he was leaving, and that he didn't have to take care of him anyway.

A. Ferris said, "You are going to take care of him."

The doctor said, "Well, I've gotta go to a fire first." And they had to wait there for five or six hours until he came back from looking at a fire before he would tend to that Indian kid's thumb. And if it wasn't for A. Ferris being a white man, they never would have tended to his thumb. So that was the attitude white people had.

Grandpa said they had to sew his thumb up the best they could. The doctor pulled the skin over the top, where his thumb had been, and stitched it together. It was his right hand, too. It gave him problems the rest of his life, not that he didn't build two or three houses and a whole bunch of barns, but it bothered him. I remember when he was an old man and had to repair fences, he had to get someone else to pull the wire, because he didn't have that thumb.

Captain Jack, the Modoc headman at the time of the Modoc uprising, was Grandpa's hero, and his favorite story was how Captain Jack's position as a headman was not understood by the whites and what that led to. That whole business with Captain Jack happened about three years before Grandpa was born. He would tell about how Captain Jack was up there in his stronghold and held off the U.S. Army and how they hung him afterwards, even though he had told them the absolute truth about his role. Captain Jack had advised the other Modoc Indians not to raid the ranchers, but they raided them anyway, despite his advice.

Captain Jack told the white people he couldn't stop the young men from raiding. He had advised them not to raid, but there was no way he could stop them. If they wanted to go on a raid they were free to do that. The only thing he could do was tell them that they shouldn't raid and explain to them why they shouldn't. If they went and did it anyway it wasn't his fault, he wasn't the instigator. The white people expected tribal leaders to be omnipotent or kinglike, and we have no kings, we only have headmen, who advise people and who people trust. They tell you, "This isn't the way it's done and it should be done this way." But then if you were headstrong and had settled on doing something, there was no authority to stop you, because the headman was not their boss. He was not their conscience. He was just there to help them out. If they did not listen to you, there was nothing the headman could do. Then they would have to live with what they did. But the white people expected the headman to be like a king, so they blamed Captain Jack, who was the headman, because the war chief wouldn't listen to him. The white people might understand a little bit better now, but they still make the chiefs more important than they were. They were respected people but they weren't the Creator.

Responsibility isn't with some tribal authority, responsibility is with yourself. You have a certain responsibility to yourself and what you do, and that is what you have to live with. Someone else can't impose their conscience and what they believe should be done on you, because in the end you have to live with it, not them. I don't think it's just Karuk. It's most of the native people in this country. Most of them have that kind of a government. You're not governed tightly. You're governed by your own moral self, not what someone else imposes on you. They teach you by example from the beginning. They tell you a story about what happened to someone. Someone did this, and this happened. Someone did that, and that happened. If you steal, no place will ever want you and no people will ever want you around, even your own people. That's what they always told me. You can't find a village to stay in if you lie. They don't want you around, because if you lie, you will steal. These lessons start when you are very young and are told these stories, and the consequences of what you do are made clear.

They always tell you from the beginning, life is good, it isn't easy. I don't care what happens, life in itself is good. It's just not easy, because of sickness and the other hard things that happen. It got harder when we had to put up with the judgments of another culture on ours. The judgment was that our way was wrong, not that our way was different. But we had to look at their way as being different and not wrong. Our way isn't wrong either, it's just different. The white people were the more judgmental of the two societies. They thought that the Indians were wrong and that they were right. Actually, in life nobody is really wrong or really right, as far as I can see. It's just their way. It might not be your way, but it's their way. It's their way of leading their life. You can't change that. Even if it's your child, you can't change it. You have to just let them go their own way and find their own life and pay their own consequences.

The white man's way has put a lot more temptations in front

of us. Because they're always telling us we are wrong and we're no good, they give Indians a bad viewpoint of themselves and that makes it easier to pick the wrong path, taking dope and drinking and beating women.

Grandpa saw Orleans become a town of half-breeds as a result of two races meeting, two civilizations coming together. The Forest Service wasn't here yet. My grandfather had his homestead and his wife got her home and they started building up their lives together.

My aunt Caroline said Grandpa built the ugliest little house she ever saw. It was made from secondhand lumber and there were two rooms in the front about twelve feet wide and probably twenty-five or thirty feet long. A stairway went up outside to a loft upstairs, where the boys slept. It was like a story and a half high. Then behind that there's another twelve-foot by twelve-foot section flattened out along the hillside that is going up at about an 8 percent grade. This flat became my grandparents' bedroom. After my aunt Caroline was born Grandpa built another twelve-foot by twelve-foot room, for her, onto the house. She said this house was like little twelve-foot stairsteps going up the hill. Later, around 1910, he dug another flat step into the hillside and built another room for their other daughters. The girls had to walk through his bedroom to get to theirs.

Grandpa was more of a dreamer than Grandma. He loved machines. Any new machine that came out, he just had to have. He even bought a car and learned how to drive. He had a drag saw and eventually ran a sawmill. Then he got a small generator. He always wanted to have enough money so he could put electricity in his house, but he never got there. He always had something else come up that used the money. He did have a little Pelton wheel powered by water that he connected to a generator, and he used that to charge up people's discharged automobile batteries for a little cash. With his Pelton wheel generator he could only power an electric light in a little shed, but he had an inside bathroom way before anyone else around here did. He also had a bathtub so early that it was carved from a tree.

Grandma made the children wash their teeth using a little rag with salt and soda on it, but they couldn't spit in the sink, because she thought it was dirty to do that. Auntie said they still had to go outside to clean their teeth because Grandma wouldn't let them use the sink in the kitchen and there was no sink in the bathroom, which was built onto the outside of the house—only a bathtub and toilet, so they had to go outside to wash up. To reach the bathroom you walked out the kitchen door and across the backyard.

There was no sink with running water for the children, but there was water running all the way down the hill to the barn with a faucet for the horses.

If you're a farmer I guess you think of your animals before anything else. The barn was probably as tight as the children's loft bedroom was. Even in 1950 most downriver houses still didn't have bathrooms. Many houses didn't have them until the 1970s. Some houses had nice flush toilets outside. That's how Grandpa started, with his flush toilet outside, then he got it closer to the house and finally indoors as he got older. Like Bessie said, [laughing] "Who goes to the bathroom inside their house?" Looking at it that way would make a difference. In 1976 they moved the bathroom inside an upstairs room and I could smell it downstairs, because now the bathroom was connected to the house. I put a sign up there for my boys that said, "My aim is to keep this bathroom clean, and your aim will help."[7]

Around 1880 my grandfather's brother Harry became sheriff of Klamath County and married a half-blood downriver Indian woman. My grandfather thought becoming a sheriff was the worst treachery and most traitorous thing his brother could have possibly done. He thought it was just terrible that his brother would be a sheriff. He never explained why, but he was just disgusted that his brother would be a sheriff. I never saw my grandfather disobey the law. He lived by all the laws, except for poaching and fishing. But then, he always said that he had the right to fish and hunt and he never gave up these rights. The white man took everything away, but my grandfather never gave up his rights to hunt and fish, and the Klamath River country was still his country. He always felt that he should have the right to hunt and fish on the Klamath River and not have to buy a fishing license, because this is where he came from, but if he left the river to go down by the ocean to fish, he thought it was reasonable for him to buy a fishing license, because that wasn't his country. The whites took control of this country away from us, but they don't own it.

My great-uncle Irish Evans, the son of Henry Evans, the Welsh linguist, was the medicine man in 1912. Sometime before I was born, in the late twenties or the early thirties, a group of men were drinking over by the dance hall near the school and Irish got hit over the head and thrown in the river and drowned. Nothing was ever done about it because it was only the Indians who knew he had been murdered. According to his great-niece, he was fooling around with someone's woman. He was always doing things like that. He was a medicine man, but he was really good-looking and he fooled around a lot. Grandma had a lot of nieces she talked about and I couldn't figure out who the nieces were until I realized they had to be Irish Evans's daughters, because her sisters all married one single man and had that man's children. Those were Grandma's legitimate nieces and nephews, and they were the first family. The others all had to be on the other side of the blanket, the second family, as they always called it. At the time he was killed, he was studying to be a physician, a white-man-style doctor.

I was talking to someone a few years older than me about it and he laughed and said, "Yeah, the second families really throw you." They have the first family, and the wife is a highbred Indian, and the couple stays with those children and claims them. Then the man has his second family and kind of ignores these children. The second wife may or may not be highbred, but the children and the wife don't get full recognition because they're the second family. I still don't know who all the children were from the second family. Grandma had a lot of nieces and her family was prone to girls.

I did not inherit any of Henry Evans's linguistic abilities, believe me. I couldn't even speak Karuk. Grandpa sent me down to stay with Daisy Jones and learn to speak the Karuk language, but I never learned it. I came back and Grandpa said, "You sound like a white person talking Indian." So I was no linguist and that was the end of my Karuk language lessons.

Grandpa leased the hotel in Orleans from F. W. Gent and ran it from 1890 to around 1896. The hotel was a story-and-a-half building and there was mostly just a big room upstairs with little cubicles, sort of like doctors' examination rooms, that people stayed in. The family lived downstairs, where the hotel dining room was located. After Grandpa remodeled the hotel they turned the upstairs into a series of small rooms with real walls and doors, and this is what they rented out. Abner, the oldest boy, was around fourteen years old at the time, and he stayed over here on this side of the river with his younger brother Trumer, taking care of the ranch. His parents would come over and bring food and check on him, and he and his younger brother would visit them and go to school in Orleans. The boys stayed at the ranch all the time and the younger children stayed in the hotel with their parents.

My grandmother Nancy Evans Ferris couldn't read or write. She could sign her name and later she learned how to add and subtract, but that came from working with money in the hotel. Grandma could handle money better than Grandpa ever could.

Around 1896 Grandpa went back to work in the gold mines around here. These were hydraulic mines and he operated one of the giant nozzles that were used to wash away the hills and get to the gold. He became a nozzle operator because he was a lot bigger than most Indians were at that time. Whenever Grandpa would start to gain weight and get up to 185 pounds he would drink acorn water for three days and drop back down to 180 pounds. Before the white people came, the Indian men always kept themselves really thin. When he was working the nozzle, Grandpa wrapped his feet in rags to sop up some of the water that would get into his boots. Auntie said that she just hated that Grandpa had these little wet muddy rags hanging on the hot-water pipes to dry behind the stove, all the time he worked as a miner.

Aunt Caroline's Childhood

When Auntie started school, they asked her what her parents' name was. She didn't know: "I was five years old, and I didn't know my parents' name." They said, "Well, what do you call them?" Auntie said, "Mamma and Papa." They just looked at her and said, "You have no idea what your last name is?" She said she knew what her brother and sister's names were. She told them her older brother and younger sister's names and then they realized she was a Ferris. Her parents' names were Frederick and Nancy Ferris, but no one had ever told her that.

Then they asked her how much Indian she was and she said she didn't know. They said, "Well, how much Indian is your mother?" She said half. Then they asked, "How much Indian is your father?" She said half. The woman at the school said, "Well, you're full-blooded. You're half-and-half, and half-and-half is full." The woman was serious and just did not know how to calculate blood degrees.

My aunt said she looked at the woman for a long time and knew that what she had said wasn't quite right and kept thinking, "Well, where did the other half go?" She said that in her mind she knew that something was wrong, but she didn't say anything. She just let it go. She always remembered that she was so dumb she didn't know what her parents' name was. She had never thought of asking them who they were. Well, if you just stay over here on a little ranch by yourself, who's going to tell you that? I guess she lived a very secluded life. Her mother stayed at the hotel before my aunt was born, but by the time she was going to school, they were back over here on the ranch, so that was all she knew about. And what was over here? There were her first cousins and her grandpa down the hill on the other side and that's all, and nobody would be coming by and saying "Mr. Ferris." So this was a very isolated life for a young person.

Children did not speak up to adults, especially adults who were authorities, like parents or teachers. As late as the 1950s, children did not answer back to adults. They might think something but they would not say anything or answer back. We were taught to be very reticent.

As a little girl Aunt Caroline started school in Orleans and stayed with one of the teachers so she wouldn't have to be rowed across the river when it was too high to cross, and she got into trouble with her mother for not being polite. She was over across the river, on the Orleans side, with her girlfriends, and she walked by Uncle Peter, old Peter Thom, the medicine man. It was early in the year, maybe February or March, and he was sitting naked in the sun flaking arrowheads, just wearing a little loincloth with his *uffup* [rear end] hanging out and the loincloth barely covering his private parts. She didn't speak to him. She didn't walk over and say, "Hello, Uncle, how are you?" He was her father's aunt's husband, the man who had been responsible for taking care of Vid-ik-it and who was paid her bride price.

Before long her mother came across the river in a canoe and took her home. She was in all kinds of trouble because she hadn't spoken to Uncle Peter and asked him how he was. My aunt said, "Well, my cousin Viola didn't go over and talk to him."

My grandmother said, "I don't care what anyone else does or says or anything. He's your uncle Peter, and if you see him, you have to walk over and say, 'Hello, Uncle Peter. How are you? I'm Caroline.' Tell them who you are and everything. Even if he knows who you are, you're supposed to tell him, 'Hello, Uncle Peter, this is Caroline,' so he'll know which one is speaking to him, because he doesn't see too well. That's the polite thing to do, and I expect you to be polite, and until you can be polite you're going to have to ride across the river every day. You can't stay with that teacher if you're going to start putting on airs and thinking that you're better than your relatives." Auntie said she would swear that Uncle Peter had got in his boat and went right over and told her mother when she hadn't spoken to him. He had such powers that he probably told her what was on his mind telepathically without having to get in his boat and go to where she was.

Around this time, Aunt Caroline said—she was just a little girl, about eight years old—she and her older brother Abner were home at the ranch when a stranger came over the hill on the trail and stopped at the house because it was too late to go across the river. It was getting dark and she and Abner were home alone. She said they were just eating mush, or fry bread, or a can of fruit, whatever they had around, because they were just children and they didn't really have anything to feed him. She and her brother talked about it and said they didn't know what to feed him or how to fix it, but they had some bacon. Abner said to get some of the seed potatoes and they boiled them up and made bacon and gravy for him.

When their dad came over the next day they were afraid they were going to get into trouble for using the seed potatoes, but they didn't get into trouble for it, because you fed everybody that came to your house, don't care what. You offered everybody something to eat. Even if you didn't have anything to eat, you found something to offer them. If it's the last thing in your cupboard, you're supposed to give it to them, because it's your way of showing faith that tomorrow God will give it back to you. They always told me that when you trust in the Creator, if you give the last thing you have to eat, he would give it back to you, so that was your trust. I don't know if it's exactly true or not, but I've never starved. Actually, I've rarely been hungry, other than having to adjust to a different lifestyle after I married into a Yurok family.

That still is our custom; if someone visits you, offer them food and something to drink, and it is an insult if it is not taken. Even if you know that they have hardly anything in their cupboard, you're still supposed to eat it when it is offered.[8]

In 1896, while Grandpa was working as a nozzle man and mining up around Windy Point and her mother was cooking at the mine, my aunt Caroline and her two older brothers went to school in Somes Bar.

Auntie said her brothers would get to galloping down the trail and run away from her on the way to school, leaving her behind on her own. Some days the trail would end at Windy Point and there would be a five-hundred-foot drop, straight to the river, when the hillside caved off. The boys were supposed to be helping her down the trail, but being twelve and thirteen years old, they would just take off and leave her behind. When this happened, she had to jump to place her feet where theirs had been, because their steps were longer than hers, but she knew that these were safe places to step. She remembered putting her face into the dirt of the cliff so she wouldn't look down and get dizzy while she was trying to jump over to where their footprints were.

When Aunt Caroline was six or seven years old, around 1898, she was the pure young girl who walked ahead of the medicine man and purified the ceremonial grounds at Camp Creek for him. Her uncle Peter was the medicine man, and she said she could hear him walking behind her. She walked across the grounds ahead of the medicine man and then put her head down and stood there while he spoke the prayers, making the medicine behind her. She said she didn't like it because she just wore a little decorated apron that had no back to it, so her little *uffup* was sticking out behind when she was walking along. She wouldn't have anything behind her because little boys and girls that age, six or eight years old, still just ran naked.[9]

I hadn't known that Aunt Caroline had been the medicine girl for the Jump Dance until Bessie told me around 1970. Aunt Caroline was in the hospital after having a series of strokes and Bessie was there, I think with pneumonia. It was in the late fall or wintertime. Bessie was telling me how pretty my aunt Caroline looked in the Jump Dance, and how she wore a little white-man pink-and-white-striped dress to the dance. Bessie was bemoaning the fact that my aunt Caroline looked so old, now that she was in her late seventies.[10]

Camp Creek had that name because people would come from all over to camp there and watch the medicine man make the Boat Dance medicine. Aunt Caroline said the medicine man would be down at the river and it would be just dusk-like, and these young girls in their teens would get in the boat. The medicine man's helper would give the boat a push and nobody would paddle, and the boat went up the river by itself. What I heard was that the medicine man had the boat pushed out just where the earth tips and the water would run back upriver for a while. The medicine man and his helper would follow behind the girls in a second boat, and a man in the boat with a torch would call out for everyone to close their eyes because the medicine man was coming. They covered their eyes and didn't talk, because the medicine man had just finished walking and talking with the Creator, and if you looked on him they believed you would die. Of course, no one ever sees the medicine man, or admits to seeing him. I mean, he could stand here and talk to you [laughing], and you didn't see him.

Even though Auntie and her brothers had been going to school in Somes Bar, one day the Indian agent came up from Hoopa to the mine where Grandpa was working and told Grandpa that he was taking his children and was going to put them in the Indian school over in Hoopa. My grandpa told the agent he wasn't going to let him do this. "My children go to school. I send them to school, I support them. My wife and I support our children. We work here. We take care of our children and there is no reason for you to take them away from us."

The BIA agent left and came back about three days later with the sheriff and took away all the children, even the baby, who was only about eighteen months old and still just wearing a little dress. Five of my grandparents' seven children were taken away to school in Hoopa. Grandpa always said my Uncle Roddy was a silly person with poor judgment. That may have something to do with his not yet being two years old when he was taken away from his parents. They took the children to Hoopa and put them in the Indian school there and Grandpa couldn't do anything about it. He said that the Indian agency had never supported his family. They never gave them a pair of shoes, a blanket, any food, nothing. So he couldn't see why they had the right to do that, to take away his children, but he and Grandma couldn't get them back.

To visit them from Orleans took a day's travel on horseback, so when she went to see them my grandmother would stay for a week before coming home. At the Indian school they wouldn't let the students use any Indian words. They would slap their hands and the children would get into trouble if they said anything in Indian. Auntie said the McCovey children from downriver were going to school there, too. She remembered them because one of the McCovey children was a baby, only about six months old. I think his mother was dead. His two sisters were probably in their teens and they took care of the baby at night and the school matrons took care of him in the daytime. She couldn't take care of her baby brother, Rodrick, though. He was kept in a nursery and she could just get to see and talk to him once in a while.

When the BIA came and took his children away, Grandpa said some white people were surprised that he was Indian. They had not thought Grandpa was Indian, because he could do business as well as they could. His father, Alvirius Ferris, had been white and had been a businessman before him and had run a mill, run a mine, run a farm and sold produce to the mining companies. Alvirius made more money selling food to the miners than he ever made digging for gold. Grandpa said there was no way you could miss his being an Indian if you looked at him, other than that he was a little taller and he did well in business and made money. By the time he was forty-five he retired from the mines and the hotel to be a gentleman farmer.

Grandpa was broad-shouldered and quite strong. He was still lifting hundred-pound sacks when he was in his late seventies. The last time I saw him plowing he was about seventy-five years old and he was plowing one of the fields up above the house. He was stopping quite a bit, but he had just a single plow with one horse pulling it, and he was lifting it around at the end of the rows, so he was still pretty strong. They were a strong and hardworking people, coming from three hundred years of farming stock.

Basically, my grandparents did not get their children back for ten years. In that time they only had them in the summertime, because the Indian agency had them all winter long every year. Auntie was trained to be a nurse at Chemawa and they had her working in the tubercular ward, taking care of people with TB. She remembered that her mother had made her and her sister pretty little red linsey-woolsey dresses out of wool and rayon material, and the matron would not let them wear them because they were inappropriate. When Aunt Caroline was sixteen years old she developed rheumatoid arthritis and her knees swelled up from working in the cold on concrete floors in the basement where their tubercular patients were kept. Wasn't that a place to keep them? I thought TB patients were supposed to have fresh air, but she said they were kept in the basement. When she developed arthritis her mother came for her. Her sister, my aunt Hazel, threw such a fit that they got to bring her home, too.

Auntie said the suck doctor worked on her knees when she came back from Chemawa with rheumatoid arthritis, around 1906. She said this suck doctor would put her mouth above the part of the body to be treated and move back and forth without ever touching you with her mouth, and then she would throw up some yellow stuff, and then go back and work on the patient again. Auntie said the treatment made her knee feel hotter than it had been. Even though that suck doctor never touched her, she could feel something coming from the doctor and going onto her skin. So I think it was the same sensation that I got later from Darrell's grandmother doctoring me with her hands, around 1970, but this woman did it with her mouth. When Darrell's grandmother would clap her hands together or the sucking doctor would throw up, they were getting rid of what was infecting you.

The sucking doctor told Auntie that her knee would be better following the treatment, but that the rheumatoid arthritis would bother her all of her life. The suck doctor told her that before her knee or wrists swelled, to wrap it with an elastic bandage. Auntie worked with her hands all the time, but there were some things she just couldn't do. She couldn't open jars and she couldn't hang up laundry, so Grandpa and I hung it out for her, and if it started to rain we would move it onto the drying porch off the back of the house for her and then move it into the house to finish drying.

When Auntie came home from school in 1906, her parents were

running the hotel again, so she and Aunt Hazel worked there as waitresses and helped cook. The boys, Trumer and Rodrick, were running the ranch across the river. She had two older brothers. Abner was a good football player and he went to Carlisle Indian School, where he studied business after he had finished school in Hoopa. By the time he finished at Carlisle the 1906 earthquake had taken place, and by 1912 Grandpa was running a boardinghouse in San Francisco, taking advantage of the opportunities that the earthquake had opened up, so Abner went to San Francisco, where he worked as a bookkeeper. I've seen pictures of him and he was a big man, six foot-one or two, and two hundred pounds, but he worked as a bookkeeper. I think Abner had married a white woman down in San Francisco, and he, his wife, and their daughter died there of influenza in 1918.

My uncle Trumer came home after he had finished school in Hoopa and helped his father on the ranch. When he was twenty years old he was killed working in the woods in Forks of Salmon. He had only been doing that work for about six months when he was killed, in 1909. A log jumped over the log chute and killed him, because he was new at working in the woods and the more experienced loggers had put him in the place where logs jumped, rather than above it, where he should have been. My mother was born the same day that he was killed. They packed him all the way over the hill from Forks of Salmon, but my grandmother couldn't go to the funeral because she had just given birth to my mother. Trumer was killed in July so they buried him immediately. Hard life.

Everybody lived this hard life. You had to walk a lot, and hard work was the only way to make a living, and with all that hard work you never had much money. If you could work hard enough to keep yourself fed you were doing all right. It took a lot of work to make enough food to keep a family. They raised cattle and pigs and chickens and had horses. They had to have horses to help them do the fields, and you had to find fields and plow them. You had to raise your own grain and corn to feed the animals. You couldn't just go to the store and buy something. They didn't even bring that kind of stuff in here. They brought in flour in barrels, then sold it by the pound.

My grandfather spent lots of time talking to me about life, and about life on the river, and he wanted me to pass it on. Of course he was working all the time, because he worked constantly. He told me to remember one thing: that of all the things you can do in life, the greatest thing that you will ever do is have a family and raise it well. With the rest of the things, you can do anything you want to do and be anything you want to be if you want it bad enough, but the one thing that really matters is your family. I had my grandfather and my aunt to finish raising me after my parents were killed. Their raising me as an only child somehow influenced me to value having a family, and I did not want what I saw a lot of other people valuing. I'd rather do with less money and not have so many creature comforts and have a simpler life. I didn't want to join the rat race.

My grandfather had ten or twelve ledgers and about forty little journals that were about an inch or an inch and a half thick, but small enough that they could fit in your jacket pocket. He would write in these journals anytime. When he was haying or doing other work, he would stop working if he thought of something and write a few sentences about something he remembered. But they were all destroyed, along with around four thousand family photographs, when my house burned in 1998. He didn't tell me I should write a book, but he did say that he thought someone should write a book about what happened to the Karuk Indians. He never told me I should do anything. He said I should do what I liked doing or wanted to do and never work just for money, never do anything just for money. Do something because you want to do it, and if you make money at it that's good, and if you don't, well, that's okay too, because you like doing it. I have tended to carry out my life as he suggested.

Aunt Caroline's Gifts

My aunt Caroline picked up her medicine to become a doctor one summer when she was home from school in Hoopa. This was around 1908. She stayed in a sweat lodge outside Camp Creek, near the dance grounds at Tishaniik, and didn't eat solid food for ten days. Then she went to Doctor Rock and danced day and night for three days by herself. For these three days her medicine-woman helper stayed camped down below her and sang and prayed while my aunt made medicine. When she would hear Auntie start to sing and pray, then she would start her own singing and dancing and she would go up to Auntie's camp and keep her fire going. She tended the fire and all Auntie had to do was sit up there and pray and fast and smoke a pipe, which is part of the praying process.

The spirit world offered her gifts, like power to see visions and power to heal, the power to take away pain, the power to change someone's vision of what is going on to a more positive vision, changing their mind—we always called it turning their face around—and numerous other powers, like she could use telepathy to talk into your mind. Whether that was a gift she always had, or whether she picked it up, I have no idea. It may have been a gift she had naturally which was improved through going to Doctor Rock. Those are just a few of the things that she picked up, and she said that she picked up too much. That's why she got so sick. I don't know what all of her gifts were because I'm not a doctor and I've never had that training.

She told me about getting these gifts and bringing back too many because she kept thinking, "Well that would help if I could do that. That would help if I could do that. This would be great, I'll take this one." And she just kept gathering up gifts [laughing], like picking flowers. She said she picked up too many gifts and she tried to carry them all back to this side. She got it all back, but it almost killed her.

She understood later that she shouldn't have taken so much, but she was young and she didn't realize that, because all of the gifts are good and could help the people that she would serve as Indian doctor. So all these gifts you pick up aren't for you, they are to help the people. That's why it took her so long to come back into herself and why it was really hard. She told me, "If you ever get in it situation, make sure that you really need what you're picking up for what you're doing. Be more careful about what you pick up than I was." That was her medicine experience, but she did have a lot of power.

When she had finished making the medicine, she put her pipe under Doctor Rock like you're supposed to and came back down from Elk Valley and collapsed. She said she was semicomatose for two weeks and Uncle Peter kept her alive during this time. She was lying in the sweathouse and could see the people outside the sweathouse like there were no walls between them. Everything turned out all right.

I imagine Peter Thom probably gave her acorn water, but I think mostly he just prayed and made medicine that way to keep her alive with the prayers. And it wouldn't be him who was feeding her; it would be the woman who was her helper. The people outside the sweathouse weren't just waiting to see how she would do; they were also waiting to hear what she was going to tell them, because she would have had a vision when she came back from making the medicine. She never told me what it was that she saw. She just never went into that. She told me of a lot of things, but she never went into what she saw when she picked up her medicine.

Auntie never went on to practice being a doctor like her mother had. She had the power and the divine gifts, but someone in her family was jealous of her. She never said who, but if you have someone in your family working against your medicine…It's hard enough when everyone's pulling for you, but if someone is against you, you usually just lay it down and don't do anything. You do some things, but you don't go out and go house to house doctoring people. But some people would come and she would work with them. That work was very low-key and very exclusive, very careful.

The Ferris Children in Orleans

Aunt Caroline said that when the [Ferris] girls were working in the hotel they had to work like the dickens because the hotel gave dinners, and midnight suppers for the dancers, and people from

Forks of Salmon and all around the area would come down and dance in the hall all night for three days. Some of the Davis family would come down from Ti Bar, up the Klamath where they lived, and trade baskets to stay at the hotel and go to the dances. In the evening people would come downstairs from the cubicles they rented, have supper, and go to the dance. In the middle of the dance they would have midnight supper. Auntie said of course she and her sister went to the dance and then they had to serve midnight supper and clean up. Then they would go to back to the dance and then try to get to sleep a little while before they had to get up and fix breakfast, but that it was fun.

They had regular dances and they had barn dances, as well as the traditional native dances. Grandma and Grandpa Ferris always went to all the White Deerskin Dances and the other ceremonial dances. That was just a given. The all-night hall dances were still happening in the 1940s when I was a kid, and none of us girls wanted to dance with Ben Wilder. If a man asked you to dance and they were sober and well bred, you had to dance with them, no matter who they were. Ben was a brilliant man but he only knew that one dance, and Auntie said that the dance had only been popular for a short period and that was a long time ago. It was all right to dance with Ben, but we all made fun of the girls who danced with him because of the way he danced. He would dance by promenading around the floor, then he would stamp his feet and promenade again. It was an old-fashioned way to dance. He was always cold sober, never drank, never swore, so we all danced with him.

Around 1910 my aunt Hazel got pregnant by a local white man in Orleans and he didn't claim the child, so Grandpa took him to court and won. Although the man had to pay a settlement on the child, the court experience was very embarrassing to the family. Generally, if you got someone pregnant on the river at this time, you married them whether you wanted to or not, but this particular white man was not going to do that. The baby's name was Henry and he was raised with his mother. After my grandfather won the court case, the baby had the right to his father's name but he never used it. He always used his mother's married name. Years later when his father died, he left Henry a hundred dollars and Henry sent it back. He said his father had never done anything for him before and [laughing] he didn't want anything from him now.

My aunt Caroline was engaged to this man's brother when Aunt Hazel had gotten pregnant, and Caroline had a half-carat solitaire diamond engagement ring the brother had given her. She broke the engagement and tried to give the ring back, because she said that if her sister was not good enough for his brother, she was too good for him. Consequently, she never married. He wouldn't take the engagement ring back and she lost it somewhere in San Francisco. Many years later, just before he turned sixty years old, around 1946 or 1947, he came over to visit. I remember teasing Auntie, "Your boyfriend is here." Then I got sent to my room to play and she served him tea and they sat and talked. When he left I came downstairs and said, "I want to know what he said."

My aunt said, "Well, if you really must know, he came to ask me to marry him again. He said he wouldn't marry me after he was sixty and he is going to be sixty this fall."

I said, "Well, what did you say?"

She said, "I told him that I was too old. I have things that I'm doing, like raising you, and I am too old and set in my ways to want to change now." And neither one of them ever married. About six months later he died and left an estate of a hundred thousand dollars. I told her she should have married him, and she said that if she had married him she would have taken such good care of him that he would have lived forever.

The Ferris Family in San Francisco

By 1912 Uncle Abner was getting to be a young man and could take care of the ranch, so Grandpa took his wife and all his children and moved to San Francisco to get away from the gossip about my aunt Hazel's pregnancy and to get work in the rebuilding of San Francisco following the 1906 earthquake. My mother was a three-year-old child when they made this move. Grandpa rented a boardinghouse and got a contract with one of the construction companies that was rebuilding San Francisco. The workers stayed at his boardinghouse and the company paid their room and board.

Grandma cooked and the daughters worked in the boarding-house and cooked and helped clean. In the mornings my aunts Hazel and Caroline worked as chambermaids in San Francisco hotels to make extra money for themselves. Sometimes they only had sugar sandwiches to eat, just butter and sugar on bread, because food supplies would get low since so little could be bought in San Francisco after the earthquake and fire. Grandpa had Uncle Roddy take the ferry across the bay to Oakland and then go to Sacramento by horse and wagon to buy food. On these trips he had one of his cousins ride shotgun, because people would rob you for your food coming back to San Francisco. Food was really, really scarce.

The restaurants would be open for just a few hours and then they would run out of food and have to close. That's why most of the companies rebuilding the city had boardinghouses that they could count on to feed their workers. Grandpa did that for five or six years and made good money at it. His cousin was a gambler who got in bad with one of the Chinese gangs, a tong. One day the cousin was walking down the street with his three-year-old daugh-ter in his arms and a tong member just shot him dead, killed him right there on the street. Not long after that Grandpa came back home to Orleans because he wasn't making as much money as he had at first, since the rebuilding was getting done.

Some of my relatives were striking-looking people, the men and the women. My aunt Caroline was a handsome woman, she was not pretty, but my aunt Hazel was an absolute beauty. She was fair-skinned with light brown hair and had hazel-colored eyes that would change color with the light, or according to the color she was wearing. She always wore lavender, blues, grays, and greens. She liked to wear lavender and have lavender-colored eyes, and when she wore white she had pale, champagne-brown eyes.

She married a boy she had gone to boarding school with and they lived in Hoopa for a little while, but she couldn't get along with the Hupa Indians. She was very, very pretty and she knew it, for one thing. She was one of those people who just did things her own way. When she was a little girl and her mother would tell her to put her schoolclothes on and get ready for school, Aunt Caroline said Aunt Hazel would slip out the back door and run down the hill through the trees, and she could see her white dress flashing through the trees as she went to school in her Sunday school dress. She was just willful, and that's probably why she wasn't getting along with her in-laws over in Hoopa. Her husband wasn't really Hupa; he was a Yurok from Weitchpec and had been raised in Hoopa because the Indian school was there. When Hazel couldn't get along with the people in Hoopa, she and her husband moved to San Francisco. Aunt Hazel had three sons and one daughter. When her husband was a kid, he had sandy blond hair and gray blue eyes. When he got older his hair got dark, almost black, and so did my aunt's. When they had children, only two of them had dark eyes and dark hair, and three of them were blue-eyed with sandy blond hair. Aunt Hazel said that when the family walked down the street in San Francisco people would look at them like they had stolen their children.

The girl was the youngest and she and two of the boys did really well. The youngest boy grew up to be a really nice-looking man and a heroin addict. He married a call girl and she supported his habit for years. He would disappear for long periods but managed to live a fairly long life, up into his sixties, considering that he was an addict. One of the other two boys became a merchant seaman and the other went to work for the post office. Their father was a printer and died of cancer caused by poisoning from the dyes. Aunt Hazel stayed in San Francisco for the rest of her life.

My aunt Caroline was five feet, seven inches, with wide shoulders, and weighed 120-some pounds in her prime. She was black-haired and black-eyed and had a curved nose. She always said she got her Indian nose from her English grandfather. She looked like her grandfather and had the same bone structure and long face. Except for his having Indian color, her father, my grandpa Frederick, actually looked a lot like an Englishman. My grandmother

Nancy was tall like that, only she was slightly lighter built. I don't know if that was from her European father.

Aunt Caroline was in San Francisco from 1912 to 1938, when her mother died. When she was in San Francisco, Aunt Caroline got a job working as a live-in cook and housemaid for a wealthy family. She kept house for them for about thirty years before she came home to Orleans. The family owned a funeral home and had three or four houses. She had to wear a uniform, and they gave her the ugliest uniforms possible. She had brown skin and black hair and black eyes, and they gave her a mustard-yellow uniform that she said made her look like mud. In the summer she wore an aquamarine blue uniform with a white collar. This was okay for the summertime, and her green uniform was okay, but in the winter-time she had to wear a yellow cotton outfit and if they dressed her up it was in brown silk.

She said her employers had made a mistake at first and dressed her in a black silk uniform with white trim, and one of the guests remarked on how striking she looked. Caroline was a handsome woman, not a pretty woman, but she looked striking in her black uniform. So after that she had this old brown silk thing so she wouldn't outshine her employers. They always told her she should say she was Italian rather than Native American. My aunt thought, "What's so great about being Italian, when all you do is look down on Native Americans? I'd rather just be what I am. Why change from one brown race to another? The next thing, you'll have me telling them I'm Mexican." But she didn't tell them that.

She said there was something very odd about these rich people. She would be at their summer place in Sausalito with the grand-children, then she would get to come home for two months. At the beginning of the summer she would go to the summer house with them and open it up for the season. They had a Japanese cook for their dinner parties, so for the parties all she did was prepare the vegetables, clean up, and serve, and they had an extra clean-up person. She said the mother would be sitting by the baby at the table—the baby would be in a high chair—and there was no nurse at the summer home. The baby would start crying because he was hungry and the mother would not have enough sense to feed it. Caroline would have to stop serving and feed the baby, and it used to just irritate her. She said, "What's wrong with her? What's wrong with these people? They can't even see that their own child is hungry when it's fussing and sitting beside them."

She said the other thing that got to her was that they knew that she got up at seven in the morning, an hour before they did, to prepare coffee and start doing things. It took longer to get ready in the morning in those days when they didn't have the fancy doodads that came along later, but around ten-thirty at night they would ring their buzzer. Caroline was asleep, but she would have to get up, put on a wrap, and go down to see what they wanted. "Would you make us some coffee?"

My aunt said she thought she was getting too old to be a maid, because it just used to irritate her terribly. She couldn't say anything, but she thought, "You know I'm going to get up at seven o'clock. What the hell are you doing getting me up at ten-thirty at night to go fool around for half an hour to make you a cup of coffee?" She said they were nice to her, but she didn't appreciate some of the things that well-off people expect. She said they don't think, and I said, "Well, Auntie, you know they don't know how to work, how to do take-care-of-yourself work."

Auntie had become friends with an elite group of intellectuals, artists, poets, and filmmakers while she was in San Francisco. They were the avant-garde. They were also naturists and went around naked in places like Muir Woods and the Marin County beaches. They invited my aunt Caroline to go along on one of their trips, and when she got there they didn't have any clothes on, so she took hers off as well. She said this wasn't bad, because up here you swam naked until you're twelve years old and in our culture we don't wear any clothes when we are young children. The children run around naked until they are five or six years old. We don't put a lot of clothes on them unless it gets cold. So she wasn't much concerned about the naturist part of things, but she did think that it was sort of odd that these people were supposed to be doing something that was so different and sophisticated and it was just going back to nature, which was something she had only been away from for a generation or so. She never elaborated on what happened, just kind of mentioned it in passing, but Grandpa didn't like her talking about it anyway.

Some of Aunt Caroline's artist friends came up to the river and were making a movie up at Somes Bar, and she and my grandma and then Hazel were extras, but the filmmakers got to drinking wine and drove their Pierce-Arrow over the bank. That's when Grandpa told her that if she came up to live with him she would live by his rules and she wouldn't bring any of her big-city friends up here. The film was supposed to be about Indians in the redwoods, and the woman who was making the film made it look like there was a background of redwood trees, and then she rubbed the film with rubbing alcohol so that it looked like there was fog and it looked like they were in the redwoods, but they were actually just up here at Somes Bar. [Laughing] He didn't like her bringing her big-city ways back up here.

Back to Orleans

Grandpa came home from San Francisco and went to work running the Orleans Hotel again around 1916 or 1918. He tore down his old stairstep house and started building Grandma a beautiful house with marble countertops and maple floors, silk wallpaper, bay windows, French doors, the whole nine yards. It must have cost him [laughing] at least nine hundred dollars. The French doors opened out onto the porch, and when they had the grand opening of the house, a woman who was there as a young girl told me, there were doors from room to room and they danced through the doorways out onto the porch. She thought that dancing out on the porch was very risqué. About a month after it was built the house caught fire and burned down. That was just a couple of years before they started remodeling the Orleans Hotel.

Toward the end of his life, A. Ferris had the property he had worked for all his life seized for a grocery debt that was probably only a few hundred dollars. To make it worse, Ernie Anderson, who seized the property for Gent's store, was the husband of Alvirius's granddaughter. It broke Alvirius Ferris's heart. My grandfather felt like his father was betrayed and that they should have just waited and let him die before they seized the land, because he was up in his nineties at the time. After his land was taken, A. Ferris stayed with his oldest son, Harry, for a time, but his daughter-in-law was kind of an ornery woman and he said she was mean to him, so he moved in with his daughter Ellen Hotelling. He lived with her for a time and I think that got to be too much for him too, so he moved down the hill and stayed with Harry toward the end of his life. He lived to be ninety-eight years old and could still get around pretty good.

A. Ferris died soon after Grandpa's house burned, in 1920, but the new house was already up and it was almost the same design as the one it replaced. They milled their own lumber and threw the house up in six months. Some of the lumber was a little green, so the boards got cracks in them, and some of the lumber was from old flume boards. They called it a balloon-style house and put flume boards up with two-by-sixes on the bottom and top of them. The flume boards were twenty-foot-long one-by-twelves. Then they put the framing boards on the outside of this flume-board structure that held the house up. This way they built the house like a shell with a dead airspace between the inside and the outside wall. It helped keep the house cool better than it helped keep it warm, because the winter wind tended to break up that dead airspace. And there were three layers of flooring—there wasn't insulation in this house, so it took three layers of flooring to keep air from coming up from beneath and cooling the house.

Uncle Roddy had made a mistake in building the floor, and by the time his father caught him, it was too late to do anything about it. All the boards were sixteen feet long and he had laid them evenly, so that there was a seam running across the house sixteen feet from the wall. He said Grandpa never told him that the way to do it was to put down a short board and then stagger them back and forth, weaving them into each other. Grandpa said Uncle Roddy was always running out of nails and he used to complain that Uncle Roddy put so many nails in the house that it could stand by nails alone. Once, when my son Long Gone was in bed with mumps, he looked at the ceiling of that old house and figured out there were twenty-two hundred nails in the living room ceiling. If there were that many nails in the ceiling, think about how many there were [laughing] in those three layers of flooring on the first floor of the house.

Every day, Grandpa would come over and cut the lumber for that day's work and tell Uncle Roddy what to do that day. One day Uncle Roddy was lying on the floor reading a little pamphlet from the church and he heard Grandpa coming with the team, hauling something up the hill for him. He stuffed the pamphlet in behind the frame and hammered the frame into place so his father wouldn't know what he had been doing. What he had not been doing was any work.

About the time he was building the house, Uncle Roddy married a quarter-breed Indian girl from Oklahoma and they had one child, Calvin Orville Ferris, who was born in the early 1920s. It cost my grandfather five hundred dollars this time to rebuild a two-and-a-half story, five-bedroom house and Uncle Roddy used the left-over lumber to build his house. Around 1944, when my grandfather was up in his seventies, he said that before it's over, the inflation is going to be so high it will take a wheelbarrow full of money to get something, and it looks like it's getting that way.

My Mother, Beatrice Ferris

Grandpa and Grandma continued to live in Orleans, and around 1924, my mother, Beatrice Ferris, went off to high school in San Francisco. She was a coloratura soprano in the Concord High School arts program and she sang with the San Francisco Opera Company, starting when she was about sixteen years old. The opera company discovered her when she was in school and began training her in a progressive program in the arts.

Sometime before she moved back home, she was here visiting her mother, and while she was out for a walk she met a doctor's wife and they struck up a conversation. My mother told her how she was just home on vacation, and that she had been singing in the San Francisco Opera. Now that the season was over she was home visiting her mother. She told the woman that she had gone to Concord High and was in the arts program there. Then the woman's husband comes up from the river bar and sees my mother, who is wearing a straw hat and a plain old dress. The doctor starts talking to her in broken English. "Me...you..."

My mother just kind of laughed a little bit to herself and started talking back to him in broken English. "Me um come over town, walkum..." The wife didn't say anything for a minute, but she was so embarrassed. Finally she said to her husband, "She attends Concord High in San Francisco and she sings in the San Francisco Opera!"

After my mother completed school she sang with the opera company during the season. When the opera season was over she worked as a chambermaid in the hotels, like a lot of the Indian women who went to San Francisco. If you needed money and were Native American, the Native American women in San Francisco would get you in the chambermaids' union and you could get work in the hotels. It was something Native American women could count on all through the 1950s. Both of my aunts and my mother worked in the maids' union. A lot of women from up here worked in the maids' union in later years. It was either that or possibly prostitution if you had to work and make some money to live on. There are always people around who would give you an "easy" way to work. But the women from up here would get you into the maids' union so you could make some money to live on. When you got to San Francisco, you met with some other Native American women and they got you right in there to work as a chambermaid. I went to San Francisco as a teenager with a cousin, and an Indian woman there who was a friend of my cousin's offered to get me a job through the chambermaids' union. I told her that I was still in school and my cousin said, "She's not as old as she looks, she's only sixteen."

You would go to work early in the morning, cleaning up the rooms until around noon, and then you were off work. My aunt said the guests left good tips if you cleaned well and you could make as much in tips as you did in salary. So that's what my mother did. She sang opera and worked as a chambermaid. When my aunt Hazel wasn't pregnant or having babies, she worked as a chambermaid on up through her fifties in certain hotels.

My mother was in San Francisco, being a flapper and having a great time being an opera singer and working as a chambermaid, and her older sister Hazel was sweating blood trying to keep track of her. Hazel had a job and a husband and children. In 1928 my mother came home from San Francisco to take care of my grandmother, who had had a heart attack. My grandmother had been in the agency hospital in Hoopa and was considered by the BIA to be a Hupa Indian. Because of this, even though she was a Karuk, she got to stay in the new agency hospital in Hoopa. The Indian Health Service would not let the Karuk use their hospital, even though Karuk funding had gone into building the hospital so that Karuk Indians could use it. Karuk people still couldn't use that hospital until around 1950.

My grandma was in the hospital for a while and when they sent her home they put her on digitalis and a shot of brandy a day. She would have fainting spells and had to lie down and rest. She did a lot of resting because of her bad heart when she was in her early sixties.

If it had not been for her mother's health, my mother probably would have eventually married somebody in San Francisco. Grandpa had bought her a new car when she was sixteen years old and still lived in Orleans, so she had her own brand-new four-door Chevy. When she came home she took care of her mother and just ran around up here and had a good time. She was engaged to various men off and on. She was engaged to John Bennett at one time and it broke off. Then she was engaged to someone down the river and that broke off. She was really spoiled, as you can tell, having her own vehicle in the 1920s. She was my grandparents' youngest child and she was a very happy person. She was upbeat all the time. As a mother she was really strict, but as a person she laughed a lot and had good times. She was fun to be around and people liked being around her. She loved to play cards.

My grandpa always thought my grandma Nancy Evans Ferris and her mother, Iptapue, both had diabetes. Iptapue lived in a little Indian house up on the Reese place where her daughter Laura Reese took care of her when she got old. She would lay down by the fireplace in her Indian house and go to sleep, and you couldn't wake her up. Iptapue died in a fire there. I think she was sleeping by the fire and her dress caught fire and that set fire to the house.

My grandpa used to make brandy for my grandmother because she had heart disease. She would faint and couldn't breathe and just a thimbleful of brandy would bring her around. It was probably congestive heart disease secondary to diabetes. I suspect this is true, since fifteen of her twenty grandchildren were diabetic and heredity always tells. After Grandma had eaten she would fall asleep and they couldn't wake her up. I became diabetic when I was nine years old, possibly because of a pancreas injury, and possibly because of a predisposition.

I guess Bessie Tripp must have been around sixty years old in the late 1930s when she became diabetic. She was cooking at the Steelhead Restaurant, in Orleans, when she started getting sick. She just didn't feel well, couldn't breathe and just didn't feel good, and she didn't look good. My grandpa talked with his friend Mrs. Young, who had been his classmate in school. Grandpa said that no one really knew how old Bessie was. She had a year for when she was born but there was no record, so they should make out an affidavit for her and swear that she was born in 1876. That would make her old enough to be eligible for Social Security. Mrs. Young agreed that Bessie shouldn't be killing herself working at that restaurant when she wasn't well. So my grandpa and Mrs. Young did that, and Bessie got five years older all at once. Maybe she had been born in 1876 after all, but after my grandpa and Mrs. Young gave their statement to the Bureau of Indian Affairs [laughing], that was her official birth year. Sometime after that they found that she had diabetes.

When she wasn't working at the restaurant any longer, eating all that fried food that she was fixing all the time for people, hamburgers and stuff like that, she went back home and started eating fish and beans again and got just fine. Bessie was a Donahue before marrying Bill Tripp. The Tripp family traded Ike's Falls to the Donahues, and they traded Oak Bottom to the Tripps, and that is where Bessie lived most of her life.

My Father, William Shirley Smither

After my mother came back to Orleans to take care of Grandma, she met my father and they were married in 1932. My father, William Shirley Smither, was a miner, about six feet, three inches tall—a lot taller than most of the men on the river. He was slender, good-looking, and a very pleasant person, talkative and affable, the kind of man who never met a stranger. I always say my dad was the kind of fellow who could get somebody's last pair of clean socks off of them, and they would be glad to give them to him. Everybody thought he was white because he had blue eyes and his hair turned white by the time he was forty years old. He could pass for white and evidently did. Grandma Smither would pass herself as white even though she had black hair and eyes and brown skin. The majority of his Indian blood was a Miwok tribe, with some eastern blood, Seminole.

He was a hard worker but he didn't work like the Ferrises worked. They thought he talked too much and took too much time visiting. Grandpa and the rest of his family were such hard workers that they always looked at my dad as being kind of lazy. They gave him the benefit of the doubt because he had TB, so he had an excuse of being sick, but I think he worked pretty hard, because even though he had tuberculosis, he worked in a mine and he built onto his dad's cabin in Somes Bar, and then came into this country from Mariposa and built another cabin and built another house before I was three years old. I think they kept him pretty busy. I think Grandpa and my mother might have been pushing him a little bit. But my mother really worked. She took care of me and worked for the WPA as a seamstress and had a sick husband. She was always busy. My son Long Gone reminds me of my dad and procrastinates about things.

My father was a barber. He had been married once before he and my mother met, and even though he was forty-two years old he had no children. His first wife had died of tuberculosis. His family lived in Blue Lake for a while, early in the Depression, then they bought the mines up near Somes Bar and moved to the Salmon River. My grandfather John Smither and my father, William Shirley Smither, who they just called Shirley, bought three mines at Steiner Creek and two at Wooley Creek and they lived where Merlin Tripp lived later, at that old bench by the second Salmon River bridge.

They were working at one of the mines when his father had a stroke and was paralyzed on one side of his body. After that my father had to take over running the mines. Around that time my father and mother met, and after three or four months they were married. My father had been living in a two-room cabin, and after he and my mother were married he built on two more rooms. The cabin was like two cabins built together. The front room was a living room–kitchen and behind that was my grandparents' room. Then he went around behind and built on two more rooms, one for himself and my mother and another behind that for his sister, so you had a little house with four rooms, one after another.

My Father's Family

My father's family was already in Georgia and Alabama in the late 1700s, early 1800s. My grandfather said the name wasn't Smither, but they changed it to Smither. Grandpa Smither was of German descent and my grandmother Edith May Shirley Smither was French and Dutch and Indian. Grandma's grandfather, John Shirley, had a totally made-up name too. He never existed, ever, anyplace in the world, before he showed up in Missouri. He left from around New Orleans and came into Missouri and suddenly there was John Shirley, a new person. Nobody knew who he was, what he was, who he had been. He had brown eyes and hair and light brown skin and said he was French. Two days after the Trail of Tears Cherokee people reached Independence, Missouri, he married an Indian woman who had two half-grown Indian children.

My grandma May on my father's side said that story was just a little too pat for her. She said her thoughts about her grandfather was that he was part Cherokee and sold his farm, like some of them did, and went to Louisiana to pretend he was a white man for a while. Then he came up the river and waited for his wife-to-be to show up. She had gotten caught and sent on the Trail of Tears. He came to Missouri probably six months before she got there and set up a farm. She got there as a part of the Trail of Tears, and he married her, so she never got to Oklahoma.

It's all hypothetical, but Grandma May said it was more logical and figured out better that way for her. She found it odd that he fell madly in love with a woman who was as ugly as a mud fence and had two half-grown Indian children. She said they could trace other people in the family, but they couldn't trace him, her grandfather John Shirley, before he arrived in Missouri. By then Indians had been mixing with whites for three hundred years and he could have been a quarter-breed, so he would have been a dark white man, but he would have been an awful light Indian.

Grandma May's father, William Shirley, came across the Plains with his father's wagon train from the Shirley ranch. He guided people west, at first to cities like Denver and then to California, where people were trickling in before the gold rush. Her mother and father didn't meet until after the gold rush. After coming to California, William sold out his interest in the wagon trains and bought wagons to haul ore from the Sierra gold mines to San Francisco. So he was there and gone and there and gone all the time. That was his pattern, and then he married her mother, and they had my grandmother and her brother William. They were living in Merced, and after their children were born he didn't want to go so far anymore in his guiding work, so they moved up to Mariposa, California, where they got an allotment, and then his wife died.

Grandma May said that with the death of her mother, her father had been worried about how he could take care of her and his boy, William, when he was gone a week at a time, taking ore to San Francisco. She said her father really got everybody gossiping, because he went to his wife's funeral and came home with a new wife. This was his first wife's younger sister, Mary, who was about fifteen years old. With her sister dead, he and Mary decided to get married and take care of the children. He was worried that people would gossip about his marrying his wife's younger sister and that it might cause trouble for her, being the sister and being so young. They decided that they would go ahead and get married and then people could gossip all they wanted to, but she would be a married woman and it would be none of their damn business whether he was sleeping with her or not.

All the time that I was a kid and visited my grandparents, they would always mention this crazy Smither family. The younger Smithers drank and partied a lot. When somebody would mention those crazy Smithers, Grandma would say, "Well, there's always Aunt Belle," and everybody would laugh. I never paid any attention to that, none of us kids did. Then when she got to be really old, about ninety I guess, I was having my last child and I went over to Blue Lake to visit her. I was living in Arcata, so I would just go up and spend the day with her every once in a while.

I said something about that crazy Smither bunch and she said there was always Aunt Belle. I said, "Who in the heck was Aunt Belle?" She said, "Oh, my aunt, Myra Belle Shirley. You probably know her better as Belle Starr." Grandma May thought that her grandfather, John Shirley, rewrote family history by ignoring his first family. He took Belle Starr's boys and his son, William Shirley, right out of the family history. William was a half-breed with an Indian mother, and John Shirley's other two children weren't. Belle and her brother were not part Indian because they had a different mother from their half-Indian siblings.

After his Indian wife died, John Shirley married a ritzy white woman from the Carolinas who became the mother of Belle and her brother. Eventually Belle got into trouble for supporting her two boys, who were having problems because of some horse rustling they had done, and came to Merced, California, to be with her brother. Belle wasn't an Indian, but her boys were because their father, John Starr, was a half-breed with a large ranch that lived next to her. Grandma said people wondered why Belle's father, John, let her marry a man who was part Indian and then write him and his children out of the family history.

When I went back east to South Dakota in 1978 to take some classes for my tribal work as a community health representative, I met people who were from down in that area of Oklahoma and learned from them that the boys had rustled cattle in the Indian Territories and driven them back onto the reservation. Belle got into trouble sticking up for them and came back to California to stay with her brother in Mariposa until the heat was off.

Grandma said that history had it wrong about Aunt Belle. Aunt Belle never drank, but she was very eccentric. She would ride a horse down the streets of Merced shooting a pistol, but she was also fanatically religious. According to Grandma, the only trouble with Aunt Belle was that she was a religious fanatic and thought that her boys could do no wrong.

Because she was a descendant of that mysterious Shirley who passed as white, Belle Starr was not known as an Indian in Missouri. I don't know what Shirley did with the Indian woman who came on the Trail of Tears, and who he had Belle and her brother with. I don't know how he arranged that these children would pass as white, but evidently he did very well for himself.

Grandma said that Belle really did go around with Black Bart, who was unknown at the time, and he was religious like Belle was. They went to church together a few times and that helped her reputation as a nefarious woman. Grandma said that Aunt Belle stayed with them for about six months, until things cooled off, then she went home to Missouri and Grandma never saw her again. A few years later Belle was murdered, and they said her stepson did it. Grandma said her stepson was hung for it, but he was devoted to his stepmother and the family never thought that he did it. They thought a preacher killed her who was trying to get her land away from her, because by then her father was dead.

Aunt Ollie named her daughter after Aunt Belle. She named her May Belle rather than Myra Belle. I said, "All these years I've been looking in my Indian family for a renegade, and you know what, Grandma? You folks are supposed to be my white family, and there's the renegade." My grandma said the reason Belle passed herself as white was that it was too dangerous to be an Indian in Mariposa, California. Grandma said that when she was a girl the Indians would bury their girls to the neck in sand so the miners wouldn't rape them. Grandma had passed herself off as a black Dutch person because she was dark-skinned. Then in the 1970s the government made a law that if you had been passing yourself off as white you could redeem yourself and become Indian again.

When my grandfather Smither came up here, everyone thought he was white. He and my father both had blue eyes, kind of gray-blue eyes. Everyone thought he was white and if anyone asked, he would say, "Well, I got a little Indian in me."

My father and uncles in the Smither family would all say, "I have some Indian in me." But they wouldn't say, "I am an Indian." I became a half-breed after a woman with the BIA ran down the percentages of my Indian background for me, using a computer. I told her what I thought I was and gave her the names of the people and their approximate birthdates. Before she started, she told me it was iffy and hard to find. I had to go back to the BIA office the next week, and she said, "Oh, by the way, you are three-sixteenths Miwok, one-sixteenth Seminole from Alabama, and one-quarter Karuk, so I changed your certified Indian blood degree."

I said, "How did you do that?"

She kind of smiled and said, "Oh, it was easy. They all had allotment numbers." Now the Karuk Tribe has adopted my other one-quarter Indian blood and made me one-half Karuk.

So all those Smithers had allotments back there. I know they lived in a place called Bootjack, on Indian Hill in Mariposa. The

Miwok up there are lucky because they still have their dances and their ceremonies. In order to make sure their children would be tough enough to live, they took the babies to what is now Yosemite National Park as soon as the snow melted in June if a baby had been born the year before, and dedicated it. They did this by holding the baby under Vernal Falls with that ice water coming down in June. That was part of their belief, and Grandma did that with her children and all but one of them lived. They lived!

My Early Childhood

I was born nine months, four days after my parents were married, and I was the only child they ever had. Just before I was born my parents moved from where they had been living on the Salmon River down to Orleans because my mother was having problems with her pregnancy. My grandpa Ferris had lumber around, and my father built a little house for them on the ranch. Also, my mother was still taking care of her mother and that may have been another reason why they had to move down to Orleans.

As long as my father lived, when he was around I don't think my feet ever touched the ground. He packed me around all the time. I wasn't very heavy. I only weighed around thirty-eight pounds when I was nine years old, but I was a little taller than most of the other Indian children.

They were just making a living with the mine, because the price of gold was low at that time. When I was about one year old, my father went back to work in the woods. I remember seeing a letter he wrote to my mother in 1933 saying, "The check is five dollars short because I had to buy a pair of logging boots." Five dollars for a pair of boots that would cost two hundred dollars now! When I was around two years old, his TB became active and he had to come home.

My parents had been living in my Uncle Roddy's house and my mother decided she wanted to have her own house, so my father and grandfather built a new log cabin for us. According to my aunt Caroline's diary, as soon as they moved into that cold new house, my father came down with active tuberculosis. I know from my mother's letters that she blamed herself for this, because it was cold in the cabin. After that my father had to go to Eureka to the hospital and then to San Francisco for lung surgery. Aside from six weeks when he was able to come home, he was in tubercular hospitals for the rest of his life. Even when my father was dying of tuberculosis and coughing up blood, he still smoked cigarettes. I remember him sitting at the cribbage table, holding his cards in one hand and rolling a Bull Durham cigarette with the other. That is one of the reasons I never smoked and never had any desire to smoke.

By the time I was four years old, he had to have his lung collapsed. To do this he was hospitalized in San Francisco for about six months. When my mother and I drove down to visit him, we drove through the redwoods down to Ukiah. It took us all day to get from Eureka to Ukiah in early 1937. We stayed in one of those new-style places that weren't yet in Humboldt County. It wasn't a hotel, but a motel with little cabins that had their own garages. My mother must have said something to me about motels for me to know that. The San Francisco Bay really impressed me. My mother was still driving the little car that she had gotten from the time she was working in San Francisco and enjoying herself being a flapper. When we got to Oakland she handed somebody a ticket and we just drove down this ramp and right onto a ferryboat. There was no Golden Gate Bridge at the time, and I thought it was fascinating to drive a car onto a boat. After we crossed the bay we drove out to my aunt Hazel's house in the Clay Street district of San Francisco, where she lived in a Victorian flat. My aunt Hazel had a whole bunch of boys, and they had these little play cars that looked like motor cars, and they would go careening down this long Victorian hallway, banging into the walls. Aunt Hazel was always hollering at them to quit banging up the walls. It didn't stop them.

Later that year, when my father was hospitalized in Eureka, I could only visit him for about five minutes, and then the nurses would take me down to the kitchen and my mother would stay on visiting with him for a couple of hours and playing cards. They would always play cribbage and she could do the waterfall with cards when she was shuffling them. If it was a nice day and we were outside, I could visit him a little longer. So with my dad in the hospital, first in Eureka, then in San Francisco, my mother and I moved back into Uncle Roddy's house that was vacant in Orleans.

Then the welfare department said that if my mother wanted to get money from them we would have to move to Eureka and she would have to go to work for the WPA. In Eureka we boarded with the Smiths from Somes Bar. They had had a store at Somes Bar which they lost in the Depression. So my mother worked and a friend of hers came down to take care of me while she was at work. My mother started running a boardinghouse for fishermen, working for the WPA, and raising her four-year-old child. This left her mother, who was still sick, home alone in Orleans with my grandfather, so then some of her granddaughters helped to take care of her. With my mother this busy, I went to school for half a year and then was kicked out for being too young when I was halfway through kindergarten. I remember I had already learned how to read. Then Esther got sick and her tuberculosis relapsed and she had to go back to the tubercular hospital somewhere around Sacramento or Stockton.

After that there was really no one to take care of me until my mother came home from work at noon. Between eight o'clock in the morning and noon I stayed alone. Whenever I woke up, I got up and fixed myself Rice Krispies for breakfast and waited for my mother to come home. The man who owned the house was older, in his sixties or seventies, and he lived upstairs. Although he didn't watch me, if the house had burned down he would have made sure I had gotten out. That was about it for care. The doors were locked and I just stayed in the house and played on the sun porch, reading my little books and playing with dolls and entertaining myself while I waited for my mother to come home.

As a child, I thought my mother could speak Italian and all these other languages that I heard her practicing singing. She explained to me that she could sing Italian, but that it was just a song and she could not speak all those languages. She would sing for two or three hours every day, even though she was raising me, running a boardinghouse, and working for the WPA and not singing at the opera anymore. She would sing scales when she was cleaning our house, doing dishes, making beds. She would start at Middle C and go up and down the scales, and then she would go one octave higher and sing the scales, and then she would go another octave higher and sing them again. She would do that for quite a while, and then pretty soon she would start singing "The Bear Went over the Mountain." And she would sing that up the scales and down the scales. When she got through with that she would start singing songs after working on probably an hour of vocal exercises. If she was getting ready to sing for the church or at some program, she would sing for days, hour after hour, practicing.

In May of 1937 my grandfather went to San Francisco to celebrate the opening of the Golden Gate Bridge by walking across the bridge with several thousand other people. He came back to Eureka and my mother was supposed to bring him back home to Orleans on Friday when she got off work. But on Wednesday we were driving on G Street in Eureka—myself, my mother, Grandmother Nancy, and another little boy who was a friend of the family—when a drunk driver going sixty miles an hour broadsided us. My grandma flew out of the car and hit a telephone pole. The little boy got all cut up and fell on top of me. My mother got thrown out of the car too, and landed out of sight in a bunch of berry bushes. We thought at the time that I was pretty lucky to have only gotten one bad cut on my face, but my back was badly hurt and we didn't learn about that for thirty-five or forty years.

I came to, lying on the street, and started screaming for my mother, and people were telling me she wasn't there. My grandmother had been knocked out too, but she finally woke up for a little bit and asked where my mother was, then passed out again. At that point they began looking for my mother. They hadn't believed me and had thought I was hysterical. I was hysterical, but I knew what I was talking about. It's like they say [laughing], just because someone is crazy doesn't mean they are not telling the truth. They finally found my mother up in the bushes and took us all to the hospital.

In the hospital they had to sew up the cut in my face without using anesthetic, in order to make sure they got the nerves connected correctly so that my face would not be stiff later on. You try sewing up a five-year-old's face with no anesthetic! I kept screaming and waking my grandma up out of her coma long enough for her to tell me I would be all right, and then she would pass out again. It helped calm me down a little bit, that at least she wasn't dead. I had thought for certain she was dead; she had been so still and gray-looking in the ambulance. She had broken her femur and her hip. Grandma lived for a little less than a month after the accident. My mother used her ten-thousand-dollar insurance settlement money to buy a little Victorian boardinghouse in Eureka. After about three months, my mother thought she was pregnant and my father got well enough to sign himself out of the hospital in Eureka, and we all moved back home to Orleans. My grandmother had died, so my grandpa had been alone until my aunt Caroline had quit her job in San Francisco and moved back to Orleans to take care of Grandpa. It was around Christmastime, and I remember my mother singing "O Holy Night" at the Orleans school Christmas pageant in her beautiful soprano voice. That is the last thing I remember hearing her sing.

My Parents' Deaths

I was six years old and we had only been back in Orleans for a short time when my father needed to have a procedure on his lung that had to be done in Eureka. My mother didn't want me to stay at home, because I had a bad cold and I would be fussy. But my aunt said that since I had a cold I really shouldn't go out in the rain with them and be in the cold car, so my mother finally left me with her. My aunt was very clairvoyant and she told me later that she did not feel like her sister was going to come back from that trip. I didn't think she was going to come back either. I don't know if it was childishness or my gifts or why, but I didn't think she was going to come back. So my parents went to Eureka and stayed overnight with my father's mother, who lived nearby in Blue Lake. The next morning they got up early and started driving home. My mother always drove. They made it as far Willow Creek and then somehow drove off into the Trinity River in my grandpa's brand-new 1939 Plymouth. They found my father washed ashore in upper Hoopa Valley about six weeks after the accident, but her body was never found. Grandpa searched diligently for her and spent a lot of money having the river dragged for her body, then for a couple of years he continued searching the riverbank.

Because of the nature of roads along the rivers in this country, deaths from accidents have taken a real toll on us from the time cars first came on the river. Between the limitations of the roads, cliffs, rock slides, and ice, driving can be very dangerous at the best of times, and if speed, alcohol, or bad luck are thrown in, it is a lethal combination. Hardly a year passes without a death by automobile accident and unfortunately, the deaths often happen several at a time, even with single vehicles, because once you go in the river or are thrown from a car in this country, a person is lucky to survive.

I don't know how I knew, but I knew they were not coming back. I wouldn't accept that my mother was gone for quite a while, because I kept seeing her, and I didn't know that what I was seeing was where she was, where her body was. After they died, I didn't learn much in the rest of the first grade. My teacher said that I daydreamed too much. My thought on it is that I was just insane. I feel like I was insane there for about two and a half years after my parents were killed, but finally I started to learn in school again.

I kept seeing her at the place on the Trinity River called Sugar Bowl. They were looking everywhere on the river for her body, and dragging for her, but I knew that she was at Sugar Bowl. She was on this mountain across the river from Sugar Bowl and I kept thinking she was lost there. I just kept seeing this place on the river that is about three-quarters of a mile long, and I knew she was there somewhere.

After I got older and learned more about my powers, I realized that her body was probably in the Sugar Bowl area of the river and that she was buried in the water someplace and I could see that, but at that time I didn't realize what it was, I just thought she was really alive, and there, and they weren't finding her. That bothered me for quite a number of years. It's really hard to be somewhat psychic. Later on I realized that I could see where bodies were if someone asked me to, and with my own family I don't need to be asked. But if other families ask me to, I can see where the bodies are. The thing is to interpret what you see. I have had it happen thousands of times and I still don't know for sure if it's real, because it's so vague. The thing that happens isn't vague, but the way it comes to me is and has to be interpreted.

Sometimes it just comes out of my mouth, but I know it wasn't my thought. It wasn't me talking, because I didn't know about what I was going to say until I said it. I have no thought on a subject, and all of a sudden I know something about it. Like when a woman died down at Bluff Creek, Leaf Hillman brought the drowned woman's husband to me and asked me to use my powers to look for his wife, and he paid me to look for her. In my vision I saw her cross the creek on a bridge, using a flashlight, and she went up the hill and fell down, and I could see the light rolling on the pavement. Then she went down and picked up the light and then started back towards her car. Then I saw her sliding down the hill and slide into the water and kind of laugh a little bit and then get scared, and then the current took her and she was gone.

After I told them my vision, Long Gone and Leaf and Sonny Buck went down to Bluff Creek to look. I told Long Gone he should go up on a trail to a high spot and then he should look down from that high spot and she should be in the water, right underneath where he would be standing. I told them the last place I had seen her was there behind a rock, and if she wasn't there then she had been washed out into the Klamath River.

Long Gone did as I said and was bending down to look into the creek and got vertigo so bad that he sat down. He thought he had seen something, but then he couldn't see it, and he looked and looked, but he couldn't see it again. He said that when he was bent over, leaning forwards, and got vertigo, he remembered me telling him to be careful because if he started sliding there he would slide clear down to Bluff Creek, because all of that rock is rotten shale and nothing would hold him. Long Gone said that when he was leaning over he thought he saw something, but after that he thought it must have been just a stick or a rock, because he couldn't see it again. Then eight or nine months later a fisherman spotted her body there, caught under the overhang behind that rock where I had last seen her go in my vision. But then the water was higher when Long Gone was there and she may have just been laying beneath the surface when he was looking for her.

I didn't know where she went. I thought that since she was in the water she had to go to the river, but the voices kept telling me she was in Bluff Creek: "She's right there at that slide where she went in the water." And that's where they found her. She was on a bench in the creek under the slide, hidden from view on a little shelf behind a rock underneath an overhang. In my visions all the clues are there, but it's murky and I'm not smart enough to follow them, or it's not meant to be.

Another time, my sister-in-law drowned in the Trinity River, and before she died I felt I was in someone's body and I thought it was my sister-in-law. In my vision I was in the backseat of a car that was going fast and I was getting scared. Then the car went flying off into an abyss. I didn't know who else was in the car, but I went on down with the car, and in the vision I never hit bottom. I don't know if she died before the car went into the river, but she was washed out of the car.

My brother-in-law kept going to the cops and asking if there was any report on these people who had disappeared, and the cops told them that there was no report and that they were just off drunk someplace. He told them that his son did not stay away that long and if he was going to stay away he would have phoned him. The cops never once said that they had been chasing a car in that area and it disappeared. When my brother-in-law had the car pulled out she was not in it, and the Trinity River is awfully swift there.

I was over in Redding when this happened, around 1978 or

1979, and in the middle of the night this vision comes, and it's my sister-in-law just calling me, and she says, "I'm right here. I'm stuck right here." And then I saw her stuck in some fir roots out of the water, and there are willow trees hanging over the water. I didn't know if it was on the Trinity or the Klamath, I just knew that she was telling me that was where she was. They were looking for her when I came back over to Orleans and I described for them the place that I had seen her. I told him that I knew that was where she was supposed to be, but I couldn't tell if it was on the Klamath or the Trinity River. They found the car and they found the bodies of my nephew and his girlfriend, who had been thrown out of the car before it went in the river, but they never found my sister-in-law.

The vision gift doesn't bother me as much as it used to. As you get older I guess your power wanes, so you don't have this constant interference. When I was younger—and this is awful—I used to wish that this damn thing would quit interfering with my life. Isn't that terrible? "I don't want God interfering with my life! I want to live my life without him throwing all these other things into it."

So when we have impressions, it isn't all drawn out, like you see a woman wearing a white dress. You don't have a full picture, just impressions. It's like the profilers that detectives get to help them sometimes, people who are somewhat psychic, and they may see something white, and when they get there it's the body of a woman wearing a white dress. They see those things the way I do. It isn't a full picture, it's just a hint.

Growing Up in Orleans

After my parents were killed, Grandpa took care of the mine as long as he was able. He was seventy-two years old in 1940, when they were killed, and I moved in with him. The mine wasn't doing much because gold was only thirty-two dollars an ounce. My grandpa talked it over with my father's parents and they decided that it was all right that he and my aunt Caroline would raise me. Most of my aunts and uncles who were married had big families to take care of and didn't need an extra child, so Grandpa said he would keep me and send me to school up here in Orleans. Most of the students were mixed-blood children, more half-bloods than anything. That was unique because there was actually no racial prejudice in Orleans, because there were so few white people around, or if they were around, many were married to Indians.

After the decision was made that I would be raised by my grandpa Ferris and my aunt Caroline, my grandmother May, on my father's side of the family, didn't come to see me very much and she didn't have much to do with me other than to write to me and send me a card at Christmas and on my birthday. She said she did that because if another family was raising me and they were doing all right by me, she shouldn't come in and interfere, because someone from the outside will always think that they're not doing it right. Then the child gets confused by one family pulling one way and the other family pulling another way. Because of this, when my mother's family started raising me she just let me go, even though she thought they were spoiling me, but it wasn't her call. She was busy raising her other granddaughter.

When I was growing up in Orleans, if an adult in any one of the families, any one of them, caught any of us children into something and they told us to quit doing it, we had to mind them or we would be in all kinds of trouble. If someone told me not to do something, I had better quit whatever I was doing or I would be in big trouble. They would tell my grandfather that I hadn't minded. You just had to do whatever they said.

If they said, "Don't do that" or "Don't go over there" or "You're on the wrong side of the street," you paid attention to them. We couldn't walk on the same side of the street as the Steelhead Bar, because there were drunks walking in and out of the bar. So to avoid the bar we walked as far as Delaney's store, then we walked across the street and walked on the other side. Then, when we got up to Gent's store, we crossed back over again. We couldn't walk in front of the bar, because one of those drunks might say something to you or do something to you. Everyone in Orleans, as close as the Indian families lived to each other, knew each other as well as you know your own brother and sister. I knew what they did, what they thought, how they acted, and their basic nature. Nobody could get away with anything. That's the kind of society I grew up in; there was nothing you could get away with.

The old ladies wouldn't tell you not to do something if you weren't doing something wrong. Like if you were playing too much in the creek, splashing another kid, and it was getting to the point where they couldn't breathe or they were scared or too upset, and they told you to quit, you'd better quit. If one of those old women who was sitting there by the creek told you to quit doing something, you quit. The usual punishment was that they would take a little switch and switch your leg if you'd didn't mind when they told you to do something, and then you didn't do it, and just refused to do it. So it was like the whole town of Orleans was taking care of you and raising you. The whole town had something to say about what you were doing.

After my parents died and I was living with my grandpa and Aunt Caroline, I used to write little simplistic stories as a way of entertaining myself because there were no other children around. I had to do things that I could do by myself, because there were only three children on this side of the river at Whitey's Flat, which had been named for a powerful albino Karuk headman. I couldn't go to anyone else's house, but they let me run around in these woods anywhere I wanted to. Grandpa told me to be careful of the trails. "Don't go following some trail without looking back all the time. Check your back trail, because sometimes these little deer trails just disappear, and then when you look back, there's nothing behind you either." Usually I followed the ditch line that had been dug to bring water across to my uncle Billy's house in order to be able to mine below.

My problem was I would play and come home late from school. If I got home late my aunt would switch me. My grandfather never did anything. He never spanked me or switched me or anything. He just had to say my name and I stopped whatever I was doing. I don't care what I was doing. I just stopped dead and never did or said anything more. I was like a startled deer, but that was not because he ever did anything to me. My aunt did everything he said, and [laughing] I sure as hell wasn't going to argue with him.

In those days you didn't talk back. I learned that from my aunt Caroline. I never talked back to my grandpa. If he said something, even if I thought it was wrong, or I didn't think it was right, or that it could be interpreted more than one way...I never said a word back. He never spanked me or shook me or even hollered at me. If I was playing and carrying on, he would just say my name. He would say "Mavis," and whatever I was doing, I would stop. I knew by the tone of his voice that I was doing something he didn't want me to do. I didn't ask him what, either; I just stopped doing whatever I was doing. Whether I was bouncing around or jumping around too much or talking too much, whatever I was doing, I'd just stop doing anything at all and he never said anything more. He never told me it was wrong or right, or "Don't do that." He just said my name and I instantly conformed. Aunt Caroline never answered him back either. She never said anything. He'd say something, and whether she liked it or not, she didn't say anything. It was his house. It wasn't our house, we didn't run it and we didn't support it. Aunt Caroline supported herself with her own retirement and there was some money in the bank from the accident that killed my grandmother Nancy that partially supported me.

I had learned to cook at a very young age. Because I was weaker than I should have been as a child, I was not very good at working in the gardens. My aunt and my grandfather both worked in the gardens and we sold produce to the hotel in Orleans. We had a couple of acres of gardens, and four or sometimes five acres of corn. We'd raise feed corn and pick it slightly green to sell it. What was left over we would dry and feed to our pigs and chickens.

When I was eight years old, Grandpa had already milked the cows before daylight. Then he and my aunt Caroline would be out there in the morning, working in the fields, and since I could do less work, they would send me into the house about nine o'clock to cook breakfast. It would take me about an hour to build a fire, make hotcakes and refried beans, cook eggs, and make coffee, and when it was ready they would come in and eat around the time the day was starting to get hot. After breakfast they would go back to working in the fields for a while and then go back again in the evening and run water down different rows in the garden. I could do that, change the rows water was running down, but usually Grandpa and I would do it together. By the time I got married I had been cooking for ten years, so [laughing] it must have gotten progressively better.

My grandfather would go over to town and pick up the mail at two o'clock in the afternoon, about the time that I got out of school. Even though I was mollycoddled and spoiled by my grandpa, he still wouldn't wait five minutes for me to get from school to the post office. He would get in his little car and drive home, and I would have to walk the two and a half miles home. This shows you the difference in how children were raised in those days.

Since my mother had come from this area, a lot of the towns-people were actually my relatives. My aunt was fifty years old and my grandpa was seventy-two when they took on raising a six-year-old child. I thought that was kind of brave of them. My grandpa was in good health, but my aunt had had rheumatoid arthritis since she was about sixteen years old, so she was in a lot of pain, but she didn't show it. She was a trained Indian doctor and she seemed to be able to set aside pain. It may have plagued her, but it didn't stop her from the activities of daily life, and she still kept an immaculate house.

When I was growing up with my mother taking care of me, I had been left to fend for myself a lot of the time. When I came to live with Grandpa and Aunt Caroline, it was different. I remember Auntie telling me to get dressed for dinner, and I looked at myself and thought, "I am dressed." I didn't say anything, but that's what I thought. Then she said, "Go wash your face and hands and put on your Sunday dress." So I went upstairs and changed my clothes and came back wearing my Sunday clothes for dinner. I learned that was what was expected in this setting, which was very different from when my mother and I had a bunch of fishermen for dinner in a boardinghouse in Eureka, with things being slammed on the boardinghouse table.

In Orleans we had a spoon, a soup spoon, a salad fork, a dinner fork, a dessert fork, a plate, and a salad plate. When the salad was finished I would have to get up and take the salad plates and forks into the kitchen and put them away. Then I would come back and sit down and then dinner would be served family-style, from bowls and platters on the table. When those plates were taken away, my aunt got up and brought in dessert. After dinner the adults had tea and sat and talked, and I drank my milk, had dessert, and listened to them. I didn't say anything unless I was asked how my day was or how school had been, and then I would tell them. Actually, I talked quite a bit, because I was a talkative child and they were sort of quiet people, so I talked more than some children did who were raised that way, but children didn't get to talk out of turn. You couldn't just start talking unless they asked you to add something to the conversation. If they didn't ask you, you sat there and listened to what they had to say. That is how a Victorian person was raised.

Their main meal was not in the evening, it was dinner in the middle of the day. Supper was leftovers from dinner with a different dessert. Since dinner was such a large meal, it was usually followed by fruit, with dessert like cobbler or cookies following the smaller evening meal. They also ate a large breakfast. Grandpa's breakfast was really large. He would have cooked cereal, potatoes, beans, toast, and bacon. But then, by breakfast-time he had already worked two hours. He would have been out and milked the cows, fed the horses and chickens and given them fresh water in the summertime, and probably hoed a couple of rows, because my aunt and I got up at seven.

The War Years

During World War II the Indian Health Service sent a doctor up here to see the little half-breed children in Orleans, and they would hold a clinic to give us our immunization shots, look at our tonsils and stuff. They would line us up, girls and boys, and we would all have to take off our shirts so they could listen to our hearts and lungs. They would make us take our shirts off and stand there in line in front of everyone like a bunch of cattle all lined up, even the girls who were about twelve years old and had breasts.

In 1942 there was a whooping cough epidemic and they gave us shots. Of course there was the fear that the Japanese were using germ warfare against us, and they had found some of the balloon bombs up in the mountains around here that had floated across the Pacific on the jet stream, so the government sent more whooping cough shots for us to take. I guess the vaccine had gotten warm or old or something, and we all got great big boils on our arms where they gave us the shot. Big blue boils. Big, the size of Ping Pong balls, and everybody got sick and headachy, the whole school. Everyone who got a shot got sick. Most of the boils broke and children got a big ugly scar on their arms. I was one of the unlucky ones, mine did not break and I got pancreatitis and was sick for three weeks.

I remember weighing forty-nine pounds and wanting to weigh fifty pounds so bad because my cousin Laverne weighed fifty pounds, and she was a year older than me. I wanted to weigh fifty pounds because she kept laughing at me and saying she weighed as much as a sack of spuds. You know how children get; they just have to do what the other children do. But when I got sick, I lost eleven pounds and weighed thirty-eight pounds when I was nine years old. I was just devastated because I had lost all that weight and couldn't weigh fifty pounds like my cousin.

Years later, when I was twenty-three, the doctor told me that that was when I had developed diabetes, because after that I had signs and symptoms of the disease. I would throw up my breakfast, and they tried feeding me acorns, of course, and bitter yucky stuff, probably milk thistle tea, but I still threw up. Auntie had a vision that if she gave me oranges, half an orange cut into little sections, when I felt like I was going to throw up, that it would keep me from getting sick and I wouldn't feel like I was going to faint. She was right, but she didn't know what the sickness was. She only had this vision to treat me by.

Around 1943 they took all of us over to the agency hospital in Hoopa and took our tonsils out; there must've been ten or twelve of us. All of the children were mad at me when I woke up. They all just growled at me, because I had a reaction to ether and the nurse had to take special care of me and I didn't wake up right away, being sick and with a raw throat. I didn't wake up for eight or ten hours, and they all had to go through that recovery by themselves, and I had the nurse taking care of me. My cousins were all mad at me: "You got out of half of it."

During the war years, between 1941 and 1945, there were no ceremonial dances because so many of the men who danced had left for the war. Almost every family had young men gone to war, because most of them were in good health. I don't know anyone who stayed home because of 4-F status, but I only remember two men from Orleans being killed in the service. After the war a lot of the servicemen never came home, because of the economics of the river. There was just no work up here. First there had been the Depression, and then there was the war, and things just didn't open up for about twenty years after the war, until they started logging up here and the economy got good. A lot of the Karuk men moved to the coast and worked as loggers in the redwoods.

Karuk people who have moved away come home to visit when the fish are running, so the whole family would be here in August, and Grandpa would have his twelve grandchildren for most of the summer. They had to work in the garden and I had to help, but I didn't do much, because I wasn't very good at garden work. I learned to do it but I wasn't very productive.

I learned a lot of things in a kind of dreamlike state, an altered state of mind. You recall your training after you have fasted and done a ceremony, or done something for someone. You fast and pray to get into an altered state of mind and the training comes back to you, but when you're in your regular world it's hard to remember the training and the teaching. When I was younger I always thought that the medicine women were telling me something, then when I got up in my forties I realized that they were talking into my mind so that I would have a greater understanding of what they were saying than if they just talked to me, because they put the whole thought in my mind and the feeling that went with the thought. The other way, if you just talk, you don't have that instant full understanding. They put me in a trance so they could talk to me with a better understanding on my part, otherwise I would not have a good understanding of what they were telling me. So what I had thought was talking, when I was younger, wasn't really talking—it was telepathy. Also, communicating that way, nobody else could hear what they were saying.

They thoroughly frightened me so that I never said anything about the training or being trained to any of my contemporaries. They said that if I told anyone, that I could possibly be killed, because people are killed for having this blessing. The white-dominated society that we were living in by the time these medicine women were young did its best to get rid of them. This society didn't really understand what medicine people did, but they wanted to put an end to it, so it was kept very secret. I imagine it was more open a generation or two before me. I was growing up in the thirties, which was just after they were still killing people, in the twenties. The medicine people were mostly killed by miners, but they were also harassed by the Army. We would be in their way, and we spoke out against what was happening all the time, so they would do their best to get rid of the medicine people who provided leadership in resisting the miners and the Army.

The medicine women put me into an altered state so they could talk to me better. They did this by looking into my eyes and then walking into my mind. All I remember is their eyes. You're not supposed to ask anyone anything about what is happening. You just do as you are told. When I came out of this state, many times I knew something that I never knew before. That is the way things happened to me. That lightly altered state of mind was not a trance, because if someone walked into the room I would immediately pick up on their vibes and what they were talking about. I was aware of the other people around me; I was just more focused on what the medicine women were doing. They would slip me into this slightly altered state of mind so they could talk to me with a better understanding on my part. I had been taught not to ask questions, so I was at ease knowing that I would be told everything I needed to know.

When they talk to you telepathically, it is more emphatic than ordinary speech. You feel what they feel about the subject. It isn't just telling you about a subject, they give you the complete essence of what they think and their feelings about it. The telepathic communication is more complex than speech because you know what they're saying and you know what they're feeling.

Nettie Ruben lived next door to us, about a quarter of a mile away, and she was a renowned basket maker. She would see me on the road coming home from school and get me to come down and help her strip her woodwardia ferns out for basket material. I would come to her house on Saturdays because I was going to school during the week. We would strip the green part off the fern and take the little strip in the center and lay it in little flat piles to dry. I would do that all day long with her. I would get down there around nine-thirty or ten o'clock, when it was warm enough to sit outside, and I would do it all day long until it was almost getting dark, and then I would come home. My pay was five dried eels. When I got home, the first thing I would do was build a fire up in the kitchen cookstove and take the lids off the top. I would warm my eels up over the stove and get eel grease on the stove, and my grandfather did not like to smell burnt eel grease. He wouldn't tell me I couldn't do it, he just told me he didn't want me to get any of the grease on the stove, because it stunk. I did this for two or three years with her, and then I went away to Indian school.

Sometime in the mid-forties, when I was about nine or ten years old, my aunt Caroline got sick for about two weeks and she asked Nettie Ruben to come up and nurse her, and paid her probably a couple of dollars a day. After my aunt got well, Nettie came back and brought her six flat baskets that white people thought were placemats. Actually, before white people came, they were patterns that Indian women used to lay out the design of their basket, but then white people used them as placemats. She brought her these placemats in payment for the honor of being asked to take care of a medicine woman.

As a girl I studied piano and learn how to play, but I realized I had no talent and sounded like a player piano—atoonka-toonka-toonka-toonka. I didn't give up, even after I realized I had no talent, and I learned to read music. I guess I could have kept on and tortured everybody with my playing, but my grandfather would not have liked listening to that, and I gave up on playing the piano. He played the violin and was musically very talented. I knew he would have been quite perturbed with me if I had kept on playing, because I had no musical talent and would have always played badly, but he didn't say I couldn't play.

He played the violin by the time he was five years old and would have been a violinist if he hadn't lost his thumb. By the time he lost his right thumb, when he was around eight years old, he was playing classical music. After he lost his thumb he could still play, and played the rest of his life, but he couldn't play the way he had before, because you just can't feather the bow and get the classical sound with no thumb. He had a really fine violin that he had paid sixty dollars for in the 1890s, and after losing his thumb he just played the violin for the fun of it. He tried to teach me the violin, but I had no talent for that, either. My mother played the organ and sang, and my uncle Roddy played the violin. A lot of people in this country played music at that time.

When we were kids, my friend Juju and I would get up way early, about five o'clock in the morning, and walk the twelve miles up to Bessie Tripp's and go swimming. Bessie was Juju's grandmother. One of the reasons to always feed people was that you walked a long way between houses. It would take half a day, about five hours, to walk the eight miles to Somes Bar from here.

Of course we were kids and [laughing] we probably walked more back and forth across the road than we did up the road. By the time you got to the next place, it would be time to eat again. Juju and I would walk a couple of miles past the swimming place to get to Bessie's and get something to eat, then we would turn around and walk back to Langford's store, where there were kids to play with and a place to swim.

A lot of the Indian children couldn't swim at that time, because they weren't supposed to play by the river because the water babies would get you. I have no idea what a water baby is [laughing], but that is what would get you. Since my grandfather was raised half-English, he believed that we should all be able to swim, because we lived close to a major piece of water. When he was young and there were no bridges and you were going across the river in a small boat, if you fell in you had better know how to swim. We were around the river all the time. We picked basket sticks near the water. We got roots from under the water, so if you fell in you better know how to swim, so most of us half-breed children down here learned how to swim.

In the evening, when it began to get cool, we would start walking home. My grandfather always told me, "Whatever you do, don't ride home with those Grant boys." After the Grant boys got off work it would take them about fifteen or twenty minutes to drive the old road from Somes Bar to Orleans. They would just come flying down the road to get a beer in town. I don't think there was a time that Juju and I came walking back down the road that the Grant boys didn't come along. "Do you girls need a ride down the road?" We would jump in with them, of course. They would take Juju to her house and drop her off, but when they brought me home they had to let me off at the foot of the hill because Grandpa would just really growl at everybody if he knew I came home with the Grant boys.

Sherman Indian School

I attended Sherman Indian School, near Riverside, California, for one year and got along really well there. I could have stayed with my uncle in Eureka and gone to school there, but Grandpa thought it would be better for me to go to Indian school because I was spoiled. I was really spoiled and he knew it. He thought it would be better if I had some little adversities to deal with, something to overcome in my life. Because of his misgivings, Grandpa decided to send me to Indian school, where I would learn something about other people and other cultures.

So when I was fourteen I left for school at the Sherman Institute and met a lot of kids and had a lot of girlfriends. The government paid for a bus ticket, and my cousin Laverne and I went down together. This was Laverne's second year in Indian school. When the bus got to San Francisco we went to the park and went to the beach. Then we ran out of money and had to borrow from my aunt Hazel, who lived in San Francisco, to get another bus to take us to Los Angeles on the way to Sherman. The bus company lost all my clothes for ten days, so I had to live out of one tiny little suitcase.

When we first got to the school we stayed in the girls' dormitory. It was a beautiful place with a Spanish influence, a big circular drive with two boys' buildings and two girls' buildings—two-story, great big Spanish-looking buildings, beautiful oak floors. There were probably about a thousand students, and more than half were Navajo, with about three hundred California-Nevada Indians and the rest were Hopi and Navajo. The classroom building sat between the girls' dorms and the boys' dorms. The boys had a smoking area but the girls were not allowed to smoke. The school had a Protestant church and a Catholic church, and you went to church twice a week. Darrell said that when he went to Sherman the boys could walk to church with the girls and hold hands. I told him I didn't get to hold hands with anybody, we had to walk with a matron. But I probably wasn't as old as he had been at Sherman.

I was raised going to High Episcopal church in Orleans, so for me the Protestant church seemed different. Tuesday and Sunday evenings, students would come down from a religious school in San Bernardino and teach religion classes to us Indian children. They were trying to make us be like white people.

The Navajo and Hopi children were always in trouble. The Navajos had head lice and would not get rid of their bugs. The school wanted them to get rid of the head lice, but the Navajo children believed that the bugs had a right to live on you. You are their home and that was it. So they wouldn't comb the lice out of their hair or pick their hair, and they wouldn't try to get rid of the lice. The Navajo girls had long, black, thick hair down to their hips, and after three weeks of not getting rid of the lice, the school cut it off short, around their ears. Of course they didn't believe in getting their hair cut either, because they wore their hair in big rolls stuck up on their head. I think the school administration was stricter in the earlier days, before I was there, and became less strict after World War II. They had two matrons, who were both white. The assistant matron was a Native who had gone to school there.

The school had counselors, who were students responsible for groups of other students, making sure that they came in on time, and that their rooms were clean, and they were out at lineup on time in the morning and in the evening. Counselors got a room of their own, all by themselves. I stayed in a dormitory room in the Minnehaha Home, the younger girls' place, for about three weeks. The older boys stayed in the Alexandria Hall and the younger boys stayed in the Wigwam Lodge. After a while I decided that I was going to get a room for myself, so I put in my name, saying that I wanted to be a counselor, and after a couple of weeks there was an opening and I became a counselor.

I did get my own room, but I wasn't very good at monitoring the other children. I was too lenient. Invariably we ended up with the messiest dorm [laughing]. I had eight girls under me. They were all Navajos and they spoke English, kind of, maybe, sort of. Mostly they talked in Navajo to each other. I wasn't supposed to be letting them talk Navajo in their rooms, but I never said anything. Then the authorities got after me for that, so I told the girls that they had to keep their rooms cleaner and keep most of the things put away. They had all kinds of little Navajo fetishes and jewelry and blankets. I told them they had to keep everything cleaned off and put away, then they wouldn't call us messy. They were better after that. I told them, "When I come in, you have to quit talking Navajo. I don't care, but I get in trouble if I let you talk Navajo, so just don't do it in front of me, that's all." After that, whenever I would walk into a room for a room check, about once a week, they would talk English.

Vera Davis, a Karuk girl from the village of Ti Bar, was another counselor in the same building. It took a long time for Vera to become a counselor, and I always thought it was because she was dark. I thought I got to be a counselor really easily since I could pass for white, with my reddish brown hair and pale green eyes. My skin was dark but my hair and eyes were light. I always felt that this was the reason I was made a counselor, not because I deserved to be, but I did get my own room.

The school was run pretty much military-style. In the morning and again in the evening we lined up in front of the matron with all our little charges. They faced the matron and you faced them and when the matron called out your name you turned around and responded, "All accounted for."

In the morning, the kids in the tenth grade and higher learned the various trades—carpentry, cosmetology, business courses—and in the afternoon they went to school for their regular academic classes. The freshman year, you just took general education. You could work in the kitchen to learn to become a commercial cook. Every quarter they changed where you worked, to give a range of experiences. I worked in the hospital, the kitchen, and cleaning the teachers' dormitory.

I had to leave the school after that year because the BIA closed it to California and Nevada Indians. They felt that we had more opportunities for education than the Navajo and Hopi, so they reserved the school for these Indian children. The next year we were trying to get a school bus to take Orleans children down to Hoopa for school, and I stayed home, because they needed a ninth child in order to get that school bus. For six months we nine children and the driver rode in a little station wagon from Orleans to Weitchpec to get to school. After that they got a school bus for us and I went to school in Hoopa for the next two years.

My Grandfather's Death

When my grandpa was close to eighty years old he still plowed three- and four-acre fields with a single horse and a plow that he had to push while the horse pulled. When he was in his prime he was just a hair below six feet tall, but by then he had shrunk to about five feet, ten inches. That's about the time he sold the mines, too. He said he couldn't do the assessment work for us anymore.

My grandfather was fascinated by mines, and on weekends we would go around and look at the different types of mines. I remember crawling through mines and caves with him. He took me with him because he couldn't hear real good, and when he traveled he couldn't understand what loudspeakers were saying, so I went along with him for that too. He had so many little notebooks filled with tales of lost mines, like fairy tales, mining fairy tales.

Luther Hickox, up at Somes Bar, had a mine that he kept selling to white people who didn't know better. The story went that somebody would say, "Well, Luther has sold his mine again." After a while people would miss a payment on the mine and Luther would have his mine back and then sell it again to somebody else. None of the miners ever made money with the mine, but Luther made money selling the mine. Shrewd. When we visited Luther and his family we had to walk across a swinging bridge all the way across the Klamath River. It was built of boards laid across two cables with two more cables for hand railings. I hated the way that bridge swung, and if you stopped partway across, then it would start swaying worse than ever, and that was really scary.

One of my grandparents was related to Luther's wife, Elizabeth Hickox, and that's why we visited them all the time. By "all the time," I mean three times a year. If you took the time to go all the way from Orleans to Somes Bar, eight miles, just to visit in those days, and walk across that swinging bridge, three times a year is quite a lot.

Mrs. Hickox made beautiful black baskets with white designs that she is famous for now. She made them that way because there were lots of ferns behind her place that supplied the black material for the baskets. I don't know which of my grandparents was related to her. If they say she's a relation, you just say yes; you don't ask questions and you always speak to them, because they are your relatives.

My grandpa was in Sacramento being treated for kidney disease when he had a stroke that killed him. The first sign of kidney disease was when he was eighty-one years old and went hunting with another man up in the mountains at Salmon Summit. They stayed at one of the little cabins that were around in the woods in those days. When they had been out there a couple of weeks it snowed, and my grandfather's legs were starting to swell up, and he was having a hard time getting around, so he started breaking trail through the snow to come in. He walked maybe a mile from the cabin they were staying in and made it to the ridgetop, then he let the other fellow break trail on the downhill shot, probably about four or five miles. Well, this fellow just took them in a circle, and they ended up back at the trail Grandpa had broken. When that happened Grandpa said he couldn't make it, so he sent the other man on ahead and went back to the cabin to build up the fire and wait for help. Grandpa gave him his compass so he wouldn't get lost this time. He made it on into Orleans with Grandpa's instructions. He went to the Forest Service station and got a group of five other men and a stretcher, and the six of them packed Grandpa in. That was three or four years before he died.

When he was up in his eighties, Grandpa was staying with a relative in Sacramento while he was being treated for the kidney disease. He was still in pretty good shape and walked a mile or so to the doctor and back twice a week. He would get up around six-thirty and fix coffee every morning, but one morning he was not around, so my cousin that he was staying with knocked on his door, and he hit the wall with his foot, so she came on in. He had had a stroke and could not talk intelligibly. She brought him a pencil and tablet, and he wrote that she should get hold of his children. He wanted them to come down. Nancy wanted him to go to the hospital, but he wrote on his tablet that he was not going to the hospital, that he was going to die today. She tried to tell him no, and he wrote down that the stroke was on his left side. Everybody made it to Sacramento to see him while he was still conscious, and about four o'clock that afternoon he slipped into a coma and passed away three hours later. Uncle Alvie had taken his pickup truck down because he knew his father was dying. It took him two or three days to get home with the body. He had to stop in every county he went through and get a permit from the coroner's office to transport a body through that county. Now one permit would do it.

My grandfather only came back once after he died. It was like he hollered my name, and I looked, and I could feel him there, and then he was gone. I didn't see him, I just could feel him. I thought he came back to say good-bye to me because I had not gone to Sacramento to see him before he died, like Aunt Caroline and his children had. I had had to stay home on the farm to take care of the animals, and of course if someone had to stay home it would be his granddaughter and not his daughter.

TWO

Marriage and Children, the Happy Years
1950–1965

THE FIRST TIME I SAW DARRELL MCCOVEY, I was fifteen years old and didn't know who he was, so I asked somebody and said that I wanted to meet him. She said, "You don't want to meet him. He's no good," because he drank and partied around.

I told her, "Well, I'm going to meet him." Darrell's brother Cart had told him that I would be perfect for him. He said, "You will like her. She's crazy."

Darrell told him, "I don't want to meet no crazy woman."

My girlfriend Juju had been dating Cart for about six months, so he had heard about me but we had never met. The day we actually met, I was walking down to the agency hospital. I was wearing a black coat and black shoes and a black sweater and a black bandanna. Darrell was with his brother-in-law Frank Trimble. Frank and I had met before and he called out to me, "Wait up, we'll walk down together." They caught up with me and we walked along together. Darrell didn't say much, he was real quiet. We got down to the hospital and Darrell stopped me and said, "Are you in mourning or something?"

I just said no.

"Well, you are wearing all black clothes," he said. So I unbuttoned my coat and showed them I had a red plaid skirt on under the coat.

Then he said, "When you get through at the hospital, I'll walk back up with you," so I said okay. Then I went in and saw the doctor and got my shot. When I came back out I didn't see them, so I started walking back up toward the school. Darrell caught up with me when he saw me and said, "I thought I said I was going to walk up with you."

I said, "Well, I didn't see you." So we walked along together and talked, just getting-to-know-each-other talk. The next weekend he came up to Orleans and that's when I really started going out with him.

After that we dated for a couple of years, but I was busy going to school. Then the next year my grandpa had died, so I had to go to work for my cousin Nola, taking care of her daughter, because Auntie didn't have the money to keep me. First we went to San Francisco looking for work because her sister Ida was living down there and so was my aunt Hazel, and we could stay with them while Nola looked for work. When Nola couldn't find a good job in San Francisco, she came back to Eureka and went back to work in the woolen mills, where she had worked before, but that work wasn't as good as it had been.

When we got back to Eureka I began taking care of Nola's daughter Rita from two o'clock in the afternoon until two o'clock in the morning, when Nola got off work at the mill. Then I would get up in the morning and go to high school and Nola would get up and get Rita ready for school before she had to go back to work. I had more than enough credits to graduate from high school, but I did not have civics and U.S. history, so I took those courses in Eureka and I took a family living course too. With those courses out of the way I was ready to graduate. I didn't do very well in Eureka High because I was sick a lot. I had to walk a good distance to and from school every day, but sometimes Darrell would give me money to ride the bus. My side hurt so badly that I went into the hospital a couple of times. The white blood cell count would go up and they thought it was chronic appendicitis. (Years later, in the 1960s, neurosurgeons found that there were nerve problems in my back and head that accounted for the white blood cell count, but they didn't know why.) Around that time Nola lost her job, so I came back to Orleans to live with my aunt Caroline because I was through with school and Nola couldn't keep me anymore.

When I was a girl I used to see movies and dream about how I would find this romantic figure on a white charger who was going to pack me away like the singing cowboy who always gets the girl. Grandpa would tell me, "That isn't real life. It's a story, but that isn't what life is like. Life isn't that way," so I kind of got the idea. When I grew up and life wasn't that way, I wasn't surprised. Even though I married for romantic love, it wasn't like the movies. It was never that romantic, no white charger...[laughing] no car! We had to walk. If Darrell wanted to see me or we wanted to meet, he had to walk seventeen miles each way. But he and his brother Cart both did that when they were courting Juju and me. About the third time he did this after we met, I finally asked him, "How come you always smell like wood smoke?"

He said, "Well, when we walk up here, we walk probably ten miles or so and then build a fire and camp for a while and sleep, and then we walk on up the road." So I was smelling his campfire smoke.

Sometimes Juju and I packed a picnic lunch and took the school bus down like we were going to school, but we would get off at Weitchpec and meet Darrell and Cart for a picnic down at his cousin Ada Jones's place. Juju's brother Woody would hop off the bus with us because he wouldn't go to school without us. But usually Darrell would walk all the way up to Orleans.

When I was seventeen and Darrell and I wanted to be married, my aunt Caroline objected, but my grandfather was dead by then and she gave me her permission, even though she did not like me marrying back into the hard life that went with my marrying Darrell, because the Yurok Indians, who were Darrell's family, were poor and had hard lives on the Yurok reservation. They had to work harder and go further to find work than we did up here in Orleans, where logging had opened up a new veneer mill and jobs were available. She wanted me to marry a white man, because she thought

I would have an easier life and she wanted me to pass for white. I had green eyes and my skin was light enough that it was dark for a white person, but it still was in that range, and my hair had a lot of gold and red highlights and looked lighter than it was. I didn't like her attitude. It was very subtle but I was aware of it through my intuition. I am attuned to certain very slight variations and I always felt like white men thought they were better than I was. It would be hard enough to get along with a man if he thought he was better than you because he was a man, let alone if he thought he was better than you because of your race, too.

With the new-world Indian marriages, you went to the preacher and married who you chose, kind of, who your family approved. Sometimes they would object and you'd do what you wanted to anyway. That was what I did [laughing].

I had a couple of cousins who married white men. One of them was very light-skinned and the other very dark-skinned. They didn't make it with their white men. One of them later married a Portuguese man, who would also be considered white, but he was a more real person than her first husband and didn't consider himself to be better than she was. The other cousin didn't get along with her white husband at all. He was an overbearing horse's ass, but they come in all races.

Darrell and I and two other couples were married in 1951 after Darrell was paid his share for land taken from California Indians by the government—$150. In 1972 the interest was finally paid, and this was six times as much as had been paid for the land itself, which was something like a penny and a half per acre. The fight for the settlement on land began in the 1920s and went all the way until 1951 before the first payment was made. Then in 1972 he got $638 for the interest. After he had gotten the $150 payment, Darrell sent his sister Dee and his cousin Joe Reed up to Orleans to pick up Juju and me because he was working at the mill and couldn't come himself. They took us downriver to Darrell's house and we left for Reno that night, with Darrell paying for the trip. It was a little old car and the three couples getting married and our mother-in-law, Sadie, were packed into it. Two of her sons and one daughter were getting married, and Sadie came along because [laughing] she wanted to see her whole herd get married at one time.

Juju sat on Cart's lap most of the way and Darrell and Lawrence drove. When Darrell drove I got to sit in the front seat and Lawrence and Dee would sit in the back. We slept in the car somewhere around Lake Amador that night. Typical of him, Cart had spent his money on the car and partying, so he did not have any money to get married on, and Darrell had to buy Juju's marriage license and our marriage license, and he had to buy Juju and me rings. About two weeks later Juju got mad at Cart and threw the ring away. [Laughing] When Darrell heard about that he said, "What do you mean, throwing my ring away?"

Going up the courthouse steps I realized that I was really hungry and said that I needed to get something to eat. Darrell said, "Did we come here to eat or to get married? I came to get married." Then Sadie said she would buy us all lunch after we were married.

I looked older than I was. Juju and I were both seventeen and we were marrying brothers. When we got to the Washoe County courthouse, Juju said she was eighteen and they gave her a big hassle. They questioned her, and my soon-to-be mother-in-law had to come over to the counter to verify that Juju was eighteen and had permission to get married. I was standing in line watching when I saw that happen. When it came time for me to get my license and the county clerk asked me how old I was I said, "I'm twenty-three." They never batted an eye [laughing]. I could look older and more mature than I was. I was mature enough to know not to say I was eighteen [laughing]. Since Darrell was twenty-seven, it was reasonable that his wife would be twenty-three. It's consistent. Not that he was marrying a child bride.

The judge asked, "Do you want the long service or the short service?"

Darrell says, "What's the difference in price?"

The judge says, "It's the same."

[Laughing] Darrell says, "We'll take the long service, I want to get my money's worth."

I started crying after we got married. When the judge was saying, "With this ring I thee wed..." I started crying and I couldn't stop. I cried all the way down the steps of the courthouse and Darrell says, "I don't know why you are crying." I said, "I'm crying because I know what a hard life it's going to be." [Laughing] That was me being facetious.

The *Sacramento Bee* ran a story [about May 19, 1951] captioned "All in one day—California Indians married in Reno." It told how Sadie had been a witness for the marriage of two of her sons and a daughter. After we were married, Sadie bought us hot turkey sandwiches at a luncheon counter and we walked around Reno for a while, looking in the windows at things. We didn't go into any casinos because we were too young, and Sadie wouldn't want to go in one anyway.

On the way back, Darrell bought all seven of us fried chicken dinners in Weaverville. It was about eight o'clock in the evening and we were starting to go over the Weaverville grade, and there was a woman walking along the side of the road whose car had broken down farther up. We couldn't put any more people in the car, so we all got out and stood alongside of the road, and they picked up this woman because they didn't want to leave her walking alone all the way to Weaverville. They took her back into Weaverville and then came back and picked us up, and we went on down the road toward home.

When we got home, the children had gotten into Darrell's cot and it was half knocked down, and they had strewn stuff all around. Darrell tried to put up his cot a couple of times and it just kept falling back down, so he kicked the end that was standing up. It fell down on the floor too, and we lay down and [laughing] went to sleep on it. By then it was about five o'clock in the morning and he had to go to work that day.

About two weeks later we had our honeymoon at this little village, Hyampom, out in the middle of nowhere in Trinity County. Darrell had a brother-in-law who lived there and there was a big dance nearby, in Hayfork, so that's where we went on our honeymoon. I told Darrell that I bet we were the only people ever to have a honeymoon in Hyampom and he said, "Well, you're supposed to be alone on your honeymoon." There was a little bar there and somebody said that we were newlyweds, and they treated him to so much beer that Darrell wasn't even able to go to the dance. We rode over to Hayfork and Darrell just slept in the car. I guess we were the first people that they had seen honeymooning in Hyampom too [laughing]. Then the people in Pecwan gave us all a big blowout wedding reception with a potluck dinner down at the school.

Darrell McCovey's Story

The day Darrell was born, in late August 1923, his mother and grandmother, Sadie and Aussie, were working at the fish-canning plant, filleting fish down at the mouth of the Klamath River near the town of Klamath, and his father, Charlie, was setting nets in the river and catching salmon to be canned. Around noon Sadie's contractions were getting harder, so she and her mother got in a dugout redwood canoe and paddled to an island they were camped on, where there was a camp for people working at the fish plant and for men catching fish to be canned at this plant. This was Sadie's fourth child and she would sit down and rest for a while and then walk around, waiting for the baby. About eight o'clock that evening the fish plant whistle blows, signaling that it is time to hang the nets out in the river, and she was delivered of the baby. They weighed him on a fish scale and he weighed seven pounds even. Sadie said he was born jaundiced and he peed all over like a little boy does, and then he didn't pee again for the next three days. When Charlie found out he had a little boy, and because this was his first boy with Sadie, he went on a two-day drunk.

Darrell was born on about the last day of the fishing season, and the third day after his birth Charlie came back, and the family of two adults and three children all went back up the river in a dugout redwood canoe. They had filled the canoe up with two or three hundred dollars' worth of groceries and two adults and three little children, going up the river in this dugout, and the baby quits breathing. His mother said to Charlie, "He quit breathing." And Charlie scoops up some water out of the river and throws it in the baby's face, and he gasps and starts breathing again. Then he pees, and after that he is okay. So that's [laughing] the trauma of Darrell's birth. I guess taking him up the river in the sunshine didn't hurt, because they treat jaundiced babies by putting them under ultraviolet light.

With the boat loaded down like that, it took a couple of days to get up the river as far as Johnson's, where they lived. They rigged little sails on the boat so the wind coming in from the coast would help blow them up the river. They did this every year, and the boat was so heavy going home at the end of the fish-canning season that all the bigger children had to get out and walk along the river bar, and the parents would pole the boat upriver. When they reached a point where the river bar gave out on one side, the boat would come over, pick up the children, take them across to the other side, and then they would walk up the river bar on that side of the river. Darrell said that for the children it was like walking all the way home from Klamath.

They lived in one of those little BIA-built Indian houses with one room, and a loft up top, and a dirt floor. A lot of these houses had wooden floors, but their floor was dirt and the other Indians kind of stuck their noses up about Darrell's family living in a house with a dirt floor. They had put down a clay floor and pounded it in like the old Indians did in their houses, so you could sweep it up easily. Darrell's uncle had a house and was married to Darrell's grandmother, and Darrell's mother was married to the uncle's older brother, so his uncle was both his uncle and his grandfather. Darrell always called him uncle, because he was Darrell's uncle by blood relation and his grandfather by marriage. Then his uncle's house burned down and he moved his family in with Darrell's parents, who already had six or seven children. His uncle had four children too, but they all moved into this little one-room house with a loft, so there were two families, totaling about fifteen people, living there in this little BIA house.

Darrell's aunt Lillian said the people in the village were always talking about those naughty McCovey girls, because it was a long ways to the outhouse from their house, and there was a little wooden porch across the front of the house, and the boys would go out there and pee off the porch. And Lillian said she and her niece Bernice were the oldest girls, and [laughing] they would go pee off the porch too.

After the families had lived in this crowded little house together for a while, they decided to move up to Notchko to the old McCovey place, where there was an old, fallen-down house that they could fix up and live in. The government had given them some lumber and, because there were no roads, they had to pack it up from the river on mules to where they built two houses for the two families. Sadie said they got a man to help them who knew something about building, and one day she walked into the house and started to say something and the men told her, "Woman, get out, we know what we're doing. We don't want to listen to you."

She said okay and went on out. When they had finished doing what they were doing, she came back in again and told them, "Boy, you've got tall people in this country!" They had built a house with an eight-foot ceiling and two inside doorways [laughing] eight feet high. These were doorways between rooms that didn't have doors. The government hadn't given them inside doors with the lumber and they had no money to buy doors. They didn't have enough lumber for all of the inside walls so there was just two-by-four framing on the inside, with two finished inside walls, and there were partitions between the bedrooms. They had wood-fired cookstoves in the kitchen and a wood-fired heating stove in the living room.

The first time I went down to Sadie's house after I met Darrell, it was in the evening, and Darrell wasn't there. I had gone down with Juju to see Cart, and Sadie was getting all her grandchildren ready for school the next day. They had to pack water from the spring, about thirty feet from the house, and way around on the other side of the house, about fifty feet away, was the outhouse— on the other side of the hill so that it was in a different drainage system. She started with the youngest kid and they all took baths. She would be drying one off and another would be taking a bath, all of them bathing in the same water, starting with the youngest. Darrell said nearly every kid had a tattoo of one of the letters from the word "Volcano," which was on the side of the heat stove, burned on their butt, because they all bathed in a little washtub and then dried off by the stove.

At home kids were free to say what they saw and what they thought was kind of dumb out in the world, but you would never say that to the person outside of your family. As a child, or even as a young woman, I wouldn't say anything because I could see their take on life might not be my take on life. They may have a totally different life than you have. But I'm not one to talk to either, because I was spoiled and wayward. I didn't always act like I was raised to act and I didn't always behave the way a lot of Indian people behaved. I was more outspoken and more spoiled. Most people gave their husband more respect than I did—like if Darrell said he wanted me to do something and I didn't want to do it and we would kind of bicker about it, not really arguing, but bickering. Once he wanted me to dig potatoes by myself and I wanted him to dig potatoes with me. He had something else he wanted to do, he wasn't going to help me, and I was bickering with him about it, and he said to his aunt Lillian, "You see that fencepost out there? That fencepost will go out there and dig potatoes before Mavis will. That's the way she always is. I could talk that fencepost into digging potatoes and it would do it before she would."

So Lillian just laughed and I went out, mad as a wet hen, and started digging potatoes. Darrell stood and looked out the window at me and told his aunt Lillian [laughing], "Boy, she can work hard when she's mad!"

Lillian picked up a basket and came out and helped me dig potatoes.

When I was going down to Sadie's in the 1950s, you could see fires going clear up on the Hoopa Bluffs, where they got their basket sticks. Down by Martin's Ferry would be all on fire. They burned one area one year, and the next year they would burn another area. Sadie used to burn down the hill above her house. She would wait until the wind came up, about two o'clock in the afternoon, and burn from the bottom of the hill up through the hazel sticks. It will go up one draw, so that you burned between the ridges where the hazel grew, and the next year you would burn on the other side of the ridge. The fire would not come up over the ridge and burn on the other side, because there was not enough brush to carry a fire that way; because it was burned all the time, the fire would only burn up so far and then quit because the brush above it was all burnt out. When the fire got to the tree line, it would die down because there was nothing beneath the trees for it to burn. You could ride up the road down at Martin's Ferry, and when you looked up, you could see way up the hill under the oak trees where they burned out all the time. Of course if there were deer up there [laughing], you could see them too.

When the Forest Service came in, around 1920, my grandfather was always arguing with his brother-in-law Billy Hotelling about the Forest Service and their crazy restrictions. He said to him, "You are just growing brush and making kindling underneath the trees so the forest can burn."

His brother-in-law would argue back that the ecology needed the brush to hold water in the ground, so it shouldn't be burned. Grandpa would tell him, "Well, there was always water here before, when we burned all the time." There used to be great, huge, old oak trees in the field where the school is now, and there were no bull pine or fir trees. From what Bessie and others told me, around these villages, clear to the top of the hill, there were no fir or pine trees, because for generations the Indians of this area had burned the brush back every couple of years. They burned the brush clear up to the top of the hill. There would be fir trees on the other side, but not on this side of the hill.

We burned clear to the top of the hillside and no one ever worried about fire getting away around your village. Everybody had a little fire outside, and they cooked outside in the summertime.

They had fires all around their places, and they never worried about it. They would make pits and cook the salmon on stakes around them. They never had any running water, so they couldn't have done anything if there was a fire. They made sure that if there was a fire it would burn right there and not go anywhere else.[11]

Sadie used to talk about things that happened before the white men came and before the roads got down to where they lived. She would talk about the dances or something that had gone on, and Darrell would tell her that those days are gone forever. "That isn't here anymore. It's gone." I used to think he was being mean, but she would get upset about the way it had changed, and I guess he was just telling her that there is no way to go back. There is no way to go back to what it was before. You can't go back to yesterday, ever. What's done is done. It's done today and it's done tomorrow and just keeps on going from there. You may be sorry it's gone, but...

There was a wagon road down at Wautec that went up to Pecwan Creek. Darrell said the first time he rode in a car, they had brought a car across the river on a raft, then you could ride the mile from Wautec up to Pecwan Creek and you could ride back down, and that was all the road they had. That was the big road [laughing]. Around 1936 or 1938, they built a road from Kepel on down twelve miles to Johnson's. There was a little tiny grocery store six miles away, at Pecwan, and they had to walk those six miles to go to the grocery store, or else they ordered groceries with the mailman. The mailman would take the grocery order up to Pearson's store, in Weitchpec, and then deliver the groceries with the mail for a little freight charge. In order to do this, someone would have to be there at the road, waiting for the mailman, about two o'clock in the afternoon. When Darrell was younger the mailman only came by two days a week. When we first met and I was writing him, he would get mail on Tuesdays and Thursdays, so those were the only days you could get groceries delivered.

The doctor came up the river by boat once a month to see the children and everyone, to see how they were. They got immunizations at the school once a year, so the little children didn't get those shots until after they started school. After his family moved from Johnson's, Darrell had to walk six miles to and from school everyday. There were little schools all along the river in those days.

Only a couple of people had cars, and we would hire them to take us up to Weitchpec to get groceries or cash our checks. There would be three or four adults and our children, all piled in this car. The road would get really muddy and slick and sometimes run along in the creekbed. The cars would spin out going up the hill, so we would have to back down the road to start over again. The men would all get out and start pushing, and the women would walk up the hill, packing our children. When they pushed the car to the top of the hill we would all get back in and drive again to the bottom of the next hill, when we would have to do it all over. It would be pouring down rain and we would be walking along with our kids. That was fun.

Upriver and downriver, the Jewish peddler came by twice a year in his little panel truck, around the end of May and again in the late fall. He had socks and shirts and work pants, wool underwear, stocking caps and dresses, and all kinds of things. He even had Trojan condoms. You name it, he had it. He loved to come to Grandpa's place, because there was our house and four cabins around there, so he could just lay everything out underneath the walnut trees and people could come from the cabins to look over what he had.

The first time I went downriver to visit his family, Darrell whistled, and pretty soon his three little sisters came running barefoot up the hill to see what he wanted. He talked to them for a little while and they giggled around a little bit, then went running off down a kind of wide trail. The next time I was down, his cousin—who always drove too fast—was driving, and all of a sudden we just went flying down the hill, and we were on that little trail. It about scared me to death [laughing]. I told Darrell that I thought that was a trail, and he said no, that it was a little road. It was a little road indeed, because the car just barely fit on it.

Darrell's family started speaking English at home when he was about three years old. The reason for that was that one of his older brothers had not started school until he was eight years old because it was a long ways for a six-year-old to walk to and from school every day, and when he started school he couldn't speak English, even though he was very bright. He was more book-smart than Darrell, but he had a hard time because he couldn't speak English, so Sadie and Charlie stopped talking Yurok to each other and started talking English because they didn't want Darrell and the other children to have a hard time in school. They always spoke English after that, but Darrell's first language was Yurok. He was the last of the children whose first language was Yurok.

Dolly was Darrell's other full-blooded Yurok grandmother. His grandfather, Charles Alfred McCovey, was an Irishman who had joined the American Navy in Singapore when he was seventeen years old. After getting out of the Navy he got a job as a mail carrier, bringing the mail to Orleans. When he got to the Yurok reservation he settled down and continued to work as the mail carrier in Orleans. Then he met Dolly and after some time won her in a card game.

Alfred and Dolly had four sons, and each of the sons married full-blood Indian women who fell in love with them. Now, that's a true romantic story. Their sons were nice-looking, hardworking men, so they got good, full-blood, hardworking Indian wives. So when Darrell was a boy all his relatives from his father's family were three-quarter Indian, like he was. I remember Darrell's mother and grandmother talking about their fathers and grandfathers having ten wives, so when you talked about fidelity with some man, it wasn't the same as it is in monogamous cultures, and I can understand the Mormons' point of view.

Darrell had heart disease when he was a little kid, because he had rheumatic fever. The doctor who came up the river in a motorboat treated him so he got better, and when he was around fifteen years old he started boxing. He saw other people boxing and he would have to just sit there and watch them, because he was sick. He kept watching them, and he thought, "I could do that." One day he tried it and he could box. Darrell never turned professional, but for three or four years he won the Northern California Golden

Gloves championship for the welterweight division. He had to fight people all the way down to Stockton, including all those tough little Mexicans. Darrell gave me one of his trophies, but I never got one of his little Golden Gloves pins, because he had given them away to his little honeys before I was around. The *Blue Lake Advocate* had a front-page picture of Darrell posing in his boxing trunks. Looked pretty good to me. I should say looked damned good to me.

I never saw Darrell box, because he was in a bad wreck before I met him and was out of his head in a coma for about three days. His grandmother Aussie prayed for him and told me she knew he was going to be all right because his face was shining like a light was coming out of it when she was praying. After that he coached his brothers when they boxed.

When Darrell was courting me, we would go to the fights and all his family would be there. I would sit with his aunt and uncle, and Darrell would walk back and forth all the time, or else he was the corner man for his brother, when he was fighting. Old man Bill Tripp, Bessie's husband, said that for Darrell, an Indian, to win a fight in Humboldt County, he had to knock the other fellow out. I was told he knocked out one fellow in fifteen seconds of the first round. He was good at knocking them out. Someone asked his uncle who he thought was the best fighter on the team Darrell fought with. His uncle said Milton Obie, and everyone was kind of surprised, and Darrell's uncle said that Darrell wasn't mean enough. "He doesn't have that killer instinct to keep beating on somebody." Once he had them beaten, he would back off.

When Darrell was a boy in school, none of the children had ever seen a bicycle until one of the boys got one and the teachers let everyone out of school to watch him ride around the playground, since it was such an unusual sight. After Darrell had learned to ride that kid's bicycle he wanted one too, so he earned his bicycle selling seeds. He walked house to house and sold seeds from the American Seed Company to people downriver because there was a prize of a bicycle if you sold enough packets of seeds. After he had sold so many seeds, his dad bought enough for him to get his bicycle.

Darrell went to work in the woods for Hammond Lumber Company when he was just a kid, only sixteen years old, because his dad had died. He and another kid who was sixteen were setting choker. They wrapped cables around logs to skid them out of the woods to be loaded on trucks. He said that they were such kids that they would drag their cables down the hill and up the other side, just running and jumping and hollering all the way. When they got their lunch at the cookhouse in the mornings, they would fill their lunchboxes up with candy. The first week at work he almost starved to death because he was sitting at a table where he didn't know anybody, and everybody was grabbing so fast and hard that he would just eat what was right in front of him. After that he moved to a table with Indian guys that he knew, and then he got to eat. One of the men had said that they had to get that little Indian kid at their table before he starved himself.

World War II Service

When Darrell was drafted into World War II, he went into the Navy because his grandfather had been in the Navy. They asked him if he had ever been in trouble and he said, "Oh, disturbing the peace once." And they told him that was okay [laughing], that wouldn't keep him out of the Navy. His brother Cart, who was fifteen years old, saw Darrell in his uniform and got his grandmother Aussie to sign her X on a piece of paper saying that he was her son and was eighteen years old, so he joined the Navy too.

When he was in the camp they had a boxing tournament and Darrell was way up there in his weight class, winning all the time, and they wanted him to stay for the finals, but he wouldn't do it because that would have separated him from the division that he was with. Before he shipped out, Darrell's aunt died and he came back up north for her funeral. He stayed around partying for two or three days with his uncles and friends, and then he didn't have enough money to get back down to his ship in San Diego, so he went over to where they held the fights and asked them if they needed him. They paid him forty dollars to fight, win, lose, or draw. So he fought and got enough money to get back to San Diego, but he got back late and the executive officer brought him up on charges, and he told them what had happened. They ended up taking away six liberties to go ashore when they were in port, for being late.

He was a gunner on an aircraft carrier and was in the battle of Leyte Gulf, in the Philippines. Darrell's division was on one side of the islands and Cart was on the other side with the main part of the fleet and Admiral Halsey. Darrell said he got up one morning and came up on deck and he saw an armada and thought that Halsey's fleet had caught up with them, but it was the Japanese fleet. He said, "I took one look at them and thought, 'Today I might die.'" About the time he realized these were Japanese ships, the general quarters alarm started ringing and he ran for his battle station and started shooting at the planes coming at them. The ships had to turn to face the enemy, and he said this seemed to take forever. He said that his piece of the fleet broadcast to Halsey's piece of the fleet in uncoded plain English, "We're meeting the whole Japanese navy over here." Cart said he heard that and thought, "God, my brother's over there," and then his part of the fleet picked up and started sailing over toward Darrell's, but they were already fighting away. He said one of their ships broke in half, and it didn't take a minute for the whole damn thing to go down and disappear. Then all at once the Japanese fleet just turned and took off.

Darrell said he didn't like the service, but there sure were a lot of nice people there. He made a lot of friends and had a lot of fun with them. One time they came off shore leave and one sailor had his booze taped to his leg under his navy pants. The Marine guards were tapping around on the sailors coming aboard, and when they found the bottle taped to this fellow's leg, they just jerked it off and pulled all the hair off his leg where he had had it taped. Darrell said, "God, that guy hollered!" Darrell was next in line and he had a big bulldog doll that he had won throwing darts. He said to the Marine, "You want to look up my bulldog's ass, too?"

The Marine said, "Shut up and get the hell in there, smart ass."

[Laughing] Darrell said he did have a bottle up his bulldog's ass. Then they all went out by the fantail and got drunk. He said when the Marines got shipped out they had big, good parties, and he would get invited and party with the Marines.

One time some great big sailor got smart with him and Darrell knocked the shit out of him and had to go to the captain's mast for a hearing. The captain kind of looked at that guy and said, "You mean you brought this to a captain's mast and that little tiny guy beat you up? I would be ashamed to admit that. I think you guys need to go down and put the gloves on and settle it." The guy never did go to the ring with him. He didn't want to take two beatings.

When Darrell was in the South Pacific, his ship moved out of the war zone and they were all initiated as Shellbacks, for having crossed the equator, and Golden Dragons, for being across the international dateline. First they had to crawl through garbage, then they had to run the gauntlet between two lines of sailors who swatted them with paddles. When they had finished that, there was a big fat guy with grease on his belly and they had to kiss his belly. When the initiates did that, he would rub their face into his belly. Darrell said some of the sailors would get mad and fight back when they were running the gauntlet and they really got the hell whacked out of them, so he just walked through the line and let them hit him without ever saying or doing anything but what he had to do. He said that two or three days before there was going to be an initiation, you could watch the sailors getting the word from their records in Washington, DC, that they had already been across and been initiated, because they didn't want to have to go through that a second time. Right in the middle of the war, they left the war zone and did that, and then went back into the regular shipping lanes and went on about their business after taking a whole day out for the initiation.

The swabbies were responsible for sweeping and mopping different sections of the deck four times a day, and every time, they collected large pans full of dirt. He always wondered where it came from out in the middle of the ocean.

Once when Darrell was in the service he and some big tall Texan were over the side of the ship, standing on a scaffold board, scraping paint off the side of the ship. He said unless you are in a battle, scraping paint and swabbing the decks went on all the time. They had a bucket with a long rope on it that they could get water in to throw on the side of the ship where they had been scraping. The scaffold had a little chain running around that to keep them from falling into the ocean. When the bucket was empty, this Texan threw it over the side of the scaffold and just about the time it comes tight Darrell hollers, "No!" But it's too late, and the line pulled the Texan right over the top of the chain because he was so tall. Darrell reached down and grabbed him by his belt, pulled him back up over the chain, and stood him up. He said he didn't know where he got the strength to do it. The Texan kept in touch with Darrell as long as he lived.

On his way home from the service he was in some town in Texas, walking down the street, and a black guy walking toward him steps off into the gutter. Darrell says, "What did you do that for? Don't do that."

The guy says, "I'm black. I have to do it."

Darrell says, "I'm darker than you are."

The man says, "Yeah, but you're not black." That was a shock to him, and it was a shock to see toilets and drinking fountains labeled "Colored" and "White."

The Bright Lights of Klamath

For the first year of our marriage, we lived in the little town of Klamath, at the mouth of the river. Darrell's aunt Mindu was pregnant at the same time I was pregnant with my first baby. I was about six months pregnant and we were going across the river, getting driftwood to build cook fires because Darrell was working and he did not have time to cut wood. Mindu was paddling a Yurok dugout canoe—I never learned to paddle—and we would gather the wood in gunny sacks and pack them down to the canoe, go back and fill up another sack and pack it back, both of us pregnant, with her expecting in a couple of weeks. There we were, getting wood, and Darrell came by on the trail and saw us and felt sorry for these two pregnant women packing gunny sacks full of firewood, so he came down and packed the wood over to the canoe for us, then he unloaded the canoes back on the other side of the river and packed all the wood to our houses for us.

When I went into labor with Beavi the doctor for prenatal care at the agency hospital said he was going to give me a spinal and I told him that I wasn't going to have a spinal.

"Oh, you won't feel any pain."

I said, "I've never heard anyone in my family complain very much about the pain they had having a baby. They seem to all have their children fairly easily. I'd rather just have it naturally, and if I need some pain medication at the end, I will take the pain shot."

"Oh no," he said. "It isn't good to take those pain shots. I'm going to give you a spinal."

I told him, "No, you're not."

He said he was and I said, "Then you won't be delivering my baby, because [laughing] I'm not going to have a shot in my spine in order to have a baby."

At this time Darrell was working in a mill out on the coast, so I went over to Eureka and stayed with my cousin Nola and got set up with a doctor who had delivered the babies of a cousin of mine, and who [laughing] was also Darrell's fight doctor when he was boxing Golden Gloves. He took me on as a patient, and although I didn't know it, I was already in labor and he just didn't tell me. So I walked around town with Darrell all afternoon, and I thought I was having false labor pains. Darrell went back up to Klamath to go back to work and I went home to my cousin Nola's and started cooking dinner. I'd invited my aunt Lottie over, and she was watching me cook. I'd cook for while and then I'd stop. Then I'd cook for while and stop again. My aunt said, "You are in labor and you're getting so close that I'm afraid to leave you to phone the doctor, because you might have your baby while I'm gone."

I told her I couldn't be that close, but about that time Nola came home from work and phoned the doctor. He told her if I was anything like my cousin whose babies he had delivered, I had better get to the hospital. We took a cab to the hospital and met the doctor. He checked me out and said that I was going to have the baby in a half-hour, but he had not eaten all day, so he was going to finish his supper and come back to deliver the baby. He just made it back to his house when they phoned him and said, "She's delivering." And I did not need any spinal shot.

Darrell was working in Klamath and somebody phoned up to the bar there and told them we had a baby girl, so Darrell came back to Eureka. He stopped by Nola's on his way to the hospital, but I opened the door because I was already home. I got out of the hospital in about two and a half days. They tried to send bottles home with me, but I figured I was going to nurse the baby, so I didn't take any. No bottles, no spinal.

When Beavi was born, in 1951, Darrell made twenty-two hundred dollars in three months, peeling redwood logs for one of the mills. We lived in a motel in town and paid eighty dollars a month rent. I didn't have a crib, so we put Beavi in a dresser drawer with a pillow for a mattress. At that time you could rent a house for twenty-five dollars a month, but living in the motel was fun for us, as a newly married couple. Darrell worked right across the river from where one of his uncles lived. His uncle had built a new house, so next door to where his uncle lived there was the old empty house and we could have stayed there for probably ten dollars a month, and Darrell could have gone right across the river to work. But no, we had to live downtown because it was fun. People kept asking Darrell's uncle why we didn't live in his house, and he said that he thought we liked living uptown with the bright lights. Other than Eureka, I'd never lived in a real town before, but when I was living in Eureka I was taking care of my cousin's daughter at night and never had enough money or time to go anyplace or do anything.

Klamath must have had around fifteen hundred people, and a lot of them were Native Americans. There was a theater, four bar-rooms, two big grocery stores, about four restaurants, three churches, and a malt shop. There were three or four motels right in the town of Klamath. I don't think an ordinary little wage earner could live in a motel anymore. Our old friend Nadine Starritt was there working in the Busy Bee Café, and when we first came into the restaurant one morning she said, "Darrell, give me my quarter tip now. I know you're going to give it to me, but I want you to give it to me now because I'm dying for a pack of cigarettes." That's what cigarettes cost out of the machine. From a store they were even less, of course. Klamath was a tourist town, so things were more expensive, and we could still eat ham-and-eggs breakfast for the both of us for less than two dollars at that time.

The theater was across the street from us, and we went to a movie almost every other night. After Beavi was born one of Darrell's relatives babysat for us, and we would go to the Busy Bee Café and have milkshakes and banana splits and drink soda pop after Darrell got home from work. Other times Darrell would babysit and I would go to the movie. He would go Monday night and I would stay home with the baby. I went on Tuesday night and he would stay home with the baby. On Thursday night we got a babysitter if we both wanted to see the show, because they only showed the Thursday night movie that one night.

Married Life in Yurok Country

After living for a year in Klamath, we moved back upriver and lived for the next fifteen years in several Yurok villages. We moved away from Klamath because I was getting sick a lot. It was too damp for me out on the coast, and it was a cold, cold year, and I kept getting pneumonia. The doctor said I needed to move inland where it was drier, because he thought that damp weather was going to kill me, my lungs couldn't take that weather. So we moved back up to Pecwan even though Darrell earned better money on the coast.

Darrell's family did not eat three times a day, the way I was used to. They only ate twice a day, in the morning and again in the evening. They worked throughout the day and might have a piece of fish or a piece of jerky, but they didn't stop and cook a meal in the middle of the day. It sure was hard for me to get used to that. And most houses on the Yurok reservation had outhouses when I first went there.

I finally learned how to drink coffee so I wouldn't be so hungry all day. Sadie melted cheese in coffee so it was more like food. Between those two meals you would just take whatever food was around. Sadie had twelve children, so there wasn't much around. She also had three or four grandchildren she took care of, and about five of her own children were still living at home, so to eat without cooking was a chore. They got busy working on things, and never stopped and wasted time cooking, because they would be away from the house, gone picking sticks for baskets, picking up acorns, or doing the other things they had to do in that life. Sadie had so many acorns stored in her attic that it broke down the ceiling in the back of the room. She made baskets and tried to teach me, but my hands weren't strong enough to tighten the woven roots and sticks together. Wood for the cookstove was a never-ending chore.

Darrell was always shocked that I was so weak, but I don't think I would have been if I hadn't been in that automobile wreck when I was five years old. It shocked him that as big as I was, at five feet, four inches and 120-some pounds, [laughing] I couldn't push cars as well as his sisters could. But he didn't marry me for my strength, so that is one of the good things. He thought I was smart. I wasn't as astute as he was, but he thought I was intelligent, and naive.

Darrell has always been sensitive to emotional situations. When he would come into a house and people were arguing about something, having some kind of altercation, he would sense it right away and say, "Let's go," but I wouldn't feel anything. He'd say, "Don't you ever feel when things aren't quite right?"

I told him, "No, I don't sense that. I don't know anything about that." So even though I was born with certain sensitivities, I was really stupid about these feelings because I had been protected so I wouldn't react to things like that, because the medicine women believed that, being this spiritual medicine person, I'm supposed to make the world a happy place. And to do that, I have to be content and happy. That is very simplistic, but it is what they believed and they worked hard to try and keep me happy.

Among the Yurok, the females were left with the females. After Darrell and I were married, I was left in the house with his female relatives—his sisters, mother, his grandmother, and his aunts—all the time. I didn't have much to do with the men except to cook for them and clean for them, because women didn't go fishing or hunting with the men. I remember his uncles teasing Darrell about me in Yurok so much that I cried when Darrell told them, "At least she can cook."

I thought Darrell was awfully bossy to his mother, and it used to really bother me. I never said anything, because it was none of my business, but I used to think that. I didn't know what they were talking about, but it seemed that he had an awful lot of say about things, and he was awfully bossy to his brothers and sisters and everyone else in his family. Sometimes they would not like what he said, but they wouldn't say anything back. I guess I had been married quite a while, probably ten years, before I realized that he was the head of the household, and that he was in the place that my grandfather had had in our household. There were so many men in Darrell's family that I didn't realize that he was the "chief," and that explained his behavior.

Of course Juju and I were married to brothers, and we all lived in the same house. When Darrell would come home and start giving orders, we called him Chief Give-Um-Orders. Our nickname for the second brother was Grumpy, because he was always growling about something and it seemed like he was always trying to catch somebody doing something so he could tell on them. Leonard, Darrell's half-brother from his father's other family, was somewhere in the family logistics, but he wasn't a major player. I felt that he was catered to and had things done for him, but it didn't seem that he had much say. His grandmother and his mother just kind of coddled him. This was all very interesting to me because I came from a family of one child, so all these logistics were brand-new to me. Juju came from a large family, so she knew all about these things, but it was all brand-new to me.

After Darrell and I were married and living with his family, he began acting differently. He wasn't so romantic as he had been before, and he was kind of standoffish-acting. I didn't understand it and my mother-in-law would say, "Oh, he loves you. He's in love with you." And then, later on in life, I learned that Yurok people didn't believe in marrying somebody that they loved, because it made the family too volatile because the couple would be too centered on their love, and that wouldn't make a stable, quiet, balanced family life, because their emotions would be too entangled in this person that they were romantically involved with.

Then I realized that he was acting like he was supposed to act as a Yurok married man, involved with his family, his wife, and his work but not that emotionally entangled, and that's what he was doing. He was acting like a Yurok husband was supposed to act. He was still romantically entangled in his heart, but he didn't act that way because if he did, then men would tease him and make fun of him for being so involved with a female. It took a while for me to get used to that.

My mother-in-law let me eat with him because Darrell wanted me to. She knew I wasn't raised in the Yurok way, so I got to eat with him. My mother-in-law never ate with the men. She ate after all the children had finished eating, and sometimes there wasn't much left. You could tell how well your husband treated you by how much food got left for you, because he could eat it all up like a lion and leave you with nothing. In the old days, when a boy got to be twelve years old he left the women's house and could eat with the men. He didn't get served first, but he could eat with the men, so he got to eat before the women—the grandmothers, the mothers, and the daughters.

A lot of things were like that. For instance, if your husband was angry he could tell you to shut your mouth, but you could never tell him to shut his mouth. I don't care what you were, as a woman you could never tell a man to shut his mouth. You could have had the female power of the Creator and you could not tell your husband to shut his mouth. Actually, you would wait on him hand and foot. He would eat first and get the best food and his wife would eat last.

It was a custom of both the Karuk and Yurok that you never talked back to your husband in public, ever. I don't care what he was doing, other than flirting around with another woman, and in that case you could hit him if he dared to do that in front of you. I liked the downriver custom that my mother-in-law, Sadie, told me about. She said if you see your man making eyes or flirting around with somebody at the dances or some other public place, you could take a stick and beat him. That's permitted. Since I was the first family, that was my right. You could do this in front of everyone to embarrass him. On the other hand, if a woman flirted, the man could scar your face and send you back to your family and disown the children, or they could kill you and keep the children. I never heard of anything like that happening up here around Orleans, in Karuk territory, but they were less influenced by white culture downriver. They got the first road down there around 1938, and that is one reason for them being more traditional and less influenced by the [laughing] "Caucasian persuasion."

I have been told that the old moral codes were very strict. If she committed adultery, a woman would be lucky if her husband killed her, because if he didn't kill her he would scar her face, cut her hair off, and disown their children. That meant the children could never dance or marry, because being disowned that way, a child never really knew who their family was, and if you didn't know your family, you couldn't pray or get married. This is sort of what happened when Aussie went against their regulations and bought her own husband. They took the children away from her, but her father, Dick Gray, had enough money and bought the children back and raised them himself.

"The White Man Set Me Free"

I asked Aussie about the white man's coming and what it was like being around white men on the river before 1900. She said it was different than before they had been here, but she said, "The white man set me free."

I said, "What do you mean, he set you free?"

"Well, after the whites came, you could marry who you wanted to and choose who you wanted and not have to marry who they told you you must marry." So that was a difference, and she felt that they had set her free, because they let her live her life the way she wanted to live it.

When Aussie was about twelve years old she had been married to a Yurok man named Jones who was in his forties and who had already had several wives. He treated her like a little doll, dressing her up and having her sit out with his other wives, because she was pretty. She said he was always complaining about her as a wife because she wasn't doing one thing or another right. She never lived with him as a wife and he never built her a house. She stayed with his mother and took care of his grandchildren. She was lonesome and cried and cried because she was only twelve years old, so the old man got her younger sister to live with Aussie and keep her company.

After the old man died, Aussie was given to a young man in the family; since old man Jones had paid the bride price, she belonged to that family. She had two daughters with this man, and he was falling redwood and got killed working in the woods. Then Aussie decided that she was going to buy her own husband with her own money and have who she wanted. That was unheard of. Of course the Jones family was just up in arms, took her children away from her and ostracized her. Her father, old man Dick Gray, did not want the Jones family to have his grandchildren, so he went up to Weitchpec and gave the Jones family the bride price back, and they gave him his children back. Then, technically, those children became Grays and were part of his family.

I know of one story where a man's wife was two-timing him but he loved his children too much to disown them, and about three days after he learned what his wife was doing, she died mysteriously. People think he poisoned her.

It was acceptable for a man to take a new wife and take her to his mother's, then build a house and live with her part of the time and live with the second wife part of the time. The first wife always had more rights than the second or third wife had. The various wives didn't have to get along with one another, because they each had their own house and didn't have to live with each other. They just had to get along with the village, and the husband would claim all of the children. If the woman was pregnant when the man met her, that child would be his and the biological father didn't matter. But if she got pregnant from someone else after he met her, then she was in trouble. Sadie said that if your husband was making eyes at a woman, flirting around, then you'd have a right to take a big stick and just go over and beat him up in front of everyone to shame him. He could take another wife, but he couldn't go play footsie with a woman—[laughing] he had to be deadly serious about what he did with women.

These days young people talking about the old times say you could have as many wives as you wanted. Darrell always said that you could have as many wives as you could afford, and the man had to build a house for every one of his wives. These days [laughing] you could hardly afford one.

Generally, if you were in public you could not talk back to your husband. It was that way with my aunt Caroline and my grandpa. Whatever he said, she wouldn't say anything. Whether she believed it or liked it or not, she never answered her father back. It didn't necessarily mean she did what he said, she just never told him, "I'm not going to do that." She just didn't say anything if she elected not to do it.

Aussie said that the men abstained from sex for any excuse they could think of. That's how it looked to me, too. If you were going to dance, you didn't sleep with your wife for ten days. If you were going to hunt, you didn't sleep with your wife for three days. If a man was going to flake ceremonial arrows, he would not be sleeping with his wife for ten days before he started to flake his ceremonial arrows, but he could flake regular arrows and sleep with his wife. Anytime you were going to do anything that had to do with the sacred or regalia, you would not sleep with your wife, because you had to be pure [laughing]. So it seems to me they found every reason not to sleep with their wives, which seems odd. But they did not have very many children. Two or three children were a large family.

One form of birth control was that the men and women did not live together, and they only slept together every night during the fishing season when they were on the river bar. That might be why most of the children were born in the early spring or summer. They did not want to have children during the severe weather toward early spring. Sadie always called that the second winter, when it would get cold and snow and the fish weren't running yet. The big fish runs are not started by the time the dogwood blooms, around April. This is the same time the deer are having their fawns, and you're not going to kill deer then, because you want them to have more deer, and at that time of year the acorns from the previous fall would be getting low or running out, to where you had to measure out what you were eating.

When I married Darrell, my Yurok friend Alberta said, "*Awok,* Mavis."

Well, I knew what *awok* meant, so I said, "Why are you sorry for me?"

She laughed and said, "You're like my cousin Mona. When I was about five, I kept saying, '*Awok,* Mona,' and my mother finally said, 'Why are you sorry for Mona?' I said, 'It's because she's blind. She's got those eyes you can't see out of.'"

Her mother laughed and said, "No, that's just the color of her eyes." She had never seen gray or blue or green eyes. So when she saw me, she thought of Mona and started joking, saying "*Awok,* Mavis" to me because I had green eyes. I had never thought of that, because almost everyone up here in Orleans was a half-breed and there were very few even three-quarter breeds around Orleans, but there were a lot of quarter-breeds with light eyes.

When we got married, Darrell told his family they didn't have to like me, they just couldn't be mean to me.

The McCovey Family

Around 1949, when I met Darrell's grandmother Aussie, she was in her sixties and camping down at Pecwan, the village her father, Dick Gray, was from. She was camping on the river bar because there was no house left at that place. She had probably come down to clean the family graves. Dick Gray had been immensely rich, and I don't know how many wives he had had. Evidently Aussie and her sister had to be children of the first wife, because he did a lot more for them. It seems like downriver, if the first family did not acknowledge the second family or other later families, the later families didn't press it and stayed pretty separate. So it wasn't as friendly an arrangement as the men make it out to be.

One thing Aussie said was good about the white men was that they brought in woodstoves, so it wasn't as cold inside anymore. That was one thing that I was familiar with when I moved to the Yurok reservation after Darrell and I were married. I had lived up here in Orleans all my life and I had always used woodstoves, and you are always a slave to them, cutting and packing wood, then cutting kindling and feeding the fire and keeping it going, cooking off of it and heating with it.

Darrell's aunt Myrtle was a little tiny woman, about four feet, ten inches tall, with little tiny feet, about size four. She said that every single McCovey boy, by the time they got to be about eight or ten years old, would stand up by her and look and measure how tall she was or measure his foot to hers. All her life those boys were doing that, and there were a lot of boys in this family.

Uncle Walt and Myrtle had been in love with one another before he left for the First World War, while she was still in her teens. By the time he came back from the war, Myrtle was twenty years old, and they were married. They had been married for sixty-five years when he passed away, at the age of ninety-five. She said Walt had just grabbed his chest and said, "It hurts, Myrtle. I guess this is good-bye," and he died. Myrtle was so glad that she was there with him and that he wasn't alone when he died. He had lived a hard-working life, falling redwood timber, and had a nice little ranch on the Klamath River, above Klamath, California. They gave the place to her granddaughter that they had raised. By the time I met her, she and Walt had been married about thirty or thirty-five years. I remember I used to think about how old they were, and how long they had been married. I thought [laughing] that thirty-five years was a long, long time.

When I was a young mother, Myrtle said that my situation reminded her of her life. Both our husbands worked in the woods, and both wives followed them as they went from place to place working. Her mother took care of her children when she was away, and my aunt took care of mine when Darrell was away working and I was with him.

When you got married, your mother-in-law would teach you the customs of your husband's people and tell you how they did different things. "We don't do that in your way down here." They weren't saying, "You can't do that" or "This is wrong," it's just that they didn't do things that way down here. There were subtle differences in how the different tribes did things.

I went to church some when I was young, because my grandmother said that I needed to learn about the white man's religion. So I went to church and learned about Christianity, got baptized and confirmed in the High Episcopal church. Then I was down the river living with Darrell's family, and one of his cousins who belonged to one of those fundamentalist churches was preaching to me like a Southern Baptist would, trying to get me saved. I never said anything, and Darrell's grandmother Aussie finally said, "You're preaching to the wrong one. You should talk to Sony over there [laughing]. Sony's the devil."

She called me "Hony," because she couldn't pronounce the *v* in Mavis, and this was as close as she could come to saying "honey." She called most women "Hony" and most men "Sony," for "Sonny," because she couldn't pronounce certain sounds which the Yurok language didn't have. She couldn't pronounce "Darrell." It came out something like "Dowl," so she called him "Sony," and I was Sony's Hony if someone asked which Hony she was referring to. She wouldn't even try to say "Darrell," so if you asked her which Sony she was talking about she would just say "Sony" again, but in a mean voice. If one of her daughters asked if she meant Darrell, she would answer yes, but she wouldn't try to say "Darrell."

Darrell has been trying to teach me to say Yurok words here for the last fifty years, and I can pronounce some, but his language is very difficult. The Karuk language is much simpler for an English-speaking person than the Yurok language. There is just a hair's difference in pronunciation between words in the Yurok language, and I didn't realize that when I was trying to learn Yurok. Darrell was always laughing at me and laughing at me, and pointing at me because I was saying something totally different from what I intended. I didn't know enough about the language. And Sadie would get after Darrell and tell him, "She comes from a different country. If you know what she's talking about, you're supposed to be polite and just correct her. You're not being correct in your behavior. She comes from a different country. You're supposed to be polite. You're supposed to be gracious." Which he wasn't. So I gave up and told him, "Forget it, I'll never learn to speak Yurok." I just learned the word *aleke,* meaning [laughing] "I don't know."

When my children would be jumping around and running around too much, and running back and forth, in and out of Sadie's house, she would say, "Get away from my basket sticks, get away. *Ray peche, ray peche*—I'm going to spank you," but she never did. But she would holler at them. Finally, I would holler at my children and she would say, "Yuh huh, another country you've heard from!"

Aussie didn't practice Indian religion anymore, because both she and Sadie had become Indian Shakers, way before I met them, and practiced a combination of Indian and white man's religion. They were sort of like deacons in the Indian Shaker church. Indian Shakers are surprisingly powerful, amazingly powerful with their prayers.

Aussie would move her hand over your body and the hair would stand up and you could feel something coming out of her hand, sort of like electricity, when she prayed for you. She would move her hands back and forth over the patient's body and then she would clap them together lightly and take a deep breath and let it out, let go whatever she had absorbed.

Darrell used to get Aussie to pray for him when he got gout so bad that he couldn't walk and had to use crutches. She would put her hands over his legs and talk and clap her hands softly, then she would put her hands over his leg again and pray. Then she would sigh and let the air out. She didn't know what she was saying after she got into her prayer, because then she would talk in tongues— what she did was like what white people call talking in tongues. After she had finished the prayers, she wouldn't remember what she had said, but she would remember what she had been told in her vision and could see what the problem was. She would work with her hands and pray. Darrell's legs were so sensitive that he couldn't stand to have a sheet touch them. After she had prayed for him, he would get up and walk, and the gout would not bother him. It was gone, she just took it away. After her treatment, Darrell would walk back to the car without crutches.

In the 1960s when she prayed for my back, she talked in tongues while she was praying over me, but afterwards she knew what was wrong. It was like she had x-ray eyes and could see what was wrong. She told me that nothing was really wrong with my spine, but I had to be careful that my legs did not die.

Old Gram, Aussie, told me about the time a drunk kind of fell through the door and she gave him the dickens. Then she learned that he had come because he wanted to be prayed for and Indian Shakers had their own songs and prayers. She decided that even though he was drunk she would pray for him, and so she started praying, and she prayed and she prayed, and a song for him came to her. The song was "Jesus loves sinners." After that she understood that when she saw something that she didn't believe was right, she had to get another mindset, because Jesus loves sinners and she was being too judgmental and narrow-minded.

Aussie was born in 1873 and couldn't read or write, but she could stand there and just quote the Bible. Something would come to her when someone would mention doing a certain thing, and she would respond that "the Bible says..." and quote the Bible. It was as if someone had just told her what to say.

Her grandson Tim Williams was the mascot of Stanford University, where they called him Chief Lightfoot. He invited her down to watch him perform at a game and she met all kinds of dignitaries. He had gotten his master's degree in business at Stanford and worked for one of the shipping lines. They took a picture of her when she was down there, wearing a gray suit with a big flower corsage on it, and she liked that picture. There was another photograph of her in her medicine woman regalia, but she said she didn't like that picture because it made her look so old.

Stories about Sadie

Sometime after Aussie's children had been bought back from old man Jones by their grandfather, the Indian agent took them away from home again, to Indian school in Hoopa. They spoke several Indian languages, but they could not speak English because they had been raised down at Pecwan, speaking Yurok. Even if there had been English-speaking people around, they would not have been available to these sisters, who would have been home with the grandmother, Kitty Gray, who was raising them. They would be with their women relatives and not with some strange person speaking English to them.

One of the girls in that school was from up here in Orleans; she was a relative of old Redneck, the Karuk man who always wanted a silver dollar to skip across the river as a fee for going across in his boat. This girl took a chance of getting a good beating for talking Indian, but she would tell them in the Karuk language what they were supposed to be doing until they caught up in English and could understand what was being said to them, so Sadie and Ethel became fluent in the Karuk language. Sadie could talk Karuk like an upriver Indian.

After Sadie and Charlie were married and had children, they took two or three days and walked all the way up from Pecwan to Katamin to the Pikiawish with their four children. Charlie was a really handsome man. My aunt Caroline, who had gone to school with him, mentioned that to me, and he was really smart in school. Sadie was carrying the baby and Charlie was packing Darrell, who was about four years old. The oldest girl, who was eight years old, would get tired and want Charlie to carry her, so Charlie would try to get Darrell to walk a little ways and let his sister get packed along, but Darrell would just throw a temper tantrum and cry, so that finally Charlie was packing both the children. Sadie said Charlie was only five feet, nine inches tall, but he could really pack a lot, way more than you would think he could.

This is one of Sadie's favorite stories. After they had gotten to Katamin and were watching the dance, she said, she heard a woman say, in Karuk, "Who is that ugly woman with that nice-looking man?"

Sadie turned around and told her in Karuk, "I thought you knew, that's my husband."

The woman was surprised that Sadie spoke to her in Karuk, because she had thought she and Charlie were Yurok. She said, "I didn't know you were Karuk."

Sadie told her, "Well, that's why I thought you were calling me ugly, because you knew I was Karuk."

The first year Darrell and I were married, we went to a big celebration in Hoopa, and one of the events was women racing dugout canoes across the Trinity River. Sadie and one of her daughters, Cooney, were in this race. The other women in the race kind of went down the river in their canoes as they crossed the river, but Sadie and Cooney just shot across as straight as an arrow. I don't think it took them a minute to cross the river and win the race. No problem. Later there was a stick game with the older men against a team of boys sixteen and seventeen years old. This is a traditional game in which small, sand-filled pouches are thrown down a playing field using hooked sticks. One of the men, a great big fella about six feet tall and two hundred pounds, rubbed Sadie's baby boy's face in the dirt, and she didn't like that. She told him she didn't think he had to play dirty like that with a boy, and he said something back she didn't like, so she bounced right up there and socked him in the nose, all five feet, one inch of her. He took it, too, and didn't say anything else.

Traditions of Family

When Darrell and I moved out of Sadie's place, in 1956, we moved downriver a ways. I left him that year and moved back up to Orleans. We had been married five years. I told him I would give him six weeks to make up his mind. Either he was going to be a father and a husband or he was going to be a party guy and keep going out with his friends and carousing around on the weekends, but he was not going to be both, it's either-or. And I came home. He came up to Orleans, gave me some money, and asked me what I was going to do if he didn't shape up. I told him I was going to stay up here, and he asked me what I would do for a living. I told him I guessed I would find something to make a living. Then he rented his sister's place and we moved downriver and thought we would try again. When his sister moved back, we rented a little frame place that I called the cave. It had a beautiful view and you could see two or three miles down the river, but it was cold and the sun never shined on it. This is the time when it was getting hard to find jobs in logging, and when the logging company moved, Darrell got a job on the river putting logs into rafts held together with cable. He did that for eight or nine years. He used a little five-pound sledge-hammer all day, and that was the best shape I ever saw him in. Even though I didn't know how to drive a car or shift gears, he bought me a little black 1952 Ford.

Sadie made sure the young women who lived with her stayed thin when they were pregnant. She would make sure you did not get too fat, by making you get up and walk around. The way she was raised, the full-bloods' way, pregnant women didn't have to pack things around. Pregnant women didn't lift heavy things, and they made you stay thin so the baby would not grow too large before birth. During her pregnancies my sister-in-law was so sick she was throwing up all the time, and Sadie made her get up and walk around to help with the nausea, and she kept her exercising so she would not gain too much weight.

Before the Europeans came, it was kind of taboo to have twins. It wasn't something you looked forward to or something you wanted to have happen. You didn't want to have twins. The Karuk people would let one of a pair of twins die. Among the Karuk people, if the twins were a boy and a girl they would let the boy live, just in case he might have medicine power. It was different among the Yurok, and if there were twins the girl would be allowed to live, because the females have more power there. The Karuk let one child die because mothers did not have enough nutrition, enough milk, to feed both children, and if they tried to keep both children, they would both die. Through the years they had learned that they could not sustain two children. The strong one would get weak because the other one was taking its food, and you would end up with two sick babies. And this other way, you let the weak one die and the strong one live. So having twins wasn't something you wanted to have happen.

Even though we've been living in a white-contaminated society for one hundred and fifty years, there is no stigma in having a child that is not claimed by the father, or the mother, because someone in the families will take them in. I know one boy whose birth certificate says "mother unknown," but his grandmother on the Caucasian side came in and raised him. So there isn't much giving a child out for adoption. They are usually taken in by the family, like I raised my sister-in-law's child, and one of the other sisters raised someone else's child. The other thing is, things happen, things change. A couple may be way in love with each other, and all of a sudden something went wrong. There are also a lot of severe automobile accidents in this country that kill a lot of young people. Some of the accidents are caused by drugs and alcohol and others are just plain road conditions. It is almost a weekly occurrence, and there are deaths on the Klamath River highway every year.

Aussie told me that they used to see wild people, and they believed that they were people who had been born into normal families but couldn't live like the rest of us. They didn't want to dress and they didn't talk intelligently and they ate with their hands. They were the animal people. White people call them retarded. Sometimes they ran away, they just ran away and left. They didn't want to be with the rest of us, they wanted to be animals. If you saw them out in the woods, they were usually bigger than the average person, because we were tiny people. I would have been considered a big tall woman in our society, because the women averaged being five feet tall—four inches shorter than I am. I am as tall as some of the men were. Even today there are Karuk men who are shorter than I am. So these wild people wouldn't have to be very big to be considered giants. Aussie said, too, that when the white man first came, the Natives saw them as bear people because they had hair on them and they were so big.

You were supposed to ignore the wild people if you saw them. They didn't want to be human, they wanted to be animals, so you just let them go and be the animal people. My Yurok in-laws thought that Bigfoot was the wild people who did not want to live with others and had left the tribe. They all knew a fellow down toward Weitchpec whose brother had run away like that, and when white people in the camp would talk about Bigfoot he would always just walk away, because he thought it might be his brother. I'm sure that if they are who we thought they were, they would be kind to people, because they had a mother who took care of them, so they would have some feelings toward the other human beings. The families never seemed to try to keep them if they wanted to run away. The parents kept them pretty much separated from everyone because they were strong, and if they got angry about something they could hurt one of the other children.[12]

Later in my life, one of my friends had a little girl who was that way, and she said it broke her heart to have to send the child away. My friend was a big woman, one of the biggest women around, and she said the girl just got so mean that she couldn't control her when she became so strong, and if she wanted something of her sister's, she would just go over and take it, so to protect her other children she had to send her to a home. Her husband was about five feet, six inches tall and the woman was about five feet, ten inches tall, with shoulders out to here, like a classic Greek statue of a god.

My friend hated to send her child to a home, but the time is past when we can just let them go their own way. We have always been tolerant in that way. When they found a tumor on my brain, Dr. Burnett told me that evidently it was surrounding a bone shard from the fractured skull I had when I was in the car wreck at the age of five. He told me if it started growing I could go insane. I was about thirty-five years old, I guess, and when I got home I told Darrell, "I could go insane."

He looked at me for a second and said, "Well don't worry, I'll never put you away. I'll just put a high electric fence around you, and you can run around naked and do anything you want to do, but I won't put you away."

Raising the Children

Between 1951 and 1964, when our children Beavi, Carol, and Long Gone were young, we lived downriver in several Yurok villages. In those days very few people in this part of Yurok country had inside toilets. Everybody had outhouses, and the outhouses had two or three holes, sometimes with little holes set down lower for the children, so it was a family affair. Our outhouse at Pecwan had a view, and you could sit in the outhouse and see a mile or so up the river, and up the road if you flipped up the little cloth that was hanging down in the doorway.

Darrell never hunted during these years, but he did a lot of fishing. He said that he didn't hunt because deer always see you first and look at you before you could shoot them, and he didn't want to shoot a deer that was looking at him. When he was laid off in the wintertime, he and Milton Obie fished for eels and set trigger net in the river for eels. I think they got more firewood for the fishing place than they did for their houses, because they had big piles of wood thrown over the hill so they could have a fire all night long while they fished for eels, but they never caught very many. They would get fifteen or twenty eels, just enough for everyone to eat, not enough to sell or dry, but we got to eat eels all the time because he was sitting up there all night long by that big fire.

Even though Darrell didn't hunt, we had friends and family who were always hunting and bringing us deer. I remember going up the road with Darrell and Bob Obie when we saw a deer. I must've been about twenty-seven or twenty-eight years old at that time. Bob had me stop, and the deer was standing up on the bank, looking at us, when he shot it. I said, "Oh, poor thing." Bob said he thought I wouldn't eat it. I said, "No, I just felt sorry for it when you shot it. [Laughing] I'll eat it."

Sadie did a lot of praying for me. She was a religious woman and had become Christian, an Indian Shaker, like her mother, Aussie, had. In the Yurok tribe the women had the most medicine power. Up here in Karuk country the medicine men were more powerful than the medicine women, and down in Yurok country the women were the most powerful medicine people; the Yurok medicine women were the equivalent of Karuk medicine men and held the higher power. Sadie prayed for me and did all she could to help me when I was having children. I carried the two girls and lost one boy. My next boy, Long Gone, didn't threaten miscarriage like the others had. I carried them to term, but one died right after he was born. After that I wanted to have another boy. I wanted to have four children and then I was not going to have any more. I miscarried and lost the next baby. Then I miscarried again and the doctor told me not to try to have any more children.

When I first got pregnant with Long Gone, Darrell nicknamed him for Long Gone Dupree, a football player in the 1950s. They called him Long Gone after his initials and because he would get the ball and be long gone. We named the baby Loren Gerard so his initials would be L. G. Some people don't even know his name.

There's a reason why Indians have nicknames, so that you can talk about somebody without using their real name after they're dead. If they have a nickname, you won't call them back from the dead, because they won't recognize who you're talking about. We believe that you can call them back from the spirit world if you talk about them after they're dead. The dead will come back if they hear their names, and you don't want to call them back, because it's better over there, or so we believe.

Nine years went by without me becoming pregnant again, and then Darrell's sister gave me a baby boy to raise. When he was two years old I got pregnant and had another boy. I had a lot of trouble carrying him, but I carried him and he was all right when he was born. This was Daryl Dele, and he was sixteen years old when he was murdered.

The name Dele came from my middle name of Adele. The other baby's name was Darrell and I had to name this baby something different, because I had already had one son I had named Darrell, who had died. So I spelled it differently this time and his name was Darryl Dele. His brother Chucker gave him his nickname of Daypay. He was trying to say "Daryl Dele." At first he called him "Daypell," but pretty soon he could say "Daypay," and that's what stuck.

The doctor had thought the baby was in jeopardy because I had been so sick with the pregnancy. He warned us that a lot of times children in those circumstances are weak and don't live, so we shouldn't plan on this baby living, and to just buy enough to bring him home, because he might not live very long. Later the doctor said that's when good genes and good blood can tell the difference, because he was just as strong as any other baby. In fact he was very strong, so strong that he rolled over while in the hospital bassinet.

Around 1952 Darrell was out of work and couldn't get any unemployment payments. We didn't have any money, and his mother, Sadie, was working as a dishwasher in her sister's restaurant at the mouth of the Klamath River, but she had left a hundred-pound sack of potatoes and a case of peas and some onions for us to eat. At that time you could not have a vegetable garden in Yurok country, because everyone had wild pigs, it was open range. Cattle and pigs and horses just wandered around everywhere down there.

You couldn't plant a garden or put flowers in your yard or the pigs would come and root it up. You could not just shoot the pigs, because their ears were marked and they belonged to somebody. So every day, Darrell would go down to the river with his two brothers and fish. The brothers used fly rods and Darrell used a casting rod, and every time they caught a fish they would holler, "Fish on, fish on." It was okay at first. I'd eat fish and potatoes and onions and peas. We would bake fish and potatoes, we would fry fish and potatoes, and I would can fish because there was no refrigeration. There was a woodstove to cook on, and there was a stove to heat water, and that was it. There was no sink. There was a table in the kitchen and a little stand where two buckets of water sat that they fetched from a spring about thirty feet down the hill from the house. We ate so much fish that to this day fish is not my favorite food.

After a while, Darrell and one of his brothers got jobs with a logging company that lasted for three years. He would get up at four o'clock in the morning and leave without eating breakfast. I would just hear their cork boots going crunch, crunch, crunch, going up the hill to walk six miles to work, working ten hours a day, and walking at least part of the way home because sometimes they could catch a ride. The checks came out of Oregon and one payday they were about four days late. Sadie had a bunch of little banty chickens that ran around in the yard and somebody gave us some bread crusts to feed them with, because they felt sorry for these chickens that were Sadie's pets. They also gave us some commodity honey for the kids and about all we had was flour, baking powder, and salt, and some beans. We were running out of food and the check never came. Darrell and his brother were okay because they could eat lunch at the log camp cookhouse, and when they came home we could have pan bread and beans for dinner. Pretty soon we ran out of flour and the kids were hungry, so I said, "Let's put some honey on that chicken bread and feed the kids." We ate it [laughing], and the kids ate it, and the chickens went hungry. Cart and Darrell finally got paid and then we had food again.

Another time all we had to eat was canned meat, and the door

White Deerskin Dance, Panamnik, 1910. Courtesy of the Phoebe A. Hearst Museum of Anthropology and the Regents of the University of California—photographed by V. G. Duran, catalog no. 15-13563.

The first car in Orleans, c. 1912, owned by John Greese of Ferndale. Front row: Elsie Starritt, Mrs. Frank Smith, Mrs. P. L. Young, Mrs. Bob Starritt, P. L. Young, Percy Starritt, Starritt baby, unidentified girl, unidentified boy; (in car) Frederick Ferris, Caroline Ferris, Alvirius Ferris, Beatrice Ferris, John Greese; Jim French, George Salstrom, Charlie Long. Back row: Neva Ottley, Lizzie Orcutt, Pete Thomas, Earney Smith, Louise Wilder, Ella McClellan, Alice McClellan, Mamie McClellan, Frank Harley, Mrs. Frank Harley, Bill Sebring, Bill Rhodes.

The house Frederick Ferris built in 1920 after the first house he built burned down. This was Mavis McCovey's home during much of her childhood.

Nancy Evans, daughter of Horace "Irish" Evans, 1922.

Alvie Ferris with fish he caught, c. 1930.

A view of the Klamath River. Photograph by John Salter.

Frederick Ferris and Nancy Evans Ferris with their living children, 1937. Left to right: Alvie, Hazel, Frederick Ferris, Caroline, Nancy Evans Ferris, Rodrick, and Beatrice.

Frederick and Nancy Evans Ferris, Mavis McCovey's maternal grand-parents, on their fortieth wedding anniversary, 1928.

John Smither and Edith May Shirley Smither, Mavis McCovey's paternal grandparents.

Mavis McCovey at about eleven years old, near the time she was sealed off by the medicine women.

Caroline Ferris in San Francisco.

Above Left: Darrell McCovey during World War II. Right: Sadie McCovey.

Left: Long Gone McCovey working on nets; right: John Salter. Photograph by John Salter.

Daypay McCovey.

Above Left: Bessie Tripp, c. 1977. Photograph by John Salter. Right: Mavis and Darrell McCovey and family.

The crossroads. Photograph by John Salter.

was open—it was springtime—and one of the chickens came in the house. Darrell's brother Cart picked up the little rock that held the door open and threw it at the chicken and by accident killed it. The rock hit the chicken in the head and boom, it just dropped over dead. And these are Sadie's pet chickens. I said it didn't look like enough for all five of us to eat, so Cart killed another chicken. They were tough, so we boiled them and made chicken soup with dumplings. Just as we're sitting down to eat we hear Sadie coming down the hill in a car. We knew we were busted [laughing]. She came in and Cart said, "You are just in time. We're eating soup. We got chicken soup."

Sadie said, "Oh, good," and sat down and had soup with us, and she never asked what happened to those two chickens. She never said anything about those two chickens being gone, but they were pets, and she had little names for them. She never said anything to us, but I'm pretty sure she knew what happened to her chickens.

I would get one of my nephews, Buzzy, to pack the water up from the spring, and I would pay him a nickel or a dime. A nickel would buy you a Coke, and for ten cents you could have a bag of peanuts and a candy bar. One day I only had three pennies, so I told him I would pay him three pennies to pack water. He said, "Naah, what can I do with three pennies?"

I looked at them and said, "You can buy a stamp," and he said okay.

Darrell used to tell Buzzy that he would pay him to pack water when he got his bonus from the Navy. Darrell died fifty years later and he still hadn't gotten that bonus. Buzzy said that any bonus money that came was his.

Back Trouble

When I lived at the Yurok village of Techlu in 1960 I fell and hurt my back. For a couple of years it would get better for a while and then it would get worse again. The doctors had me taking pain pills because it hurt so badly I couldn't stand it, so I went to see Darrell's grandmother and she prayed for me and had a vision.

She said, "It isn't your back that you have to worry about, it's your legs. Your legs are going to die, that's what I see. You gotta get help."

After she had told me this I went back to the doctor and they took me down to the hospital in Santa Rosa and did a myelogram and couldn't find anything wrong with my back. When I came home my back pain was worse than it had been. I had reached the point that my leg was collapsing under me. This time the doctor sent me to the Marine Hospital in San Francisco because I was an Indian and that made me a federal patient. I stayed there for six weeks and they did ultrasound treatments on my back. This time the neurosurgeon decided that there was something wrong with my spine and that I needed to lose weight. I went from around 132 pounds to around 112 pounds.

They put me in a room with a woman who had burned her arm off by the electric fence when she was going over the wall, breaking out of Leavenworth prison. She had burned her arm off and the doctors had amputated it further back. They had federal guards out in the hall outside our door because she was getting better. Betty, a woman I had met at the hospital, went to the hospital authorities and gave them hell. She said, "What do you mean, putting that little Indian girl in the room with a hardened criminal?" She said, "She just came off the reservation. She doesn't know anything about that kind of life. I barely know about it, and I've been a cruise ship stewardess for thirty years!"

She got them to move me because I was a naive twenty-seven-year-old, and [laughing] they moved me to a room with a lesbian. I got to talking with my new roommate, and all at once that woman gets up, comes over to my bed, and runs her hand up my nightgown, under the covers. I was totally shocked. I had been to Indian school and there were no lesbians there, and I never knew anything about that. If I had met a lesbian woman, I didn't know it. I told my friend what she did, because I was just shocked. I said, "Do you know what she did? She ran her hand over my legs."

Betty said, "What did you do?

I said, "I just sucked in my breath because I was totally shocked. I didn't say anything, because I just couldn't breathe."

Betty told that woman—if she hadn't figured it out by then—"Just leave her alone. She has her little family and her husband and she knows nothing about that kind of life." So she saved me twice.

While I was at the hospital they were always poking needles in me and assessing me. The doctor would ask stupid questions, like "Are you happy?" I told him that I didn't know if I was happy. What did he mean by happy? I said that I was content, and he didn't think that was the right answer; he thought that I was supposed to think of "happy" as being like when you are a little kid and you are skipping rope and playing with your friends—that was what being happy meant to him. As an adult, in my culture, you don't expect to be happy, not like you are when you are a child. My feeling is that the only time that you have true happiness is when you are a child. That's your chance to be happy, happy, happy. Once you start growing up and becoming an adult and having concerns and responsibilities, you're not happy, happy anymore. You're content with your life, having times of happiness. I guess what he was looking for was for me to say, "I'm happy, I'm happy." For me, I had moments of happiness, and I was content the rest of the time.

I gradually got better with the ultrasound treatment and physical therapy for my back, so that after six weeks it didn't bother me.

I think the doctor thought I was neurotic or depressed, but I wasn't depressed. I was depressed about being sick and not being able to do what I should be doing, but I wasn't clinically depressed. It's a damn good reason to be depressed when your house is infested with ten million fleas, you have three children and a lot of work to do, and a vegetable garden going, and have been working ten hours a day, six days a week. You need to be there doing your share, and I wasn't doing my share, so Darrell hired a woman to do some of my work for me.

At that time there were lots of pigs in this country, and since some of them had slept under the house, it was infested with fleas. So every other day I scrubbed floors with Pine-Sol to keep the fleas out of the house, and I used it on the kids' clothes and the sheets and blankets. Keeping the fleas out was a lot of extra work, even though they were not the kind of fleas that bit people—they were pig fleas, and they were big fleas! They were so big and there were so many of them that you could see them crawling around on the ground, and when they got onto your body they would drive you nuts. They would get on you and just crawl and crawl and crawl, and crawl up around on you. But I finally learned how to get rid of the fleas using Pine-Sol. People had used pepperwood underneath the bed and under the mattress to keep the fleas out, but it was a bad year for fleas and pepperwood didn't do much good. This was all going on when my back was bad. Darrell paid a sweet little old Yurok lady that lived two doors down from me, a Christian woman, to come over and wash clothes and mop the floor and clean up the house for me every other day. I think Darrell paid her two dollars a day and she gave it to the missionaries.

I hardly ever went upstairs, because of my back, but one day I did and saw that my girls, Carol and Beavi, had been playing and left their paper dolls lying around. I told the children to pick up their paper dolls, and Bea tells me, "We've got a maid; she can do it." I told Bea, "She's doing it to be good, and we give her a few dollars, but she's not here to clean up our messes. She's here to do the stuff I absolutely cannot do, which is things like mop the floor." When Darrell came home I told him, and that's one time Bea remembers catching hell from her father. She still remembers that. She found out that you clean up your own mess.

Downriver Indian Devils

Sometimes medicine people can appear in spectacular forms. Darrell's uncle told me that Indian devils went through a ceremony down there in Yurok country. He said they sold themselves to the dark side, then put a burden basket on their back and walked like it was loaded down, even though it was empty. For a couple of months they walked around and wailed and cried and mourned for the dead, and wailed like the family was dying. They were mourning for their people, who were going to die and would never go across to the good place. Selling themselves to the dark side means they and their whole families are doomed forever to be on the dark side. He said they have immense power, and they can have money, and all the things in life that they want, they will have. Whether they work hard for it or not, these things will be given to them. From what I gather, Christians believe that if the devil gets a hold of you he can make you do anything. The Indians I knew who were talking to me about Indian devils said that if you had faith in the Creator and you believed in him and you were a religious person and you weren't afraid of the devil and you didn't get angry at someone for being that way, that they had no handle to get a hold of you. The Indian devils could not do anything to you if you devoutly believed they had no power over you.

As a child living upriver in Orleans, I never had much contact with Indian devils, although I was living next to someone people said was an Indian devil. She never deviled us, but I had heard the stories. Whenever people got together, some Indian devil story would come up. After Darrell and I were married and I went down the river to live with his family in Yurok country, there were people who did things like coming around and watching someone's house from the trees, and you could feel them out there. This happened to me as a young married woman, new to living in Yurok country.

I don't know if they did it as a creepy joke or if they were actually trying to devil somebody. If they didn't spook me enough by just being around and watching the house when Darrell wasn't home, they would throw rocks on the roof or shake the pole that held up the radio antenna, so that you would know that someone was around. They did this to try to manipulate you. If they didn't like something you did or something about you, then they would devil you and try to scare you and manipulate you to do what they wanted you to do. You usually knew who was trying to scare you, what you had done that they didn't like, and what they wanted you to do. They were just raising hell with me. I don't think they were angry with me; they were just raising hell with me.

When I lived down Pecwan Hill, I could always feel someone watching me when I went outside. Three different times, before I could make it to the outhouse I would look up the hill and around because I could feel someone watching me. I know who that person was, and he wasn't trying to devil me. He was peeping through the telescopic sight of his rifle to watch me, though. I know what gave me these feelings, because he got drunk and told somebody that he liked doing this because he could tell that I was scared. He wasn't trying to do anything really dangerous; he was just being creepy because he knew I could tell he was watching me.[13]

One time Darrell was home, when we heard a noise outside like a panther crying, though we knew it was somebody trying to frighten us. And his mother, Sadie, says, "Don't run outside, invite them in. But Darrell ran out and swore at them, and she said, "No, no, no. Tell them to come in and ask them if they're hungry or if they're tired. Invite them in because they can't do anything if you invite them in and you are being friendly, if you have no animosity towards them. They can hang on to your fear and anger."

Darrell had an aunt who wanted to be a white woman. She dressed like a white woman and had diamond earrings and a fox stole that she wore over her shoulder. Just really white-woman-looking, and she liked to believe the white-man way, not believing in all these myths and what they call superstitions that we believe in. She drove clear down to my house around eleven o'clock one night when I was living at Wautec, the last Yurok village at the end of the road down in Yurok country. She pounded on the door and I got up. She wanted me to make some coffee. Darrell asked her what was going on, and she said it was okay; she just wanted to talk to me. So Darrell went back to bed.

She tells me, "I was driving down by the old mill and almost hit a little yellow dog. I noticed that when it looked at me, its eyes flashed red, and I thought, 'God, that's an odd-looking dog.' I looked back in my rearview mirror to see if I could see what had happened to it, because it was so odd-looking, with these red-flashing eyes. But I thought that the car's lights had just hit its eyes right or something. When I looked back, that dog was standing up on its hind legs, looking at me with its red eyes, and it had its paw over its mouth and was laughing at me. It just scared the hell out of me and I had to come down and tell you about it."

That yellow dog was well known to be the form this devil appeared in. So much for Indian superstition.

I told her Darrell's grandmother had told me to not be afraid of it, but that is a powerful Indian devil. The woman was dead, but her devil power was still in her medicine necklace. The rocks from the necklace were around and under my bed until my house burned down. I don't know if those rocks burnt up or not, but someone looked for them. I don't know if he found them. He found quite a few things, so he looked pretty closely. I think he was looking to find them and put them away again, because the power is still in them. They are still dangerous, even if they are not strung. They were made powerful by the owner's prayers. She had gone on for months, crying for the dead, in order to get that power.

As far as I can tell, in recent years no one has stepped out and become a traditional Indian devil by going through weeks and weeks of packing a burden basket on their back and wailing for their dead. Most of the Indian devils come from a certain family, and they pass the deviling ability down to one heir. In the case of the downriver devil, the power is passed on to a female heir. The one that I knew most about, it was passed from male to female every generation, with the power having been put in a deer's jawbone. When they buried the woman devil who had owned that jawbone, balls of fire kept coming out of the ground at her grave, so they dug up the jawbone and threw it way out in the woods, where they thought no one would ever find it, although people now believe that it has been found.

Once the family has that devil power, they no longer have to carry a burden basket and wail for the family. The devil energy is just placed in a rock or some other inanimate object and passed from generation to generation. There are many inanimate objects, but I wouldn't say a deer bone is really inanimate, but then we believe the rocks can talk too, so I guess that really isn't traditionally inanimate either. We believe they live. I have had scientists argue with me that the rocks do not live. I pointed out that there are crystals that grow and multiply, and you tell me they don't live?

When you think about people and religion, Buddhism, Christianity, Indian religion, they are all telling you to be a good person, and they all have ways that show you how to be good, and rituals that you do to take part in that religion. All these religions have different rituals and different ideas of what they're headed toward, like Nirvana, or rebirth, and they all worship a supreme power, or a supreme being, or whatever they call it. I don't know if we come back again or not. There's more people all the time, so [laughing] they're sure splitting us finer and finer if we are coming back. Some people go over the edge and get fanatical about it, I don't care what religion it is. I think it is all the same God. That's my thought on it. I don't know if I'm right or wrong, I wouldn't want to argue it, but I just have that feeling.

I prayed about it for a long, long time, because Indian Shakers would say you couldn't go to the Indian dances because then you are worshipping a devil. And the Indian people who believed in the Native American Creator felt that the Indian Shakers were worshipping a false god. I prayed about it all the time, and then I went down to a Shaker meeting about fifteen or twenty years ago and I was praying about it as usual. The Indian Shakers believe that when God answers you, he gives you a song. Like Old Gram, Aussie, was given that song, "Jesus loves sinners." This little song came into my head and it was, "There is one God, only one," and I thought, "Well, God answered me." There's just him. That's all there is to it.

THREE

The Medicine Returns
1965–2005

IN 1965, AFTER FIFTEEN YEARS OF LIVING in Yurok country, our whole family moved back to Orleans to take care of my aunt Caroline. Very few men move out of their own country to live with their wife in another country the way Darrell did, and when they do, it is for the same reason. I was the only one available to take care of my aunt, who had raised me like a mother, so I had to come back here to take care of her until she died—and Darrell came up here with me because I had that responsibility. I wouldn't just leave home and come up here to live with my people. I had to have a very good reason for leaving his country and coming back to mine, and his family could see that I had to do that.

It was a different world up here. We had electricity and cars and better roads, and Darrell didn't even have a road when he was a kid. His road was the Klamath River. As it was, our daughters, Carol and Beavi, would go back and live with Darrell's family for months at a time.

When I came back to Orleans from Yurok country I started having visions and seeing things. I had also had visions while I was living in Weitchpec, but not as often, not as profound. After I got to be older, I looked back and thought that the years downriver were that time when Daisy said I would have my happiness, when I would be truly happy and not have a care in the world outside of my life with my family and friends. But when I came back up here,

I couldn't just love my family, my in-laws, and my friends, all the relations that I had loved in Pecwan. When I got back to Orleans I had to embrace people that I would have not been close with, but they were always around, needing my help with the things they were going through in their lives. The medicine women had told me, "When you get to be around forty-five years old, you will pick up your power." They kept telling me, "Don't worry, you'll pick it up pretty soon."

I do not really believe the power comes from me. I had been told that when the time came I would pick up my power, but in fact the power picked me up. So I don't think the power is mine. I think I'm like a conduit and this spiritual power is somewhat like electricity, and it comes through me when I need it or it needs to use me, but it isn't something I walk around with all the time. I think that it comes from the spirit world when I need it; the spirit world sends me what power I need at that time.

I think that most of the time when I go on the trail over to the other side, my body stays here and I come back to it, but I know that there were a few occasions...like the time I went to pick up power I went in my physical form, because Darrell said I was not here.

When someone is asking me for something I feel this power within me and then I feel myself throw it out. I think that power just came from the spirit world, came through me and went out into this world.

The White Deerskin and Jump Dances

When I say I am making the world happy, for me that is right here in this little valley; this is the world. That's the only little world I have to worry about, right here in Orleans. I don't have to worry about the other places, even around here, like Somes Bar or Bluff Creek.

When I say "happy," I think of smoothing the world out. At the White Deerskin Dance the Fatawanun prays for the fish, prays for the hunting, prays for the people. After he completes that prayer on the last evening of the ceremony, he throws the power toward Offield Mountain and I split a piece off, and it falls down on the people, and when they go back up the hill to eat you'll hear them all laughing and talking, and then I know I've done it. People go up the hill calling back, "*Yootwa*, Fatawanun, *yootwa*, Fatawanun," thanking the Fatawanun for all his sacrifice in making the ceremony. They all say "Happy new year" to one another because this is the beginning of our new year. Everyone is very happy, and we have a big feast of deer and salmon and everything else you can think of, and the young people serve the elders.

The White Deerskin Dance is done very ritualistically when the White Deerskins are brought out. This dance smoothes the world out, smoothes all the strife and the fighting. But the War Dance is not done in a smooth, ritualistic way. It is done kind of haphazardly, and there are a lot of things that make people laugh in the dance, and that is another thing to smooth the world out and make it a happy place, to calm it all down and just make it smooth.

The purpose of the Jump Dance is to round the world, integrating the people, the trees, the fish, the earth, the deer, and the birds in the sky. We all have to survive together. The red headdresses that flop back and forth on the dancers as they move their heads are to simulate the mountains. Placed down inside these headdresses are sticks that press very tightly on your head to impress the purpose of the dance on your mind. Some of the dancers have triangular cloths with designs and hieroglyphics that hang down behind their heads, and that is for the spirit people to read. The dancers hold the basket down by their manhood and they place their manhood, their family, and everything else between themselves and the Creator when they are praying for their family. Long Gone told me that he was praying hard at the Jump Dance, praying for the fish and for the world to heal, and that voice came to him that speaks to me and told him, "Don't pray for the world, the world is fine. You gotta pray for the people, that's what isn't fine. The world will heal itself. The people are what you have to worry about."

One thing Darrell never liked was the Fatawanuns and different ones touching me. He didn't like to share me. He would ask me why they were always touching me, and I would tell him it was because I was the medicine woman. I said, "I think it gives them luck. I think that's why they do it. It's like the boys staying with the medicine man in the sweathouse, men do it for luck."

There are three dance givers and dance owners in each area. They are usually a little better off, they have a little more money and a few more things. Sometimes they have regalia, but they usually have money, and they can buy food for the dance and supplies so you can camp at the dance grounds for ten days without having to worry about where your food is coming from. People bring food to the dances like a potluck, and there are three meals a day, and there is always food there for someone who just drops by and wants a sandwich. Sometimes you think you are going to eat and the dancers get ready too quick, and you have to run down the hill to the dance and you don't get to eat until you come back.

Moving Back to Orleans

My last child, my son Daypay, was born in 1965 not long after we had moved back to Orleans. Around the time Daypay was born, Darrell decided to do something about the packrats that were living in old jackrabbit burrows around our house. The jackrabbits around here got some kind of plague and died off in 1930, just before I was born. Grandpa said they were big, huge! When I was a little kid—I must have been about four feet tall—he said they were about my size, with ears on top [laughing]. He said the rabbits had been a scourge to the garden and he was glad they died. There are a couple of places down here below my house where you can see where the old rabbit holes were. There were rock outcrops with burrows underneath.

Darrell thought he was so smart that he would burn the packrats out of their burrows. He did, and they all ran right in my house! They climbed up the outside walls and went into the attic windows. Then I had packrats in my house, [laughing] on top of everything else! They would come down from the attic and go into the upstairs rooms. They got into the downstairs pantry a couple of times, but they didn't really come downstairs much, because I had walnuts stored upstairs that they liked. I would find foil and little pieces of yarn that they had traded for the walnuts that they took. Sometimes there would be a walnut with a hole chewed in it lying in with the good walnuts. They had taken it away and chewed into it, and when they saw that it was bad they brought it back.

When we moved in with my aunt Caroline, she was seventy-five years old and her age was starting to catch up with her body but not her mind. Darrell and the children and I would get up in the morning and fix breakfast and go off to our day's work. Aunt Caroline would get up later and fix herself breakfast and then take about an hour to wash the little stack of dishes that we had left and clean the table and the drain board. She couldn't get around as well as she used to. She couldn't walk to town anymore, and making breakfast and cleaning up gave her a little something to do. Her heart was still good but she was having little strokes that were crippling her.

I had been back in Orleans for about three years when she fell on the porch and broke her shoulder. With a broken shoulder and arthritic knees, she couldn't use a walker anymore so she was confined to a wheelchair and her bed. She went to a rest home but wanted to come home really badly. They wanted to keep her in the rest home because she couldn't get around, but they were giving her drugs to keep her from fretting about coming home. The doctor told me that if I took her home I would be responsible for killing her. I said to him that if she died it would be of old age and not because I had killed her, because she was old enough to die, and she would be happier at home even if my care wasn't as good as theirs.

As soon as we got her home her mind cleared because she wasn't on drugs anymore and she was happy to be home. She wasn't a fussy patient and if I was a little late attending to her because I had been doing work in the yard or something like that, I would come in to say I was sorry for being late and she would say, "Oh, that's okay. All you've got to do is just come in and dust me off once in a while, I'm not doing anything." So we took care of her, and all you can do is the best you can do.

When I got guardianship of Aunt Caroline and took over her bank account, not that there was hardly anything in it, I told her, "Well, now we've gone the full circle."

She says, "How's that?"

I said, "You started out as my guardian and now I'm yours." She just laughed.

Aunt Caroline's Last Years

Everyone has to be careful about the consequences of what they think, but medicine people, people with power, have to be especially careful. Grandpa and Auntie always told me that you can't have a temper, and that you can't get rid of your temper by losing it. It's like the time my aunt Caroline got angry with her sister-in-law, Uncle Roddy's drunken wife. She was being mean and nasty because she was drunk, and Auntie wished she was dead. She just got tired of it, lost her temper and said it: "I just wish you would be dead." This woman had heart disease and wasn't very well. She got hepatitis B in the course of surgery for her heart, and about four days after Auntie told her that she wished she was dead, she died. Auntie said she tried to take it back, but it wouldn't come back. She wondered what she was going to have to pay for that temper tantrum, but she said she was lucky; no one else had to pay.

She said, "God has made me pay for five years, because I've had to lie in this bed and be an invalid." But no one else had to die, and no one else had to pay, and she was glad of that because a lot of times if you make a mistake like that one of your children or grandchildren will die. So you can't make a mistake. She was wheelchair-bound for about five years and pretty much all I did was take care of her. Eventually she became weaker and weaker, despite everything I did, and she didn't want to go back to the hospital, so we respected her wishes and she died at home.

I didn't really realize how much she used to communicate with me telepathically until the end of her life. It didn't dawn on me because it seemed to me that I could just hear her. At the end of her life, when she was bedridden, she was talking to me all the time, telling me things I needed to know about this power that was coming up for me in the time of life which I was approaching, and I wondered where she was getting the strength to talk to me this way. I realized what she was doing after Darrell said to me that Auntie and I were spending a lot of time together with me just sitting there and her lying in bed looking at me and neither one of us saying anything. Darrell asked me, "What do you do all day when you are just sitting there looking at your aunt? You just sit in there and look at her."

I said, "She's talking to me."

He looked at me for a minute and said, "She's not saying anything. She's just looking at you." He wanted me to know that.

"Well," I said, "she's telling me something," and he didn't question me. He just said that she wasn't saying anything. That's when I realized that she had always used telepathy to talk to me when she wanted to, and since she was dying and weak she just used telepathy all the time. Until Darrell told me, I never really realized it, other than I had just seen her eyes and knew what she was thinking, or thought at me.

I have never been able to project my thought telepathically like Auntie and the medicine women who trained me could, but I could receive their thoughts. I can remember her getting after me, and Juju's mother, Ramona, hollering at her when we were children, about eleven or twelve years old. We were at a dance and had gone outside the dance hall. There were people around back, drinking, but we were just in front of the building. We didn't really have a reason for going outside except they had told us that we couldn't. Juju said, "You're so lucky that your aunt never says anything to you or hollers at you." I thought that maybe Ramona was hollering so loud that Juju didn't hear Auntie when she was telling me off, really letting me know what she thought, but I guess she wasn't talking. She was just thinking at me, but I didn't perceive it that way, I always thought she was talking to me. The other children thought it was great because I never got hollered at. Little did they know! She was really telling me off, but she didn't have to say anything—all she had to do was think. I think that I was born with an affinity to be open to this power which goes through me.

When she became bedridden and Darrell thought she was just lying there looking at me, she was telling me telepathically about the powers that I would have in the period of my life I was just going into. She didn't tell me anything about being an Indian doctor, because I never had to learn that. That's way, way farther out than what I would experience. She was telling me about the spiritual part of the powers because that's what I am, a spiritual person, not an Indian doctor. I just work on the mind and the senses. I don't work on changing the physical body. I can only change a person's mind or their mind-set. I can't change where you're at in the world, I can only change what you think about where you're at.

Medicine people like me all have a vision of our death, our end. My aunt Caroline said that she was going to go to sleep and die in her own bed. She just knew that was what was going to happen. In 1974 when the doctors tried to get her to go into the hospital, she said, "No. I want to stay home, here in my own place. I want to be in my own bed with my own people," and that's what happened. I was there talking to her and I said, "Do you want your drink?"

She joked back, "Do you want your nonnutritive, noncaloric drink?" Because it was just mineral stuff they were giving her that helped her electrolytes.

I asked her if she wanted another drink and she never answered me, she just slipped away. I said, "Well, if you're not going to answer me, I guess you don't want it." She never said anything, and her eyes were closed like she was asleep. When she didn't wake up the next morning, I called the doctor. He had already told me that there was a time to call for an ambulance and there was a time not to call for an ambulance. When the doctor came on the line I told him what was happening, and he said this was the time to just let it go. I told him her breathing was awfully ragged, and he said to put her bed down a little more and it would ease her breathing. I let her bed down, and about fifteen minutes later she was gone.

After Auntie died she kept coming back. I could feel her. She was there; she was just around all the time. She told me, "Go see Josephine Peters. She's your sister in medicine, go see her."

Josephine is a Karuk medicine woman who works in medicine and herbs. So I went over and told Josephine that Auntie was coming back. Josephine said that Auntie had been taking care of me so long and protecting me and sealing me off and making sure that nothing touched me that she was still worried about me. Josephine told me that the next time Auntie came, the next time I could feel her, "Just tell her that you are all right, that you will be all right, that you're fine."

Two or three days after that, Auntie was there, I could feel her. I told her I was okay. I was outside picking up walnuts. I said, "I'm fine. I'm okay and you don't have to keep staying here to watch out for me, because I'll be all right."

She kind of laughed, and then it was like, "All right, I will leave," and it was like she threw me a basket, a laden work basket. She threw it on my back and it was full of every emotion you could possibly feel, a great big load of feelings, every kind of feeling a human being could possibly have. She threw it at me and it was like, "And you can have this too. This is all of my power, and you can hold this." She had told me that when she left that she wasn't going to take her power with her. "I'm going to leave it," she kept telling me.

She had picked up so many gifts in the spirit world on the other side, picking up and picking up when she was getting her medicine. She picked up so many gifts and brought them back so she could deal with things on this side for people. She said she had been thinking, "This would be a good thing to have, and this would be a good thing to have." Well, she gave it all to me and then I had to learn how to pack that load my aunt Caroline had been packing.

Medicine people had been taking care of adverse feelings for me all my life, so that if somebody did something to me that was like…you know how children get into arguments? You know how someone pushes you or does something like that, mean to you? Well, I wouldn't react the same way as other children. I wouldn't react in the same way. I would just be kind of surprised and shocked that somebody would act that way, but I wouldn't do anything back to them. It was like there was a shield around me, like I was in a bubble, or something was protecting me all the time from wide emotional swings.

When Auntie died, it was the first time I didn't have that protection, and it was the first time I had all these emotions tossed at me, all these adverse things that people feel. This was much more intense than when I was sealed off as a young girl and no longer had that high level of protection from the medicine women who had been training me. It was quite a surprising load. Having to deal with that part of humanity was really hard for me because I had been so accustomed to not dealing with it before.

After Auntie had thrown me the basket filled with emotions, I could feel emotions that other people were signaling, like with their body language. After that, I was more like Darrell and could sense people's emotions and read them better—Darrell was always very good at reading people. Before that, I hadn't a clue. It was like I had been in the dark about what was going on with people. When I was sealed off, it left me freer to have a full range of childish emotions, and after Auntie had given me her gifts, I understood better what was going on with other people's temperaments.

Getting Tribal Recognition

What got us moving on becoming the Karuk Tribe and getting federal recognition in the 1960s was the conditions on the Salmon River, where the Forest Service were throwing people off their homeplaces.

They were evicting Merlin Tripp from his place, and I signed some papers that at one time I had owned that land, and that mining claim had been owned by an Indian, a Karuk Indian, before Merlin ever got there, so there were precedents and it was Indian land. Merlin got to stay on there for about fifteen years after that. I think it was in the 1980s that he finally gave up and moved off. We knew that we couldn't fight the government one by one.

The government didn't protect the Indian rancherias, which were supposed to be parcels of land set aside by the government for Indians who had been made landless by the invasion of Europeans. The Indians made them into mining claims in order to hang onto them, because the miners would come, make a claim on your rancheria, and move in, taking over the land. So the half-breeds and three-quarter breeds got educated and would make a mining claim out of their rancherias so they could hang on to the property, but it really wasn't a mining claim.

The government had made a big rancheria about two miles long and a mile to a half-mile wide up at Somes Bar, and that held until the 1950s. Then in the 1950s and 1960s the government just turned around and took back the rancherias and made them part of the National Forest, because they were not good mining claims; when they were tested for gold by the Forest Service, they couldn't prove enough color to keep qualifying as mining claims, and the government was going to take them back.

We figured if we all joined together we could fight against them taking over these mining claims. The government should have returned them to rancheria status for Indian people to live on, rather than giving them over to the Forest Service. The government was supposed to be protecting our claims to live on the land and have mining claims, but they did nothing to help the Indians. That was what got us headed in the direction of becoming a tribal organization.

We needed to prove that a lot of the mining claims which the Forest Service was evicting Karuk people from had never had much gold on them, that the Karuk had filed on the land as mining claims as a way for Indians to hold on to their places. Before they were filed on as mining claims, these places had been rancherias. They were always close to where the fish were.

That's what happened to the Yurok tribe, too. The government took the Yuroks' timber away from them. Can you imagine how much the redwood growing along thirty miles of river, one mile wide on each side, would be worth? Redwoods grew clear down to the river, but that didn't last long. And it was the Indians' trust property, supposedly held in trust by the government for Indian people, but the government finagled around and gave it to one of the timber companies. That's how Simpson Timber Company owns so much—the Indians didn't sell it, the government gave it away.

I was at the hospital one day and a black doctor asked me what I thought about the government. I told him, "I don't have any say about this country; I come from a defeated people. I don't have anything to say about it."

He said, "Well, what do you think? What are your thoughts on it?"

I said, "I may have thoughts on it, but nothing that I will say. I may say something to my own people, but we are a defeated nation and I won't say anything outside my own people. It isn't safe to say what I think."

"Wow," he said. "Where did that come from?"

I said, "Three hundred years of being a defeated nation." And he was a black person. He should have known, but he was a black doctor, so he was probably a middle-class black and had adopted the white man's way. The blacks didn't have much chance, because they were not only a defeated people, they were brought here from another country. We are a defeated people, but at least we're sitting in our own country. Even those Indians who have been moved, like the Cherokee who were moved from the East Coast to Oklahoma, are still living in their larger country.

In California, Indian tribes were moved onto rancherias that provided land for Indians who had become landless, but except for the Modoc, it wasn't that far from their original territory. At least they didn't send us to Oklahoma, and they didn't take people from Idaho and Wyoming and put them in Oregon.

I always thought it was a bunch of hooey that the Mexican Indians are discriminated against in this country the way they are. Our aboriginal lands went across the borders that are there now. The Apaches and the Pueblo went back and forth of what is now old Mexico—they were on both sides of the border. And up in Canada we have co-reservations for Canadian and United States Indians, like the Flathead Reservation, and there are a couple of others in Washington State and in Minnesota and in New York. These Indians can go back and forth across the borders, living on one side of the border for a while and then living on the other. It makes no difference which side of the border they live on, they're still on the reservation where they always live.

I was on the tribe's Constitution Committee with Dorothy Jordan and Trudy Molière, Lottie Beck, Heem Hillman, and Jack Sanderson, and we wrote the first constitution for the tribe. Because my ancestors on my father's side came from several tribes and I was not half-Karuk, I couldn't sign as one of the founders of the tribe, but we had twenty-one people to sign up initially. That was a great fight in the late sixties, but we never got back the rancherias, and that's what we had wanted. We placed the tribal headquarters in Happy Camp, which, until the 1920s, had been out of our territory, but in the 1920s the government moved our boundary to around Seiad, which is north of Happy Camp.

Somewhere around 1968 we sent in our constitution to the Bureau of Indian Affairs. The portion of the Klamath River we claimed lay between Dillon Creek and Somes Bar, and the Indians in Sawyers Bar and Forks of Salmon threw in with us when we were going for tribal status because they all lived within the aboriginal territory of the Karuk tribe. When the white people came, this is where we were. If you lived outside that territory you were generally not Karuk, or you were mixed with the other tribes in the area.

The first piece of land that Trudy Molière and Lottie Beck and the First Presbyterian Church bought as Karuk land was the tailings of an old mining claim, so that there was nothing but bare rock with a couple of little scraggly fir trees on it. I thought it was the epitome of what the government would give to an Indian tribe. Even though the government had not given us any land, I thought it was the perfect example of what the government would want us to get if we got anything. We couldn't even get a septic tank in the ground for the tribal building that we were planning, because it was so rocky. We had to haul in twenty feet of dirt in order to be able to bury the septic tanks. The county road crew was cleaning up some slides and the tribe got them to haul the dirt in to cover the bedrock so we could have a septic system and build our community building where the Natural Resource Department building is now. That was our first tribal land, [laughing] six whole acres! I went to meetings twice a week for years, working on this tribal organization.

Working as a Community Health Representative

The Community Health Representative program was financed by money allocated by Congress so that Native Americans could get health care, because a lot of them didn't trust doctors and wouldn't go to see them. They didn't have any reason to trust doctors. The CHR program got Native American people to go out and teach Native Americans the white man's way of looking at health. It worked very well and some foreign countries adopted this model of health-care program, to go out into the homes of elderly people and to assist them with their health needs and to teach them how to take care of their health.

I could not see people in their home every month, because I went from Bluff Creek to Dillon Creek and sometimes up to Clear Creek. I went up the Salmon River to Sawyers Bar, on the north fork, and Methodist Creek, on the south fork—over one hundred miles of river. I tried to see every single Indian family in my territory at least once a year and to see families that had children about every three months. The focus was on children under five and adults over fifty-five.

Up the Salmon River, they wouldn't let me drink the local water when I was the tribe's nurse and community health representative. They told me, "We live up the Salmon River here, and we know there's something in the water that makes people sick who aren't used to it. We're immune to it, whatever it is, but if you drink this water it's going to make you sick to your stomach, and it's going to give you bowel problems, and so you can only drink coffee or something that's boiled up here. We'll give you coffee to drink, but don't drink any water, just drink coffee." So every house I went to, I was given coffee.

Then the other thing the Salmon River people did when I was going up and down the river as the tribe's nurse, stopping house to house, was pass the word to all the marijuana growers because somebody might get paranoid and take a pot shot at me. "She's our nurse. She doesn't pay any attention to anything else. She's going house to house to see about our health"—because [laughing] they thought somebody might think I was a government agent.

John Bennett was one of my clients on the Salmon River, and when I drove up the river to see John, I would have to stop and eat lunch with him because he wasn't happy if I just listened to his heart. He said, "We know all of us Bennetts got heart trouble, so that don't mean nothing." I almost gave him a heart attack the first time I showed up. [Laughing] He thought he had seen a ghost. He said he thought for sure it was a ghost.

I asked him, "Why did you think that?"

He said, "Because I thought you were Bea Ferris. Did you know Bea?"

I said, "She was my mother."

He said, "No wonder I thought you was a ghost. You're a lot smaller than she was, but you move just like her, and you had gray hair and light eyes, and I just thought you were a ghost when you opened the gate. The way you move your head and hands, I just swore you was Bea, and I hadn't seen her in fifty years."

John was engaged to my mother before he met his wife. My mother was quite spoiled. She was engaged quite a few times and then would change her mind. I guess they didn't spoil her well enough, and they were too mean or too something, didn't treat her as good as her daddy did.

Les Bennett, John's brother up at Forks of Salmon, would hide from Millie and me when we drove into their yard to see the family.

I said to his wife, Lillian, "Well, if he doesn't want to see me that bad, he doesn't need to. I just want to take his blood pressure." Lillian always let me take her blood pressure because she had heart disease and she took care of herself. She outlived him, too, by a long time.

Then on one visit Lillian said to me, "He's up in a tree if you want him. He always climbs a tree to hide when he sees you drive up." And Les comes climbing down out of the tree and told me I could take his blood pressure. Years later, his son Hoss went to Redding to have his heart checked and they told him there wasn't much they could do for him, that he would live a few more years but would not be in very good health. Then they asked him if he had any questions. He said, "Yeah, I've got a question. Do I still get my beer?" He got a couple of beers a day so he wouldn't go into DTs, and that was his bottom line.

It was hard to catch the men at home when we made home visits, because they worked. They would leave home before I got there and they would come back after I got home. I would only see them occasionally, and usually it was if something happened, like they got a cut or mashed their hand or got something in their eye. I also did a lot of social service work. For example, one man's wife died, and he was on state disability, and they made him dead too. It took me three years to get this live man recognized as being alive. We were filing and filling out papers, getting affidavits for three years before he got back on disability. They had him down for dead and I had to prove he was alive. That was one of the most difficult cases I ever worked on. It was ridiculous. If you have a live person in front of you saying he's alive and the government says he's dead, it is very hard [laughing] to convince the bureaucrats that he is actually alive.

Around 1980 I took a pharmacology class in Eureka. I would get off work two hours early and then go to school out there at five o'clock. I took this class because I had a patient who went to two doctors and I noticed that her blood pressure was getting really low. Once when I went to her home I had to rush her to the emergency room in Hoopa because she was dying from taking two different kinds of blood pressure medicine. Two different medications, two different names, two different doctors doing the same thing. It almost killed her. Her heart was stopping. Because of that I went to school to learn pharmacology, so that I would know one medication from another.

Another time I took the blood pressure of a Caucasian woman. It was like 200 something over 190 and her pulse was really fast. She was getting ready to go on vacation and I told her, "I would check in with the emergency room over in Hoopa before I did anything." She told me that she would be okay and would go on her vacation. I told her, "Let me talk to the emergency room and let them talk to you first, because I don't really think that would be a good idea. I'm not a doctor or nurse, but that just isn't really a good idea." You're not supposed to scare the hell out of a person and tell them, "I think you're having a damn stroke or a heart attack and you'd better get to the emergency room."

So I called the Hoopa hospital and talked to one of the nurses that I had known and told her the situation. She knew that I had worked in the field for four or five years and that I knew how to take blood pressure and I knew what I was talking about, so she told the woman, "I think you'd better come in and let us check that over again, in case there's a mistake or something, because that is dangerously high blood pressure and we would really like to see you." So someone drove her over to Hoopa and took her in for me. Once they got her in there, she was in the hospital for three or four days. She did not go on vacation. That was one of the good ones. She made it and she is still alive.

And then there are those who come in and see a nurse and a physician's assistant and are told they are having a stroke or a heart attack. "We want you to go to this heart specialist over in Redding. We'd really like to send you by ambulance." The patient doesn't have insurance and they don't have money for an ambulance, so they don't want to do it. They can't do it. I'd tell them I really thought they should go there, and I would make arrangements for them to go. In one case we made the arrangements for them to see the specialist and I told the wife that she had to drive because her husband was having a stroke or a heart attack and didn't want to go in the ambulance. Whichever it was, something major was going on, and he had to get to a specialist. What does he do? He goes down to Bluff Creek and gets his RV. His wife drives the car and he drives the RV over to Redding and checks in about eight o'clock that evening. We had seen him at ten o'clock in the morning. The doctor is phoning me, asking why the patient isn't there when he hasn't shown up by three o'clock.

Two days later he died because he had wasted his time. He might have made it if he had gone right over to the specialist in an ambulance, but doing what he did, breaking camp and driving the RV because he didn't want to leave it out in the country, probably killed him. He stranded the RV, along with his body, out in Redding, so it really didn't do him any good. You get those people and there's just nothing you can do about it. There's no way you can get across to them that they are not indestructible. "You are having a heart attack or a stroke, and you need to get to a specialist to find out what's going on. There is a guy over there who knows vascular systems, and he will tend to you with the right medication." It doesn't mean a thing to them.

Herbicide Spraying

I got to know some of the hippies who had started moving to the river in the late 1970s through my work at the tribal clinic, which served everyone who needed medical care. I got involved with environmental things because the Forest Service started a program of spraying 2,-4D herbicides in this area in order to kill broadleaf plants, which would then make room to grow more conifers. Politics makes strange bedfellows, and politically, the marijuana growers and farmers were against the Forest Service spraying herbicides for their reasons, and me because of health reasons. People were getting strange little sores on the parts of their bodies where the skin was exposed, but not where it was covered by clothing. Most of the people affected were women and small children. The older children would be at school and the husbands would be at work, but the women and small children were home during the day when the Forest Service did this aerial herbicide spraying, and the spray drifted over them.

The first time I became aware of a problem of spontaneous abortions was when a woman came into the clinic whose husband was working for the Forest Service. She was about two months pregnant and was having a miscarriage. She said, "I'm losing this baby because of my husband's job. He comes home with that herbicide on his clothes and it causes me to miscarry. This is the second miscarriage I've had and I never had any problems when I had my first little boy and he didn't have this job." I thought she was a little dingy. I didn't pay too much attention, and she lost the baby. Between 1976 and 1978, we did not have a single baby carried successfully by anyone who lived in the Orleans area.

I told the doctor who I was working with that something was wrong because there were all these healthy young women who were having miscarriages after the second month, and that just didn't happen around Orleans. Usually the Karuk women don't have miscarriages. There were a few women, and I was one of them, who miscarried several children and had a hard time keeping a baby, but there are not very many women like that, and the rest of them couldn't lose a baby if they wanted to. They could have done anything to themselves and they would still carry that kid. So I said, "Something is going on here. Something is wrong."

Then they started spraying closer to Orleans, and other symptoms started showing up. They were spraying up above Camp Creek and people who went swimming there were getting bladder infections. I asked the doctor if he thought the spraying had anything to do with the infections. He said, "Well they're more sexually active," because the infections were mostly among hippies who were living up in the Camp Creek neighborhood. At first these infections looked like an allergy and that got the doctor interested. By then we had spontaneous abortions, bladder infections, and skin infections. By 1977 we had 3,000 bladder infections in a community of 650 to 900 people, and I told the doctor I thought it had to do with the spraying, and that it had something to do with the water. The only thing that had been happening that would explain the symptoms was the herbicide spraying up Camp Creek, and now the spraying down along this part of the river.

One day I was in the office and I could see them spraying right over the water, here in Orleans, so I called the state capitol and complained. Someone from the federal Environmental Protection Agency office phoned me back and said that they weren't spraying in that water source. I told them, "I'm standing here talking to you, looking out the window over at Whitey's Flat, and I can see them in the sunlight, spraying, and that stuff drifting down into the watershed. They are over the water."

He said, "They are next to it."

I told him, "You are not standing here looking at it, so you don't know what they're doing, but I know that they are spraying the watershed, because I can see it," and he hung up.

Some people around here got angry with me about the spraying because they thought that somehow what I was doing would interfere with their ability to grow crops, but I persisted in what I was doing. Around this time twenty-four women got pregnant in the Orleans area and all of them miscarried. Two of the pregnancies were not even real pregnancies. These two fetuses had all the DNA and material of a child, but there was no life, and the fetus grew rapidly, like a mole or a fungus. When I started reading about this kind of pregnancy I learned that in an area like Three Mile Island you should expect three mole pregnancies in a year from an incident like that. That was supposed to be one of the most polluted places on the earth, and here in Orleans we had two of those pregnancies in two years because of the spraying in this area. Here we were, approaching the mole pregnancy level associated with Three Mile Island!

My friend Millie Donahue and I started investigating things. We were pretty sure we were on the right track because all these health problems came at just the time the herbicide spraying had started. I thought it was due to the herbicides, because I could see that was the only thing that had changed in our environment. The Forest Service said, "Oh no, they're taking dope." I said that if they were taking dope, then they would have been taking dope before the herbicide spraying, so why didn't they abort then? The Forest Service was saying that the abortions and birth defects that had never been seen around here just happened to coincide with the use of herbicides that were one molecule different from Agent Orange. The Forest Service kept saying that people opposed to the spraying were way out there.

I told the Forest Service that *they* were way out there, and they said, "What do you mean?" I said, "All day long the air rises out of the valley, and all night long it drops into it. Whatever happens out there in the mountain air during the day comes down here at night." Then they wanted to spray something called Garlon that was one atom different from Agent Orange—not one molecule different, one *atom* different—and they didn't think it would hurt the environment! I said, "Why don't you just go ahead and use all of your leftover Agent Orange, then, and just poison the whole country?"

They didn't look very happy when I said that. I said to them, "Do you know that after all that spraying was done on the G-O Road you could go up there for years and not find one single bird or even a lizard crawling on those rocks where they sprayed?[14] Now they are coming back, but it took ten years." I told them, "You're trying to kill broadleaf plants in a forest, and there is nothing more tenacious than a madrone tree. You could probably kill the fir trees quicker than you can the broadleaf trees. If you cut down one madrone tree, thirty will grow back from the stump and the roots." They didn't want to admit that they were responsible for what happened, because then they would have to pay for it. I guess what we did worked, because they never sprayed us with Garlon.

In the beginning, when the basket weavers first organized themselves as a group, they were opposed to the herbicide spraying. Some of them had cancer and they thought it was caused by the spraying. After four or five years of the basket weavers being organized, the government quit spraying and started giving them funding for basket weaving conventions and for small burns so that they would have good plants to work with. After that the organized basket weavers have not been so critical of the Forest Service.

I wrote out my ideas about what was happening as a protest, and it pretty much got sent around the whole country through organizations like Greenpeace. I worked really hard and made statements on issues if they related to people's health, because I was working in health care. On political things, like construction of the G-O Road, some people would be for it and some would be against it, and since I had to treat them all, I just stayed out of those things. I needed to be involved so that people would come to me and talk to me and I could help. I couldn't help them if they were mad at me.

National Health Service representatives were coming to listen to our complaints about the herbicide spraying, and I had my case written up to explain our position when the government made me and the tribe's other community health representative go to South Dakota to get our CHR licenses at the same time. The government paid for this training and told Hupa Health that we were supposed to go at this certain time during the time the National Health Service was going to come here. I feel that they got us out of here so that we couldn't say anything, because in all the years that she and I had worked together, we never went to a conference together other than this one time. One of us had always stayed here while the other went to a conference, because there had to be someone to cover the area. But this time they took us both out of here for a month and a half. I finally ended up giving the paper to one of our preschool teachers, who was pretty argumentative and a good talker, for her to represent me to the National Health Service people. I knew she would stick to her guns. National Health came during the time we were gone and said that the health issues we were complaining about were no more than to be expected in any community in the United States. They just whitewashed the problems and left.

After that people in Oregon and further up the river won a lawsuit against the herbicide spraying. Nobody down here ever got anything, not even a free clinic visit. Finally, there were too many complaints and the government stopped aerial spraying, but Simpson Timber Company still does it on private property. Since Orleans is a community, the effects show up more clearly here than in other remote areas, where you might only have two or three children born in a year, so that the percentage of miscarriages and other health problems wouldn't be obvious. In the 1980s, after they quit spraying, these physical problems stopped happening. I said then that if they had been taking dope or drinking they would still be doing those things, and if this had been responsible for all the problems we started having when the spraying was going on, then we would still be having those problems. The only thing that had changed was that there was no more aerial spraying, and now they were carrying their children to full term.

When we were studying in South Dakota, I met a medicine man from Montana and was telling him about the herbicide spraying down here. He told me he could tell that I was a medicine person and I told him we don't have the continuity with our past culture that they still have in South Dakota. There, they still know their tribal histories and who was descended from who, so that their traditions keep going on and on, but our tribe was so small that they were able to decimate us and it just left big gaps and blank spots, and so much of our oral tradition and history is gone. There are just bits and pieces left. We don't have the level of continuity that they still have and we don't have the level of training of spiritual people that we once had. The medicine man who started our Brush Dance again wasn't quite sure about all of the details so he had to kind of piece it together with what he remembered and what the Creator helped him to know, and some parts of it are missing, but it works.

After meeting this medicine man I had a vision. I saw a person who was all painted up with red and green and yellow with little horns on his head, maybe buffalo horns, and he had little fur things around his ankles with little bells on them. He danced around and around and back and forth, kind of in a trance, and he went round and round and back and forth about a dozen times. He was singing and bending forward, and he had little rattles in his hands. Then he quit dancing and looked right at me, right into my eyes, and said, "This is all I can do for you, but be really careful," and he disappeared.

When the painted-up person spoke to me in the vision, it was the voice of the medicine man we met in South Dakota, but it didn't look like him. It was some kind of vision. I guess he did that to protect me, and I think it was about the herbicide spraying. I guess if the government is starting to move you around, it is getting dangerous. I learned later that he died of cancer in 1980, and although he looked old, he was still a young man. Those northern Plains people age quickly. I was in my mid-forties and Millie and I were laughing about our grandchildren, and someone said, "Oh, you had your children when you were that young." We told them our age and said that we were plenty old enough to have grandchildren. Then we learned that people we thought were in their fifties were actually in their thirties. I think it's that dry, cold weather there that ages them so quickly.

About twenty years later, I went to Sacramento and testified to the Forest Service on behalf of the basket makers about the herbicides and what had happened. I gave them the history of it here, where the relationship between spontaneous abortions and herbicides wasn't proven, but the spontaneous abortions ended when the aerial spraying stopped, and it didn't happen again.

Police Brutality

I usually only fight about things that I don't feel are justifiable. I was a mediator for the Karuk Tribe with the Hoopa Tribe against police brutality for six years, back in the late 1970s and early 1980s. At that time there were two or three bars in Orleans, and Orleans had two cops and Hoopa had one. I thought the police were using undue force against Native Americans. They would handcuff Native

Americans and then make them sit on their hands in the police car for hours while they looked for somebody else, instead of taking them down and putting them in jail when they picked them up. One fellow's left hand didn't work well after that treatment because the handcuffs had damaged the nerves in his wrist. So we negotiated about that kind of thing.

I didn't think that was right, and I thought it wasn't right when they would get somebody who had been drinking and under the influence and bang their head against the top of the police car. I said, "I don't even drink, and if you banged my head against the car, I'd come up fighting." I told them they were doing things that caused trouble. They were doing things to get people to fight. "When you go into a bar and walk along the bar with your nightstick out swinging, and looking hard at people, I think that's being overaggressive, and you shouldn't be able to do that." I remember one little cop who was kind of a small guy and was really aggressive. He didn't really do a lot of things to people other than talk aggressively and talk down to people, but the other two cops were always doing something physical to people.

One time our adopted son, Chucker, came into town. He was working out in Mount Shasta City with Darrell and had come home to Orleans. He wasn't in town fifteen minutes before the police threw him to the ground and said that he fit the description of somebody that robbed a bank, and they were going to charge him with bank robbery. I phoned over to the jail and talked to the jailer and he let me talk to the lieutenant. I said, "How in the hell can he be robbing a bank in Hoopa this afternoon at two o'clock when he was logging out in Mount Shasta City at two o'clock? There was no way he could be in Hoopa." I gave the lieutenant the phone number for the logging company he was working for and they checked it out and let him out of jail. They did things like that. They had people that they liked to pick on, and Chucker was one of them.

I was always arguing with one of the cops. We were always at sword points at these meetings, and some of our retorts would get quite sharp, and the mediator was always trying to keep us apart. Years later, when I was studying to be a nurse, he was having surgery and didn't understand what they were telling him about his surgery and was really apprehensive. I talked to him and said, "Well, I'll go find the information and bring it back to you." So I got the information and brought it back, and that was that. I went on working with my other patients. I had been in there and helped one of the other nurses with him a couple of times, but he wasn't one of my patients. Later he wrote me a recommendation for being helpful and being so intuitive about how upset he was. Another nurse said it didn't count for much because he knew me. I just thought to myself that she didn't know how he knew me. We had been at sword points and he didn't really like me. Sitting on the opposite side of a mediation table is quite a different thing from being a nurse and patient.

In the end we did manage to get some changes in the police procedures and how they were treating people. Then there was a ceremony in Eureka to sign the papers, and I wore a blue hat I had made. My cousin Betty saw me on the news and told me later that when she saw me in that hat she had laughed and said, "I'll bet that Mavis never combed her hair, wearing that hat."

Psychic Abilities

When I was younger, sometimes I would get into somebody's mind, and my aunt told me, "If they have their mind open, don't go in! You cannot do that. It's not polite to do that."

Then one day I was working as a nurse on one of my patients, a Japanese lady, who was really upset about something. I said, "I'm sorry your daughter is so sick with her miscarriage. She looked at me and said, "You read my mind. I didn't say anything."

I said, "I'm sorry, I didn't mean to do that. I'm not supposed to do that. I thought you had said it." I said, "Your mind was open and I just walked in. I'm sorry. I've been told not to do that." I figure the Japanese must be able to do that, because she didn't seem unduly surprised or upset that I had read her mind.

My aunt Caroline told me that her mother's father, the Welsh linguist, said that his mother was psychic, so Grandma's gift may not have just been from being an Indian. I don't know how psychic my grandmother was. She was old and tired and dying of heart disease by the time I knew her. People who had known her when she was younger said she had been a very strong, domineering personality.

Part of this psychic ability comes as a gift to a person, and the training helps you to understand and interpret what you're seeing. Say you see someone dead in a vision. They are in a coffin and you are going to a funeral, but the person you see is not the person who may die. It's going to be someone close to you, and there will be times—like when I saw that Darrell had been killed. I saw it three times and then told his grandmother, who was a very gifted woman. She said, "If you saw Darrell as the dead person in the vision, it isn't him, but it is going to be someone very close to him." It turned out that it was Darrell's brother who died. If I had been more astute I could have picked up who was being referred to in the vision, but sometimes you don't do that. I wasn't astute enough; I was still young, in my twenties. But there are all these little hints that come with a vision.

Sometimes it just leaves you totally in the dark. Like two weeks ago, I have a vision of somebody speeding up the road in what looks like a brown SUV and they get in a wreck. It looks like a white person, and they are dead. I don't even know anyone with a brown SUV. It wasn't an SUV in the end anyway, but it was brown. This person is killed upriver, toward Happy Camp. I just put it out of my mind because I didn't know who it was. It might have been some kind of crazy dream or nightmare or something, but it seemed like it was awfully clear. Visions are impressed on your mind. They are not like dreams, where you will see yourself, say, swimming in a pool and then you are floating and then you are walking across grass and then something else is happening. Dreams are kind of skippy that way. Visions are like it's happening right there in front of you and you saw it. I saw a brown car speeding up the road and when the person was killed, I saw that they looked white. Then about three or four days after the dream, someone told me about a wreck that was the one I had seen in the vision. The driver was Indian, but he was light and looked like a white person, and he was driving a brown Cherokee Jeep. That's who I was seeing, but I didn't know the driver. I didn't know who his relatives were at the time, but then I learned who had been killed, and my knowing his cousins was my link to him. I think I'd only seen him once or twice in his entire life.

The vision that really threw me came to me around 1980. Beavi was in a halfway house with some abused women. She had moved to Redding and was in an abusive relationship, so she was staying in this halfway house when she met three women. The husband of one of them was a domineering religious fanatic. The woman would run away from him and then she would go back to him. The last time, she left and she went to the halfway house and thought she had gotten away from him. She was still afraid that he was going to do something to her and even had written notes to that effect, but authorities said she was a crazy woman. I didn't even know her, but then I had a vision four or five times and I would see a black, wet, foggy parking lot, and I knew I was in a river town. I thought, "Where is this river town I keep seeing?" It looked too populated to be anyplace close around here. The next time the vision came to me, I saw a woman walking through a glass door into what looked like a little coffee shop. The shop had a hiding place behind this rack and looking back through the glass door. I didn't know who she was or where she was. I just knew it was a woman who looked like she was afraid someone was following her. The last time I saw the vision, someone touched her shoulder and she looked around startled and frightened. That was the end of the vision. Nothing more.

I told Beavi that I kept dreaming about someone who is afraid, and they act like someone is following them, and they are trying to dodge whoever is following them. I told her that in my last vision someone was touching her and she was looking up, frightened. It was a small, brown-haired, white woman with brown eyes, and I don't know why I'm dreaming about this white woman. Beavi went back over to Redding, and when she came back she told me that a woman she had been in rehab with who had come over to see me and acted weird had been found dead in the Redding Hotel. I told Beavi I didn't know what the Redding Hotel was like, and she described a hotel with a big parking lot and a coffee shop. I asked her about the newspaper rack I had seen in my vision and she said that the hotel had one of those. She also said the woman had left a paper saying that if she was found dead her husband had killed her, but that her husband had so much influence in Redding that it was not even investigated. I suppose meeting her briefly here at the house with Beavi was enough of a link to trigger the vision.

As I grew older, I got so that I would know if someone I knew of was going to drown. I don't have to really know the person, but if I knew of them, knew who they were, in my vision I would see the water where they would drown. This year was the first time I saw a drowning in the ocean, but all my life, starting with my mother, I have seen drownings in the river. I would see the river the way it was going to look when the person drowned, like whether it's muddy or murky or green, the way it was when one of the local men drowned. Before he drowned, the river I saw in my vision was high and the water was green. I kept thinking, "God, that river is so high. I wonder who I know where this high, green river is," and then I saw the Klamath had risen and the water was green. I thought, "That river looks just like my dream. I wonder who it is who is going to drown in it."

Sometimes if I pray about a vision, I will continue to see that vision for a while. I might see it once or twice more after praying, and then it goes away. But if I see it three or four times and it just keeps coming back, I know then that it's going to happen, no matter what I do. It's going to be. Sometimes I can change the vision and what is going to happen by praying about it. What I see happening will change to something else, like I will first see death and it will change to injury if I pray on it hard enough. It won't be exactly what you saw, but you can tell that it's close enough that what you saw had changed by praying about it. Sometimes the vision doesn't change and the event I have been seeing will happen like I have been seeing it.

My visions are like seeing through a glass darkly, like the Bible says. The visions are murky and not really that clear. You don't really see who it is. You see someone and know they are close to you, somebody you know, but it doesn't reveal exactly who that person is. Sometimes they are so close to you that you won't see who the person is at all, and when that happens I know that they are really close to me. If the power won't show me something about the person involved, I just know something terrible is coming to someone that I know. I pray about what I have seen in the vision and sometimes it comes anyway.

UFOs

When all those UFOs were coming around in the 1970s, I told my daughter Carol, "I can hear them talking."

She says, "What do they talk like?"

"They talk in that religious language that I can't understand. It sounds like talking in tongues. It sounds like the language that you hear when you go to pick up your medicine."

Once I saw something come down and land near the river. A blue light came down from it. It sat there for a while and *whssht,* it's gone. That's how fast it moved—*whssht,* and it was gone. Carol had seen it coming and said to me, "Something's falling out of the sky, Mom. It's coming down." She was standing in front of the window by a blanket chest, one of those hope-chest-type boxes, and I was lying in bed. I was quite a ways from the window, probably about eight feet, and all at once the room was like a kaleidoscope with lights reflecting through my room, and then Carol said it was gone. She was talking about how the lights looked. Where I was lying down I couldn't see what the light was coming from, but I could see the lights flashing around willy-nilly through the room. It wasn't any color, just bright light color. But she could see colors outside the window. Then she looked again and said, "No, look, it's moved down the river." I got up and could see it there on a logged-out flat by the river, a little thing sitting there with a light coming from it. It looked like a silver half-dome, like that [turns colander upside-down on table].

I was always knickknacking around with alternative realities like UFOs because of my experience as a medicine person seeing actual alternative reality. It's like you just step through and it is altogether different on the other side. It even feels different, and your state of mind is different. You're more euphoric, but you don't remember as much, you don't have that preciseness and stability of mind that you have on this side. Probably because that's not your reality and this one is.

Long Gone Is Shot

For months I had visions in which I could see three guys dead in the woods up above the Ishi Pishi Club, a bar in Orleans, but I couldn't see a face. Not one face, so I knew it was someone really close to me. I could feel they were really close and I saw it over and over again. I just kept praying about it and I went to Josephine Peters and had her pray with me about it. We prayed and prayed and then I'd have the vision again. I would be driving by from work down in Hoopa, and just feel it and see it when I drove through Orleans. I knew it was going to be someone I knew who was really close to me.

Long Gone was twenty years old and had just finished playing baseball at the field behind the Orleans School. He and some other young men had been drinking at the baseball field and he just came into the bar to see if his dad was there so he could get a little money to buy some booze to drink down under the bridge. The man who shot him told Long Gone, "I came up here to shoot Bart Starritt, but I think I'll shoot you." Long Gone said he had just turned to drop down when the man shot him through the right lung. At the same time Long Gone was shot, Dennis Donahue was shot in the back, both of them by a man who was an assistant warden at San

Quentin. Dennis started running towards the door when he was shot in the back, but he was wearing a big thick leather marine belt, so the bullet didn't sever his spine but just lodged in the vertebra. Dennis is still carrying that bullet and Long Gone's bullet is still lodged behind his aorta.

About this time, 1976, we moved our old house one-eighth of a mile to the west over to here, and the water, electricity, and septic weren't yet hooked up, so I was cooking over a campfire out in the yard and we were still getting our water from the spring. The telephone was the only thing connected, and I had to have that because I was working for Hupa Health Service. One night the phone started ringing downstairs, so I made my way down in the dark, and just as I got there the ringing stopped. I started back up the stairs and it began ringing again, but it stopped just as I got back to it, and I said to hell with it, I won't answer it again. Then a car came fishtailing into the yard. Roy McGains was driving and my daughter Carol was with him. Carol hollered to me that Long Gone had been shot in the chest in the Ishi Pishi Club, and he was being taken by car to meet the ambulance coming up from Hoopa. Then they took off.

I got up and got my youngest child, Daypay, and my grandson Cogie out of bed and dressed and took them over to town and left the boys there with Cogie's stepfather, and took Beavi with me to the hospital in Hoopa. Before the ambulance could get to Orleans, a woman friend had put Long Gone in her truck and headed for Hoopa to meet the ambulance on the road. When they were nearly to Hoopa she had a flat tire, but she had arranged with the ambulance driver to blink the lights at him when she saw his flashing lights coming. This way they were able to transfer Long Gone to the ambulance and save time getting him to the hospital.

The ambulance radioed ahead to the hospital and said they were bringing in a man, but that he was dead on arrival. The doctor told me that when he felt Long Gone's throat, he could feel the jugular vein barely quivering. The blood and air in his chest had his heart pushed over so far that it could hardly flicker, but it was still working—so he wasn't dead, quite. He was just a half a step from it.

Carol was still riding with Roy McGains, looking for the man who had shot Long Gone and Dennis. They spotted a car out ahead of them and Roy asked Carol, "Is that the guy?"

Carol said, "I don't know. I can't see him yet." By the time she could tell it was the fellow they were looking for he was almost out of range, and Roy just took a shot at his car and hit the back bumper.

Long Gone told me later that when that air and blood were drained from his chest by the doctor, he woke up and the doctor told him, "This is going to hurt a little bit." Then the doctor stuck a shunt into his jugular vein and he almost blacked out from the pain. When he came to again he said, "Hurt a little? I don't know what they would say if it was going to hurt a lot." Then they commenced to put in another shunt and IV lines everyplace and started pouring saline into him.

I waited for a couple of hours and one of the nurses gave me a cup of coffee, and then pretty soon one of the doctors came whistling down the hall. The nurse looked at how the doctor was approaching us and said, "Well, he's doing all right, then."

The doctor said, "He's doing very well."

"How well?"

"Well, it's a miracle. He's lost half his blood and he's stable on IVs. But the bad news is, the ambulance has a flat tire now, so we have to keep him here until the tire is fixed." It took them about a half-hour to get the tire fixed and ready to go, and they took him out by ambulance to the hospital in Eureka. Long Gone wanted to see me before they took them away from Hoopa, and when he saw me, he said later that he just knew he was going to be okay. He knew that he was going to live, because I told him I would see him in Eureka.

He said, "You know, I lost half my blood and you got me to thinking I was fine."

When he told me that later, I said, "Yeah, but Long Gone, I never told you that I would see you alive."

He said, "I never thought of that." Having me say I would see him in Eureka was all he needed to be convinced that he would live. He knew if I said I'd see him there, he would be there, and he assumed alive.

I told Carol that I had prayed all the time to change this vision I had been having of three dead people so that no one would die, and nobody died, even though in my vision I kept seeing three people dying. But as far as I knew at the time, only two people had been shot. Long Gone was hurt the worst. Nothing happened to the man who shot him, and even though Dennis was shot, it was not fatal and did not leave him crippled, so that prophecy was changed. About five years later the shooter was charged with being in possession of a large quantity of methamphetamine. In 1987 he was in protective custody in Central Prison for dealing in methamphetamines when he was killed by another prisoner. Long Gone kept track of him until he was killed, because he said the son of a bitch might try to come back and finish the job.

The Humboldt County Sheriff's Department said that because Long Gone's story and the story of the bartender in the bar where he was shot were basically the same, they had to have gotten together and made up the story and were lying. Long Gone had been in the hospital, shot through the lung, and had no chance to make up a story with the bartender. You can't collaborate on your story and get it all practiced if one of the collaborators is in the hospital at death's door. The sheriff's department said the shooter was just confused and had been drinking. They whitewashed the whole thing. The grand jury said that it was a justifiable shooting and that was as far as it went. So an assistant warden of San Quentin Prison has the right to shoot some Indian who is just standing in a bar.

Picking Up Power

When I was young, the medicine women and my aunts would tell me that I would not get my full power until I was in my forties. That's when I would pick it up. And so I always thought that one of these days I would just walk out there and pick it up. This was a misapprehension on my part, and I learned that you don't have a damn thing to do with picking up your power—nothing. There is no free will or choice in this spiritual act, because if you had free will you would put on your running shoes and run like hell in the other direction. And then on the other hand, there are people walking around seeking this power! People doing all kinds of things, hoping the Creator will bless them with this power. I look at them and think, "Are you absolutely insane? You *want* this?"

After moving back to Orleans, I stayed in the house most of the time because I could feel something calling me to go someplace, to go out. I don't know what it was—I've always called it "the power"—but it would call me to come outside. I told my aunt, "It keeps calling me. It wants me to go outside." Aunt Caroline said that if I didn't want to do any medicine things, then I shouldn't go outside. If I felt like I was too busy with my family, don't listen to it, just stay in the house. I said, "You mean you can tell it no?"

She said, "Yes, you can tell it no. If you're too busy and it's not convenient for you, then you don't have to do it."

I didn't want to deal with it, so I wouldn't go outside. I stayed in the house and it really couldn't make me go outside. But if it caught me outside, it would pick me up spiritually and I would be gone for a while, so I stayed inside and avoided using the medicine power. Then the tribe held a White Deerskin Dance at Katamin, because we didn't yet own the land at Tishaniik, so at that time we couldn't have the dance down here in the Orleans area. Richard Johnson was the medicine man. He went out on the medicine trail and did what he was supposed to do, and in doing that he lost his soul. Richard called to me telepathically and he was very insistent. The power just would not leave me alone and kept demanding that I go outside. I told my aunt that it was way past my time to do anything. "I don't know why it wants me."

She said that maybe no one else was available right now, at this place, at this time, who had been trained in a way that could help them. The trained medicine people who could have helped Richard may have moved away and be living someplace else. So I went ahead and helped him. To help him, I went out into the other world. It felt like I was flying faster than the speed of light. I was really going fast.

At Karuk funeral ceremonies the dead are always instructed not to take the road to the left—keep to the right when you're on the trail of the dead—so evidently I was traveling on the trail of the dead to where the souls are. I don't know if when I went to pick up the medicine I was on the trail of the dead. There was no reason for me to know that. I was on the trail to pick up the Fatawanun's soul after he prayed and walked and talked with God. He lost his soul because the experience was so powerful.

I think you're not supposed to step off the trail because you don't know where you are, and you might get lost. It isn't like going on a train trip and you're looking out the window and seeing everything pass by. You move awfully fast. I think that when other medicine people and I were being picked up, they were taking us up and down the trail until we knew the trail and it became automatic to stay on the trail. They had to pick me up as a child, but as I grew older and more experienced, I could just go out and get on the trail. There was a trail to the left and a trail to the right. When a person has died and is being prayed for, they tell you to take the trail to the right, so I took the trail to my right, to the place where souls are kept, and on my left I passed the coldest place I ever felt in my life. I think it was hell. It was all gray and black, and it was a burning cold, and it felt like it was burning me when I went by it.

I stopped where the trail entered a place of warm darkness. It felt like the trail continued, but I didn't really go in there. I just looked for an instant and in front of me was an area of warm, soft blackness with little yellow lights glowing in it. That was my perception of it, and it is probably a child's perception of what was really there, because I was just dropping in. Immediately, one of the lights came loose and went *whoosh*, into my solar plexus, kind of on the left side. As soon as that happened, I turned and zipped right back out. I don't remember the trip back. Just as soon as I stepped back into this reality, that light came out of my body and evidently went where it was supposed to go, back to Richard. I had nothing to do with where it went; I was just the messenger, the delivery person.

That place that the Fatawanun goes during the White Deerskin Dance exists at different levels, and very few go to the level Richard had reached. Some Fatawanun say they've seen me up on the medicine trail when they have gotten lost. They say that when they were lost, I appeared to them. I never said a word to them, but just pointed to where they were supposed to go. That's all I did. I never said anything and then I disappeared. They swear they saw me in the flesh and they all expect me to remember them and to know that they lost their way and that I helped them. I think I sense them, but I'm not like this, in my physical body. I look to them like I am there physically, probably because I would scare the hell out of them if they saw my real appearance in this spiritual form. I have had a glimpse of that reality and I know that I am not in this form.

There were times that I went to help the Fatawanun on the trail and later they would know who I was and that they had seen me up on the trail when they were confused about where the trail was, because they are also in something of a trance when they are on the trail, praying after having fasted for ten days. Some of the Fatawanun just came out and said to me, "I saw you on the trail. You didn't say anything, you just pointed me down the trail when I was standing there kind of confused. All at once you would be there and point down the trail." They don't remember seeing me leave. Some of them to my knowledge I had never met, but then later they would recognize me as a person they had seen on the trail.

I think I am in the form of the iridescent egg shape with a small head and iridescent bands of light when I am moving at the speed of light and in the other reality. I know that that is one shape I take. I imagine that soul-catching was one of my gifts as the Fatawanun's woman, but since I didn't complete that training, I did not know that was one of my gifts until it happened. But I have heard medicine people from another tribe talking about doing that. This was one of the large southern tribes whose medicine has been going on since time immemorial and didn't get disrupted by the white people. It actually came up in a CHR seminar taught by a medicine man. He said, "If you lose your soul, what do you do?"

I said, "You call a soul catcher."

He said, "She's right, and evidently you don't pick up the telephone to do that."

Different Indian tribes have different ways of describing this process. I've heard some call it shape-changing. With us, it's either you are over here or you're over there. If you're over there, then it's simple. It isn't very physical, other than the energy used to change from one reality to the other, but once you've done the change to the other state, then you move almost electronically, at least as fast as the message going through a telephone wire, from one place to another. When you go out into the other reality to pick up souls, it's like you are moving at the speed of light, at least. You know that you're going awfully fast. You don't know how far you've gone, but you know that you've gone awfully fast to get to where that place is. You have that feeling of moving fast. You just get a glimpse of something and it's gone. My aunt Caroline told me that when she was going to Doctor Rock, "I was moving over the top of the ground and I couldn't feel it. I could see the ground moving under my feet, but I couldn't feel it."

When I was a young girl I didn't know what I was doing when I went into a trance. After I was in my forties, I realized I was shape-changing. I studied it for a long, long time because I thought I was insane.

The Sioux believe you can turn into a deer or anything. I don't have that much power. Some of the medicine people that I have heard and been in contact with have so much power that it is just unbelievable. I change into an iridescent spirit shape. I don't change into a deer or an elk. I haven't got that kind of power, or maybe I don't have that need. But I have a need to be able to leave this world and go into the other world, so I have to change. Evidently I can't go into the spirit world in this form, but my husband told me that I'm not here sometimes.

One time I came down the trail one day from being out there, and the medicine woman who had died recently was trying to come back from the other side. I hadn't gone to her service, because I had to go to the service of a closer relation. I stopped because she was on the trail and the shadow people were dragging her back. She was really angry. She had a cane and she was swinging it at them, and they were trying to drag her back up the trail toward the other side. I thought, "Now what do I do?"—because I could not go around her. And just about the time I thought that, something took me, *whsssht,* as high as a treetop, and I went right over her. I felt like a chess piece that somebody picked up and moved. I must've gone a hundred and fifty feet up in the air and dropped down the other side when the power just picked me up and threw me over the top of her. This medicine woman was a real sweet woman and I was distantly related to her. I know my physical body remained here while it was happening, because when I woke up I screamed and waked up Darrell, and he asked me what was wrong. I told him I had stepped off the trail and I started laughing because I was in my own backyard. That was my spirit moving, and my body was in the bed.

I have only seen the shadow people a few times in my life. When I've seen them before, they are looking for someone. They have come over to pick someone up. The shadow people are a little larger than cats but are black and built close to the ground like a rat and they look like shadows.

Sometimes I am here, like that time I got off the trail and woke up in bed. I had come out of the spirit form and gone back into my body. Evidently I left a sleeping person there in bed and the spirit part just left, just climbed out of there and walked off. Other times, Darrell told me my body was just not on this earth, because he looked everywhere for me and I was nowhere around for hours.

I know this about the shape I assume because one day when I was about forty-six or forty-seven years old, after Long Gone had been shot, it was a freezing day and I was doing dishes when something made me go outside. It kept telling me to go outside, and I kept thinking, "I've got to finish these dishes," because the pipes were frozen outside and I still had to pack water and heat it up on the stove, because we had just moved into the house and the hot water heater wasn't in yet. I wanted to get the dishes done before my water got cold, but the power wouldn't let me stay there and finish the dishes. So I walked outside and was going to throw some garbage to the chickens. Then I didn't know what had happened. The first thing I knew, I wasn't where the chickens were. I was on the trail near here, at a place that is a power center, a crossroads, and a body made of iridescent bands of light came down, and a voice said that we were going to go.

When I shape-changed to go over to the other side with my aunt Caroline to pick up my power, I saw her in her changed form and told her that she looked funny. I think it was my aunt Caroline. It sounded like her voice, and when she left I thought it was her. I could kind of see through her and she had iridescent bands all over her. When I told her that, she said, "I?" and laughed. Then I realized I was in the same form she was.

We started going up into the air and I thought that we were just going over to Chestnut Ranch, near Boise Creek there, but I was off a little. We drifted up and I could see the town like I'd never seen it before. We drifted on up and we went over Boise Creek Saddle, so we were high on the mountain, and then we went over and I thought, "Well, is this Boise Creek?" Then I thought, "No, we are dropping down into Red Cap Creek." And then I was on this little bench on the north side of Red Cap Creek. It was wintertime and it was freezing and there were no leaves on the trees where I had left home, but where I got to, this place on Red Cap Creek, the trees looked like it was May. There were a couple of little apple trees there, and they were all leafed out, and it was a different time of the year.

Then I said, "Why are you taking me here? There's nothing here."

The guide didn't say anything and then these people appeared, a male face, mostly, and other people who were kind of like misty images, and then they faded and I could hear voices. The voice said, "We're here and we have something we need to tell you," and that's the last thing I remember. I could hear the voices, but I don't remember what they were saying. I mean, I don't consciously remember what they told me. I was in that altered state of mind and they were saying things to my subconscious mind that I had not known before. Later I came to and I was back in my body and in the woods up above the chicken house. It was late afternoon, it wasn't morning anymore. I went along back into the house and started doing dishes again, and Darrell said, "Where were you?"

I said, "I went to feed the chickens."

He said, "I hollered for you and you weren't there, you weren't anywhere."

I said, "Was the car gone?"

"No."

I laughed and told him, "Well, you know I have to be here someplace close, because you know I don't walk anyplace." That's logical. It's not logical that I'll go walking off into the sunset someplace. I travel by different means.[15]

He didn't say any more, and then afterwards I knew things about my past and other things, and somewhat of how the power works for me, and I could do things that I didn't know I could do. I had learned about powers that I didn't have before and—gifts, not really powers, but I could do things that I hadn't known I could do. This knowledge is not black and white. It is very subtle and implied.

I think that's what the medicine women were talking about when they said I would pick up my powers. I was gone for about three hours but it felt like about fifteen minutes, so there is a big time lag there someplace. Time goes slower there. After this happened I chastised my aunt and told her, "You were wrong. I didn't pick up anything, it picked me up." All that time I had thought I would just go out there and pick it up, like picking up a basket, but it picked me up. After that, what the medicine women had called my "happy time" came to an end. No more happy life.

The Fatawanun

Over all the years here, I've only had to go pick up one person's soul. Whether they get to the point of walking and talking with God depends on how much they get into the ritual, how much they expend. It requires a person with quite a bit of power to lose their soul, because they went into the altar, and that does take spiritual power. Other men who don't have that much power will get into the altar and get stuck, and then I have to go out and give them a little more spiritual strength and pull them out of the altar, back them off a little. But I don't take them back and set them on the trail, I just pull them out of the altar a little ways. They might not know I did it. I get a signal that they are in trouble and I have to get up there.

When the Fatawanun see me, when they get lost and I put them back on the trail, they see me but I don't see them. I go high on the trail, but I never see it. If the Fatawanun is in trouble on the trail and something has gone wrong, like he has stepped too far into the altar and can't get back out because he didn't stay concentrated, or he had his mind on something else and got in there too far, I have to go pull him back out because he doesn't have enough spiritual power to pull himself back out. This happens, because the Fatawanun are not necessarily spiritual medicine men. They are people from the medicine families who are Fatawanun a few times in the course of their lives. At these times they dedicate themselves to God and sometimes it is a very superficial dedication. Other times a person has more power, and it's a deeper thing that they do. In either case, there is no judgment on their abilities as Fatawanun. If he has more power, he does more. If he has less power, that's the way that is. But everyone who wishes to be Fatawanun and is from one of those families can go on the trail. Someone who is not from one of those families can walk on the trail, but nothing will happen. But the fact is that almost all of us who are alive now are related to one of those families. And a man can be a Fatawanun who is from one of those families from another tribe. For instance, my grandson Cogie is Yurok and that doesn't matter, because he comes from those people.

Some of the medicine men walk and talk with God, allegedly. The ones who go this far into the medicine don't have a soul when they come back down the hill after making the medicine. They lose their soul when they see the Great Spirit.

How far they get into the altars and how far they get into the other world when they are making medicine and being the Fatawanun is none of our business. A Fatawanun can just scratch the surface and go by the altars on the trail and not go into them, or you can get into the medicine so far that you can't get yourself out, like one of the young Fatawanun kept doing. Spiritually, he would get too far into the altar, and he didn't have the strength to pull himself back out. I don't know, maybe he didn't keep his mind centered on what he was doing, but something happened and he couldn't get out, and I would have to go and pull him out. When that happens I can't see them, but I know they can see me, because they recognize me and I never recognize them as having seen me on the trail.

Some have more power and are more gifted and go farther, and some don't have that power or are just negligent when it comes to power, but that doesn't mean that they are to be judged on those things. It doesn't matter. They just go out and do the ritual, and for some it is just a ritual. They go up into the mountains and say the prayers and run the trails and come down and do the prayers for the fish and that's the end of it. They are a medicine person, but they are not a medicine man. They are only a medicine person being a Fatawanun for that ten-day period. And others have immense power and go further into the medicine. Some medicine men are so gifted that they just walk in with so much power that they don't even have to think about what they're doing. They just walk in and do it and it is all given to them.

Of course, there are also the medicine men and the people who have been Fatawanun before who are helping them, so it's not just the Fatawanun all by himself, it is really a group effort. So if a Fatawanun did not have a lot of power, he would borrow from the medicine man and the medicine man's power could fill in for him. The medicine man would give some of his power to the prayers. If you are a person from one of the medicine families and you don't go out there and try, you might not learn that you are supposed to be doing this.

One year the medicine man for the White Deerskin Dance at Katamin got lost on the bluffs around Somes Peak. He finally got down just before dark and was talking about what had happened. He said that he started to come down and saw a tennis court, so he went over further because he didn't want to come down past someone's driveway. I told him that if he had continued coming down there and taken the road, then crossed over, he would have picked up the trail down at the bottom. He said, "Well, they told me not to be seen."

I said, "We wouldn't have seen you."

"I would have been walking down the road. What do you mean you wouldn't have seen me?"

"Believe me, you were being a Fatawanun, and if you were walking down the road and asked me where the trail was and I told you, I still wouldn't see you."

He asked why he wouldn't be seen and I told him, "To see you is to die. No one, no Indian, will ever admit that they saw you. We would know what you were and look the other way. Even if I was talking to you and pointing the way, I still wouldn't see you."

He said, "I never realized that."

In my work as a medicine woman I pray, even though I don't even speak the Karuk language. In the late 1920s and early 1930s when Orville Allen, who was going to be a medicine man, started growing up, the medicine people realized we were losing our language. Our language was going, so they taught him the prayers in English, looking ahead to that day when we wouldn't be able to speak our language—but even if we couldn't speak our language, we could still have our religion. That's the kind of flexibility you need, especially when you are a conquered people.

Now that I am in my seventies I feel my powers waning. I think it has something to do with my health. I'm not strong enough and well enough to keep using the energy that it takes to go into this altered state. I've come to the conclusion that I change, and that I'm not in this physical state during most of those times. Not only not in this state of mind, I don't think I am in this physical state of being. That may sound insane, but that's the conclusion I've come to because people will tell me…something will be bothering me, some situation. I sense something is going on. Too much drugs, too lax an attitude, too something, and in this physical state I start praying about it, and I keep thinking about it, and I keep praying about it, and I keep thinking about it, and then people will say they've seen me somewhere in the middle of the night. Of course I have no memory of being there. As far as I knew, I was sound asleep in bed. Beavi says that's what happens when you're traveling around in this world, you leave your body in place. And when you travel around in the other world you take your body with you. That's her spin on it.

The Fatawanun's Woman

The Fatawanun's women go as high as the medicine men go on the trails. The difference is that we do this in an altered state, not in a physical state, and we can't see that we are there. I don't remember seeing the Fatawanun trail. The other places I've been, I remember seeing, but not the Fatawanun trail. I see the bottom part, but I never see the top, even though I've been all over it, so they tell me. But that is where they recognize me from, because that is where they are when they need my help as a spiritual medicine person. I think it is funny that they expect me to recognize them too, but since they know who I am, since they have seen me high on the trail, they are certain that I saw them and know them from there, too. They don't understand that they saw me on the trail because they called me to be there. The Fatawanun are having a religious experience, and I show up, so they think I am part of it too, and that I am present there physically, the way that they are there. The only part I play is to make sure they stay on the trail. I think that that ability was a gift because I was trained to be the Fatawanun's woman and evidently that's what she does.

She keeps them on the trail, that's her job in an altered state of being. Sounds far-fetched to me. You could see why I would think I was insane. I was trained just to accept it. It's like one time when I was talking to my cousin and I said, "Well, I see things this way and I was taught to see things this way, and I believe in this religion and these medicine people, and I believe they can do things and they can heal people. I'm not here to convince you that this is the way, the truth, and the light. It's just my way, how I've been trained and how I see it.

That's what really makes me think I'm a paranoid schizophrenic, because it sounds like something that happens with schizophrenics. One of the things that happens is what we call "stopping time." For example, once our car was going out of control. I just shut my eyes and thought, "Oh no, this can't happen. I don't want this car to roll," and the car didn't roll. Then we are out of danger and I am looking at cars which we have already passed milliseconds before, but they are finally now just coming around the turn. There is a time lag there, something's wrong—either you speeded up or they slowed down. There is a gap in time. I don't know if these powers speeded up my time, or if they slow down the other person's time. Darrell used to ask me, "What did you just do?"

I said, "I don't know, I just shut my eyes," because there is no explanation, but it happened.

I felt that anyone who had been trained could do this, but my friend Millie Donahue, who had also been trained, swore that she couldn't. Someone was making a big fuss about my stopping time and I told Millie anyone can do something like that. I was being facetious. She looked at me for a second and said, really seriously, "I can't do that. Not just anyone can do that. I'm a medicine woman and I can't do that."

What happens is, I don't want something to happen. Logically, something is going to happen. A physical act is going on and I don't want that to follow through like it should. So I just close my eyes and think, "God, don't let this happen." In that space of time that the episode should have taken place, it is like either

I speed up to the speed of light or the other people involved are slowed down, but what was going to occur did not happen. The time becomes warped. Sometimes it's as small as something is dropping to the floor and I don't want it to hit, and someone will come from across the room, like Darrell is really quick. He will be standing right there and a little kid is going to fall off the chair. Darrell will cross the room and catch them before they hit the floor. So his actions are speeded up or the child's are slowed down. I don't know which way it is, but little things like that happen, as well as big things, like accidents in cars being avoided. That is what we call stopping time, and many of the medicine people who have these powers can do that. It isn't just me, different ones have this power. It is the same thing as shape-changing. Trained medicine people can do this. Shape-changing is like sleight of hand. The medicine person changes, but other people can't see what you become, so I guess if you had somebody watching you, you could throw up an image of a bird or anything, but your body has actually changed. The molecules change. It makes you very, very tired. Maybe other people are stronger and have more powers or can do it better, but it makes me tired.

When I think of it logically and realistically, from the point of view of this world, it sounds like the wild imaginings of a crazy person. That's my take on it, but things happen that don't seem logical or realistic from the perspective of this world. Things like stopping time and having visions have been going on for centuries, not just in this country but in other places, too. So these things aren't looked upon as being as unrealistic as they were when I was a child, because now they have them on TV and you can see them doing it. There are a lot of variables in this world.

In the training, the medicine women were always asking me what I saw and what I dreamt, and they just accepted it as truth. They took it very seriously and worked on it because I was so young. When your spirit is young, you don't understand part of what you're saying. Sometimes I wouldn't even know what I was talking about. They would work with what I had told them about my dreams by praying to change it if something bad was foretold in a dream. If they pray on it, sometimes they can stop whatever is going to happen from happening. They also called this "changing the face of it," like I did with Long Gone and Dennis and the other fellow being shot. It happened, but it didn't happen in the way it was being foretold. The prayers changed the face of it. It has been like this since I was a child, when I would tell the medicine women things I had seen and they could make medicine and stop or change what would have happened, depending on how much power they had.

I don't really remember the things I told them, but they were always picking my brain. They had power in them so that they could see things. Sometimes some of the medicine people will talk to you or contact you in other ways—I think it's telepathy. I don't have that power, that's not one of my gifts. To do that takes somebody with more power than I ever had. Some of the Indian doctors can do that. You need to keep your mind closed when you are around them, because they can walk right in and read it like opening a door. It makes you keep a little lock on what you're thinking unless you want them to know what you're thinking. This is a gift and it is also astuteness in judging human behavior.

Darrell has that astuteness. He just knows people, knows what they're up to. When I first married him, he and his brother Big Boy, who was two years younger than him, would say, "So-and-so is doing this," or "So-and-so is going to do this." I would say, "They're not going to do that. They wouldn't do that. No." I wouldn't believe them. It was usually some base thing that people do, like hoodwinking somebody or maneuvering around and gypping them out of something. Something like that. Something that wasn't quite ethical, a finagling. They could pick up on it, and I used to just argue with them when I was young and naive. I'm still naive, but I'm not young anymore, and I'm not as naive as I would've been if it wasn't for Darrell teaching me all the time. I would argue with them about it, and lo and behold, it would come true. It would happen. Somebody would gyp somebody out of a car, wheeling and dealing, or talk them out of something, or they would get something taken away from them and get little in return. Of course, no one had anything of great value.

I believe that when I went up the trail, the Creator gave me the power to be the medicine woman for the ceremonies, and that all these things do happen. These powers talk a language that I don't understand when I'm out picking up the medicine, but then when I go into a trancelike state, the powers interpret this language for me because they know I can't understand what it said before, so it has to tell me again because I can't interpret that language myself.

I go into an altered state of mind and I think that's what the starvation and purification process is about: your state of mind is altered because you are starving. For about ten days, when you are preparing to give a ceremony and make medicine, you only eat about a cup of acorns mixed into around a pint of water a day. This is what we call acorn water. The men do the same thing. I think we fast in this way to alter our state of mind so we can understand what the powers are telling us to do.

As I grow older, I see these things as being dimensional. There are things going on in this world, this is our reality. And then there are other realities where things are going on at the same time. It seems to me that the other reality has a much slower pace. You're there for fifteen minutes, but you're gone from here for three hours.

A Psychological Medicine Woman

I don't give out medicine to people. I'm kind of a psychological medicine person, and I talk to people. I can make them feel good about themselves by talking to them. Darrell says it's like brainwashing, and that I'm not going to hypnotize him and brainwash him and make him think how I want him to think. He said, "I see you talk to people, and they're thinking one way real strong, and you start talking to them, and you talk to them and you talk to them, and pretty soon they're not thinking that way no more. They've turned right around and they're thinking like you wanted them to think."

So he says he doesn't listen to me because I'm not going to brainwash him like I do these other people he sees me talk quietly to for a while and they completely change their mind about what they are thinking, a 180 degree reversal. I told him, "I don't brainwash them. What I do is what I was trained to do. They have a burden on them from whatever—their family, their job, their life, their health, their people, whatever it might be—and I can't change that situation. I can't make it go away. The only thing I can do is to make them look at it from a different perspective and give them a different attitude about what's wrong with their life. I make them feel better about the situation, whether I joke about it or whether I commiserate with them or console them or do all of the above. That's all I can do. I can't change the situation. I can only change their attitude toward it. If Darrell wants to think he's not brainwashed, that's fine with me.

When he said that, Beavi made one of her wise-ass remarks and said, "Dad, I think it's a little late for that, about thirty years late."

I laughed and said, "About fifty years."

In order to pick up their power, medicine people fast and pray and dance for three days. When they go into a trance they see things, gifts that are offered to them by the Creator that would help them to deal with people's sicknesses, like the power to see visions, the power to take away pain, the power to heal, the power to change someone's vision of what is going on with them to a more positive vision, changing their mind-set. We always called it turning their face around. When someone comes to me with a problem, I just start talking and state their problem one way. Then I would say it another way, then I would say it another way, and I'd just keep talking about their problem. One woman came to me who said she wished she had a husband like I had. I said, "You wouldn't be happy."

She said, "Well, you are."

I said, "But money doesn't mean that much to me. I can live with less. I can live in a house with a warped floor, and I would just put some linoleum down so I can clean it up and put some paper on the wall, throw up a little curtain and I'm happy. The place may smell old and kind of moldy, but that's okay. It's fine. When I have food on the table and a warm bed to sleep in, I'm okay. But you have a three-bedroom house and land, your husband drives logging trucks and makes a lot of money, and you like things like that. You like it that way. Actually, your husband pays a lot of attention to you—not as much as mine does to me, but your husband works really, really hard and he's gone sixteen hours a day, hauling logs. You do your own thing when he's gone and you're happy that way. But my husband works ten hours a day. He doesn't make that much money, and he spends a lot of time with me, and he pays a lot of attention to me, and I like that. That's what I need."

She told me her husband would come home so that he could sleep with her for a couple of hours and then he would have to leave to get his truck loaded. She thought that was a big waste of time. I asked her how she would like it if instead of coming home he found some other woman to sleep with those two hours. I told her she would not like that, either. Either he's going to come home and sleep with her or he's going to find some other woman to sleep with, some other place. She said she would have to think about that. That [laughing] is changing a person's mind-set. That's how you change their face around. That's how Darrell said he was not going to let me manipulate him [laughing].

There is the gift of seeing what's inside the body or the gift of taking the inflammation or the poisons out of the patient's system. Another gift is being able to soothe people and help them deal with the anxieties that people have when they are ill and don't know what's wrong with them and can't get well, so that they are not living their lives. They are just sick.

Now doctors and therapists give you pills and rub your back and try to make you feel better. In the old days they used hot packs and cold packs and pertussed your back and did all those things that would give you comfort in the face of whatever was going on, and you either got well or you died. Usually the people, like me, who were trained to help were born with an affinity toward being that way. It's like the time I told the nursing teacher I was having a hard time with tests because I didn't know the philosophy behind them. I didn't know where they were coming from, even though I knew what they were doing. She told me I was doing fine in class, and with my practical work I did the right things for the people who were my patients. I told her that all I did was what I would think another human being would do for someone that was ill: "It doesn't have anything to do with the philosophy. But then when you ask me the philosophy, I'm lost. I don't know what you're talking about." So I took philosophy and studied Plato and other philosophers, and then I finally understood the nursing philosophy and why they were doing what they were doing. I had read a lot and I had read psychology, but not philosophy, and reading philosophy helped me to answer the questions I was being asked in written tests, because then I had that basis to build my answers on. Well, I was just a little dumb Indian from the Klamath River.

Once a chemistry teacher said to me, "I hear you are a medicine woman."

I said, "Yes, I'm one of them. One of many kinds, and some people believe I can walk on water for exercise, and I don't mean ice water."

Mothers' Sounds and Cradle Baskets

You can't change reality. You can only change and mold the way people look at it. It is like my mother-in-law, Sadie, told me. When a baby was born they wrapped it up real tight and put it in a little basket that it could just barely fit in for ten days. During those ten days they rocked the baby and went, "Tttt, tttt, tttt," which is the sound of the human heart and is what the baby had been hearing in the dark, confined place in its mother's womb. On the tenth day they had a ceremony and took the baby out of its basket, uncovered its face, and started rocking the baby and saying, "ummm, ummm, ummm." The mother changed the sound to a human sound from the sound of the blood running through the baby's ear before birth.

Once they got to that point, the mother would rock the baby and make that sound. Now the baby was still wrapped, but its face was uncovered so it could see the lights and shadows and people moving. They kept its hands tied down because their nerves jerk when babies sleep and they would touch their face and wake themselves up, so they kept their hands bound down for about three months. During this time they would take the baby out of the cradle basket to nurse them and clean them and then put them back in this basket on their back, because they risk crib death if they are not on their backs. Keeping the baby on its back protects it, and if they are tilted slightly they won't strangle if they swallow their spit. Then they take their hands out at three months, when babies start playing with their hands. They take their little hands out so they can play with things. But they can still die of crib death, so they are still wrapped tight when they sleep and when they are resting. They take them out more often as they get older, and play with them, but when the mother is busy, the baby is back in that basket.

Then the mother starts working more. She's grinding acorns and gathering sticks and doing other work. That baby is over there in the basket, sitting up awake, and it starts fussing. The mother is busy and she goes, "Mmm, mmm, mmm," and the baby gets quiet because it's been trained. As soon as it hears its mother, it knows it's okay. Its mother is right there and she can continue her work. So they go on like that, and pretty soon the child is six or seven or eight years old. The mother is busy and the child doesn't feel well. All the mother has to do to calm the child down is to make that sound. She doesn't have to touch them. She doesn't have to get up and walk over to it. All she has to do is go, "Mmm, mmm, mmm," and the child calms down because it knows its mother is there.

From the time the child is three years old, the grandmother takes care of them, and the mother goes back out to work outside, and the grandmother watches the toddler. She watches all of her sons' children while they are toddlers; since she doesn't go out to gather like a young woman anymore, she is always available to take care of the children.

Heart Disease

In the spring of 1986 I knew I had heart disease. I was working for the Karuk Tribe as a community health representative and a client wanted me to fill out some papers. So I was working on his paperwork, waiting for him to come in, and I started feeling warm. I kept thinking, "I have to get up and turn that heater off. Then I've got to get out of here." It was almost ten o'clock in the morning and I had been there alone, working on paperwork, and I decided I was going to leave at ten o'clock. I started to stand up, and the last thing I remember was the desk coming up to meet me. I was out for over an hour before the client came in. He asks me, "Are you sleeping, Mavis?"

I told him, "I don't think so. I don't think I was sleeping. But it's sure hot in here, maybe that's what's wrong." So he went over and turned the heater down. Then I filled out the papers for him to sign and I put them in the envelope so they could go up the river to Happy Camp with the tribal stuff in the morning when the courier came down and picked it up. After that I called the office and told them that I had passed out and wasn't feeling well, so I was going to lock up and go home. At that time we didn't yet have a clinic. We were just open two days a week when the doctor would come to see patients—or they wouldn't come, it was kind of a hit-or-miss thing.

I drove myself home okay and then lay down. After a while Carol came in from her job with the Forest Service and asked me what I was doing home. I told her that I had passed out at work and I didn't know what had happened. Carol called up Happy Camp and made an appointment with the clinic there for the next morning. Their blood tests showed that I had had a heart attack down in the apex of my heart, which is a good place to have it, because there are a lot of nerve fibers there, which means that only a small place in your heart dies, where if you have it in another portion of the heart, great big sections—quarter sections—of the heart die.

I wasn't able to go back to work, because I was too tired. They started me on heart medications. To make a long story short, I slept for the next seven months and woke up in November, forty pounds lighter. For those seven months someone would have to come in and wake me up to ask if I wanted to eat. The only time I got up and went out was when I went to the doctor. The tribe kept wanting me to go back to work, but I couldn't work, because I was so tired that I couldn't wake up. Finally a new doctor came to work for the tribe and I went to see him. He said, "I heard you lost your job."

I said, "Yeah, they hired someone else because I couldn't get back to work because I have been too tired and too sick and couldn't wake up."

The doctor said that he wanted to take my chart and study it and see if he could figure out what was going on, and that he would be back in a week. He didn't wait a week, because a couple of days later he phoned and told me to stop taking one of the medications I had been prescribed, because he could see a pattern of my getting sicker every time they gave me this medication, and he thought I was having a bad reaction. He took me off the medication and in a month I felt fine, but I had already lost my job. I had also lost muscle tone from lying in bed for seven months, so I started an exercise class from College of the Redwoods that met in Somes Bar. In order not to overstress my heart I could only move my arms or my legs at one time. Eventually I got built back up.

I had always wanted to go to the Grand Canyon before I died. By then Long Gone was living in Eureka and Darrell had gotten six thousand dollars from the Yurok for timber sales that the Yurok had been bilked out of. I told them that I had always wanted to make that trip, and they took me to the Grand Canyon for a two-week vacation. I had already told Darrell that I had been thinking I would go back to school and become a nurse. So I did all the things that you're supposed to do, like talking to counselors. I told them I wanted to be a nurse and I wanted to come back here and be a nurse for the people on the river because it's hard to get nurses to work here. Unless they're married to someone or they're living here, you don't see very many nurses up here. Because I had been a nurse's aide in Orleans, I had had to be both the receptionist and a nurse because sometimes the doctor would show up by himself without a nurse and I would have to do the nurse's duties and be the receptionist, so it made sense for me to go to school and become a nurse.

Becoming a Nurse

Grandpa spoiled me and he told me that I could do anything I wanted to do. He told me I could be anything I wanted to be, but he was going on the basis of my intellect. I think that gave me the idea that after I had had a heart attack when I was fifty-five years old and my health was not good, I could go to college and become a nurse. I just thought that it would be more fun to go to school and study to become a nurse than it would be sitting around waiting to die of a heart attack. If I made it, I made it, and if I didn't make it, I didn't.

When I was young I was not interested in being a nurse. What got me interested in that was my working as a community health representative. There was never a nurse the clinic could depend on being there, so the clinic had to use me as a nurse, and one doctor taught me to be a medical assistant, so I could do all the things that a nurse usually had to do to prepare a patient for the doctor. I had planned on being a phlebotomist and I had always been interested in chemistry. As a young person I knew that since I had no mother or father to support me, I needed to go to a school where you could learn your profession for free. At that time I could have gone to work in a hospital and been trained to be a technician while I was working. That was my plan, and then I met Darrell and suddenly was wildly in love and married him. He was always asking me to go back to school because he wanted me to be a teacher. He almost had me talked into it, but then a sickly baby was given to us to raise and I didn't have time to go back to school.

In order to get into the registered nurse program at the College of the Redwoods, all the applicants had to be assessed. I passed all their never-been-in-trouble qualifications when they scrutinized my background to see if I was a drug addict or alcoholic or had any vices. I had never broken any laws that they knew of [laughing] and they couldn't prove I was a renegade. We all got up and gave a little spiel about why we wanted to be registered nurses. I said that I had worked in community health for fifteen years and I wanted to become a nurse and work in Indian programs to get nurses out here on the river, because a lot of times I had worked as a medical assistant and there was no nurse. There was just me and the doctor, and the doctor trained me to be his medical assistant. At that time a medical assistant could give out medication and everything, put labels on the medicine, count out the pills, show it to the doctor, and when he said okay, give it to the patient. That was in Rural Indian Health programs. I could dress people's wounds, although I wasn't a nurse. I was a community health representative, working on a reservation beginning in 1975. This was the Karuk Tribe's first little medical program and there were three of us. One worked up the Salmon River and Somes Bar, and I took one side of the Klamath River, and the other CHR took the other side at Orleans.

I was accepted into the nursing program because I was a Native American and I wanted to become a nurse in Indian country. I was in school at the College of the Redwoods between 1987 and 1991, and while I was there I was president of the Indian Club.

I was going to school and working really hard and getting tired, just bone tired. I kept struggling along, going to school, but eventually I failed the registered nursing program. But I had enough nursing training that with just a little more clinical training I could pass the licensed vocational nursing program. The problem was that I was taking a clinical class at night, and then another clinical class at six o'clock in the morning, and with my heart disease it was just too much stress. Two days after I came back home from Eureka, I was hired as a CHR/Clinic Nurse for the Karuk Tribe.

I came back to Orleans after finishing school, but I had become so short of breath that I could hardly walk without having to sit down and rest, so I went to Redding to have my heart condition evaluated and the next day went through five-way heart bypass surgery. I was back working as a nurse in six weeks. I don't think I would've lived without it. After the surgery I still had heart disease and got tired, but my blood pressure was under control and I walked at least a mile a day and got back in shape quickly. I was still bothered by the after-effects of the anesthesia for a while and tended to forget things, but I just worked very methodically and people trusted me.

Carol's Death

As part of her job with the Forest Service, Carol moved to San Francisco for a time. Several things happened to her after she moved. She had not been in the city very long when she was standing on the balcony of her hotel room and saw someone push another person out a window and kill them. She saw that person look up at her, and she didn't look back at them. She kind of slid back out of sight into her apartment and wasn't sure she could recognize him in the future.

Shortly after that, the doorman asked her if she knew anyone in the city who would be looking for her. The doorman was a great big fellow who was half Hopi and half Navajo. They had talked quite a bit because they were both Indian. He told her there was someone, a dark-skinned fellow who was going around asking about the girl who was either Hindu or Native American up on the fifth floor. The doorman protected her and said that he did not know of any dark-skinned woman living on the fifth floor—maybe she was just visiting. Carol told him that she had seen something that she shouldn't have seen, and the doorman said he thought it was odd that this person would be asking about her in this way. The doorman said if the man came back again he would try to scare him off.

The next month she started to walk across the street at the same time as another woman when she spotted a yellow cab and thought that she wouldn't cross the street, because her cousin Buzzy had warned her that those damn cabs would run over you. So she stepped back up on the curb and walked down to the corner to cross. By the time she reached the corner, a construction crane fell on the woman she had been about to cross the street with and crushed her.

The next month, the World Series was in San Francisco and she was going to go. She stepped out of the elevator onto the street and was going to take BART, but instead decided to get a little exercise and walk up to the city bus line. About that time the Loma Prieta earthquake struck and the sidewalk started dropping into the earth. She looked up and saw the windows on high-rise buildings bulging in and going back, and she thought, "What in the hell am I doing? Those windows are going to break."

She took a few more steps and glass started raining down around her. One piece cut the finger off a woman who was standing next to her. Carol handed her a handkerchief and she wrapped that around the stump of her finger, picked up the finger off the sidewalk, and put it in her pocket. Carol said she didn't know how the woman was going to get to a hospital, but the sidewalk was still falling into the earth around her so she started walking again. But since the sidewalk was still collapsing, she jumped out into the street, and then she spotted a bus coming toward her, but it was like something picked the bus up and threw it sideways into the building so that it missed her.

So she said she was lucky that she hadn't gotten stuck somewhere down in the BART tunnel or been hit by the sidewalk or the bus, and the glass didn't fall on her. Then she gave up on the World Series, of course, and walked over to where she lived, but the building was too unstable and dangerous, and they would not let anyone in. Everyone had to huddle outside in the street until eleven o'clock that night, when the inspectors finished their work and the building was cleared.

After that I told her that I had better pray really hard for her, because it looked like God was telling her something. "Three times now, you have had death looking for you, so you should be real careful, because God's trying to tell you something."

In December I was over in Eureka studying for nursing school, but I was just about ready to finish and come home for Christmas

when the spirit people came looking. They told me they were looking for Sandy. I asked them, "What do you want?" They said again
that they were looking for Sandy, and I told them that Sandy was
not there. "There's no Sandy here. You had better go away." I think
they were looking for my cousin Sandy Ferris, who was very close
to Carol. It felt like there was a mass of spirit people, and I prayed
about it and went to bed and prayed again, and I kept thinking,
"They're not looking for Sandy. There's no reason for Sandy to be
here."

Then Carol came home for Christmas, but she did not have any
money because her reimbursement checks from the Forest Service
had gotten lost. I told her not to worry about having money for
Christmas, but she loved to get big Christmas presents for people.
She was very generous that way. I told her, "Just don't worry about
it. Just give us little token things and you don't have to give me
anything. I really don't need anything. I have everything I need in
this world—in fact, like your brother says, at least three of everything!"

So she quit worrying about getting presents for everyone and
when one of her checks came in January, she got retroactive presents for everyone to make herself feel better. Her boyfriend wanted
her to come over to Eureka, but I just had this feeling and told her
that I didn't think she should go. Beavi told her the same thing.
Carol said that she had been promising him she would come over
and she hadn't seen him for a long time, because she had been in
San Francisco working. Even though I had a feeling she shouldn't
go, she went over to Eureka and saw him and they went to a party.
On the way home from the party they were in her dark red 1950
Buick that he had rebuilt for her. She was really jazzed up because
she had always wanted a fixed-up old car. She had kept my Mustang
for years, thinking someday she would get enough money to fix it
up. It was really icy that night, and just after the party they were in
a wreck and both of them were killed.

We were here waiting for her to get back from Eureka when
the sheriff pulled up in the yard. He said that he had bad news and

told us that Carol had been killed in a wreck sometime the night before. We didn't have a telephone here in Orleans at that time, because I was living in Eureka, going to school, and that's where I had my telephone. Darrell was the only person home and he never phones anywhere. I drove into town and used the pay phone to call someone in Eureka to tell them to pick up Kit, Carol's teenage son, and take him away so that people wouldn't be phoning to tell him that his mother had been killed before somebody could be there with him. Darrell and I started driving over to Eureka, and it was still pretty icy, because I spun out a couple of times, even driving my Volvo. So it was very icy, and I don't think they had been driving very fast. I think they just hit a patch of ice and flew through the air like a hockey puck.

Kathy and Long Gone had driven over, too, and they picked up Carol's son Kit and took him on a drive and told him about his mother dying. We all stayed in Eureka that night, and the next morning went to the funeral home and began making the arrangements. Long Gone asked me why I picked a little green tin-can-like casket. I said, "Because I knew Carol. It's pale green with baize down the side and pink roses on the edge. And it's all white satin inside. Carol would like that casket." She had always liked things that were flashy and shiny and rustly. The morticians made her look good. Like we say around here, she looked good for a dead person. It's kind of crude to put it that way, but sometimes you have to be practical.

Most of the time, when someone dies, I just hold back and accept it and don't show emotion in public. When Carol died I was busy going to school and busy taking care of my grandson. There were crises in Beavi's life and in Long Gone's life, and I just went totally to pieces at the service. I cried and cried and cried and cried. I thought, "I'm just going to throw it all out there and just get it out and get this over with, because next week I have to go back to school and go back to the same old grind, and I'm so tired. I'm almost at the end of the schooling and I know I'm not doing well. I just have to do that and let it all out so I can go on with my life."

When Kit turned twenty-one he was able to cash Carol's life insurance policy and use the money to buy himself a place to live. He had been ready to squander the money, but I told him, "Your mother is not going to die for you to squander that money! You are going to get yourself a place to live with it."

Then I went on the second vacation in my life, up to Glacier Park and over to Wounded Knee and Yellowstone.

Indian Country Nurse

It was interesting working as a nurse in Indian country, because something was always happening. The only problem was that you knew everyone that it was happening to, so I probably had more empathy with the patients than I should have had. After a while you know which families have which problems—heart disease, hypertension, lung disease, or diabetes, so that if their symptoms look like one of these things and it comes from that family, you don't have to go to a lot of extra tests to know what the problem is. And everybody always knows everybody else's business. It's just the outsiders who don't know—the insiders all know. Small communities are like that. The families are all tied together.

Working with Tom, the clinic's physician's assistant, was interesting. He was a flighty doctor who had no connection to native people. It took two months to teach him how to approach Native Americans. He could tell he wasn't getting it, so at least he knew that much. He did real well with the hippie types because that's what he was, but he had no understanding of Native Americans.

Norman, our medicine man, just bowled him over. He couldn't figure out why that man acted so haughty, although over time Norman came to think highly of Tom and probably took his advice on eating healthy and living a healthy life better than anyone. Once when Norman and Christy brought in their little girls to see the doctor, Tom came in and they said, "You said you were bringing us to the doctor." [Laughing] I was the doctor, according to them.

I told Tom that up here they tend to spoil the medicine people, and we can get awfully full of ourselves at times. Darrell's tribe, the

Yurok, doesn't do that. They are more demanding of their medicine people and expect them to be exemplary, so they have to toe the line more closely. If the Yurok medicine person doesn't do right, they will call you on it and you have to pay a fine for not acting like you're supposed to. Down there, in that other country, if the medicine person does not act just exactly as they are supposed to, they have to pay money to people who find out they did something unacceptable in making the medicine. The medicine people have to pay like they had wronged their patients, like if I used my medicine for my own gain, for anything other than just bowing down and accepting whatever the Creator is going to give me.

Tom couldn't understand why the Indian patients wouldn't tell him anything when they came in sick. I think Hoss Bennett was the most open with him, but then Hoss knew hippie people really well. He got along well with Tom right away, but Tom didn't like his philosophy—his total disregard of the effects of his drinking, for instance. Tom would say, "Doesn't he know that he's just killing himself?"

I said, "Well, that's his life and he's not interested in addressing his drinking." Then someone blew my cover and Tom found out that I was a medicine person, and he was on me with more questions. I told him, "Indian people do not go into somebody's life and tell them, 'Your life would be better if you quit this, and did this, and did this,' like you want them to when you tell them that's how they have to be. They are the way they are, and you have to accept them that way and try and keep them healthy, even though they are that way. That's where Indians are different. You can't just pick somebody up and make them do something. Indians are stubborn, and if you try to tell one of us what to do, we will just set our mind to not doing it."

That's what happened with Captain Jack. He was hanged for something he had no control over. Sure, he was a leader, but leaders in Indian society are not all-powerful. There's a group of leaders. There are war leaders, religious leaders, the people who take care of the headman, and others. They are all leaders and they are all part of the whole. When Captain Jack advised the war leaders that it wouldn't be good to leave their stronghold and raid the ranchers, the other leaders made up their minds they were going to do it anyway, and they did. Captain Jack had no control over that and that's just the way it is. You have no control over what people do. You can tell them what would be best, and that's the best you can do.

Eventually I saw changes in Tom's approach to Indians. He was not so affronted by them not cooperating in the way he thought they should. Before, it was like a testosterone contest, two bull elks meeting.

As a nurse at the clinic, I used my training for things like taking blood pressure and then advising patients as to what they should do. Things like try not to eat too much salt, watch your diet, don't eat too many fats. Just do your best. Try to eat a more traditional diet. Eat oatmeal in the morning, eat fish, and don't eat a lot of meat. Try to eat more acorns and fish. They knew how to eat, and I just advised them to go back to eating that way, the way they had eaten when they were children—beans, mush, fish, eels, acorns, deer meat. Don't eat the pizzas and spaghetti with all the starches that we didn't have in the old days. Back in aboriginal times, we had one starch, and that was from the acorns. That was the mainstay of our diet, and it was very rich in proteins and complex carbohydrates, so beans fit in pretty well with that to partially replace acorns in our diet, because beans supply starch and protein too. Acorns have more protein, but they are similar foods. Both take a long time to digest and the energy stays with you awhile, so you don't get hungry again right after eating. Our digestive systems don't do well with fast-digesting carbohydrates, because in a short time you will be hungry again.

I also told my Indian patients to go back to Indian medicine, because we have diseases now that we didn't have before the invasion, when the Europeans brought their diseases with them. Before that, we had pneumonia and that was about it. Pneumonia killed people, and of course there were injuries, but we didn't have mumps and chicken pox and colds and flus. When you lived in such a cold house, probably 55 or 60 degrees, the women and children avoided going out and getting wet. They stayed in the house, [laughing] where it was cold and wet. If you live in warm houses and go out in the cold, you have a greater tendency to get sick because your pores are open when you go outside. If you live in a cold house and go outdoors you're not as likely to get sick.

A lady lived down below me whose kid was always out of school with a bad cold. She said, "I see those little McCovey kids. They go over and play in the creek in the pouring-down rain and then walk home soaking wet, and they never stay home with a cold."

One of the children's teachers asked me about that one time. I said, "Well, the house is cold. The thermometer on the wall by the window in the living room says it's 55 degrees, so when the children go out into the cold they are acclimatized to the cold, and they don't get sick as easily as if they were coming out of a hot house.

I fell and hurt my back in January of 1999 and never did go back to work as a nurse. In June they gave me a retirement party and I knew they were going to give me some present, but I told them I didn't want a computer [laughing], so they gave me a Pendleton blanket. Then in November of that year I had back surgery. After the surgery I recuperated for about six months but I still had three hundred dollars a month to pay on my truck, and I only got four hundred dollars a month in disability payments, so I took a job as a cook's helper with the tribe's senior program. I did all the little running-around things and wiped the tables, made the coffee, chopped up the vegetables, and fixed up the lunches that had to go out, and I did that for two years. It was really enjoyable. I liked seeing the people. I have been working with these same people for a long time, so I liked working at the elders' program and being around them again.

In Sickness and Health

In June 1964, Darrell was in the hospital for three weeks with a burst gallbladder. He was well enough in three weeks to come home, then it took him about six more weeks to recuperate. He tried going back to work, but he was still too disabled and had to come home. They didn't give him any state disability, because he had gone back to work, even though he couldn't make it. They figured it was just a gallbladder problem and he should be able to get over that in a certain number of days. They didn't take into account that he had had peritonitis and he almost died, even though he never did get on the critical list.

While he was in the hospital the doctor had asked me, "Well, when are you going to tell his family that he has five chances out of a hundred to survive this?"

I looked at him and said, "Well, is he on the critical list?"

He said, "No, he's not critical."

I said, "If he gets on the critical list, I'll tell his family. But if I tell his family now, his sisters are going to come, and they're going to be hysterical, especially the three younger ones, and probably the one that's two years older than him too, and then he'll know how sick he is, and he may give up and die. This way he doesn't know how sick he is." I didn't tell him and he got well in three weeks, and then I told him.

Darrell said, "I'm never going to trust you again. Here I was, dying, and you were feeding me Jell-O and laughing and talking to me. I was dying and you just sat there and fed me Jell-O. When I'm dying! You didn't say anything. You just fed me Jell-O, and you knew that would make me think I was okay. I'll never trust you again."

So he didn't trust me so much, until he got run over by a logging loader in 1981. I wasn't working, because I had been sick, and Carol and I were home. Darrell was living at Mount Shasta City with Long Gone, Kathy, and Chucker, and they were all working out there. I had been really sick all summer with what turned out to be heart disease. I told Carol that I could feel Darrell calling me out to Mount Shasta City to be with him. He wanted me there so badly, but I didn't have enough money from unemployment to get there. I could have borrowed the money to get there, but I hated to go in the hole with all of the expenses we already had in keeping two places together. Carol thought I should go if he wanted me so badly that he was calling me to come.

We drove over to town and someone drove up and said he had a phone message that the hospital at Mount Shasta City wanted me to phone them because Darrell got hurt and the nurse wanted to talk to me. We called the hospital from the pay phone in town and the nurse told me that Darrell had been run over by a logging loader and had a broken femur. He wasn't stable yet, but he was all right. In other words, he was alive.

I made it to the hospital and stayed with him every minute of the time he was there. Then he trusted me again. He would ask me, "Am I hurt?"

I would say, "Yes, Darrell, you're hurt really bad. You got run over by a log loader and your legs are all broken up and your hips are broken." I was telling him the truth. I didn't tell him how critical he was. He was in the intensive care unit, so I guessed he would be okay.

Sometimes Darrell can't stand to live with me. He says I always do what I want to do. I realize that I'm hard to live with, especially for a traditional person like Darrell. Here you've got this woman who never seems to pay any attention to what you are saying or what you want to do. She's going to do what she wants to do.

I joke with Darrell that I fell in love with his beautiful black Indian hair and he went gray on me. He fell in love with my green eyes and I still have green eyes. One evening when Darrell and I were up in our sixties and didn't drive around so much anymore, he told me that they had named a magazine after him. Of course I had to ask, "What magazine?" and [laughing] he told me *Ladies Home Companion*.

A Shifting Population

Starting in the 1940s, hundreds and hundreds of Okie logging families came into this country, and that went on until the mid-1970s. There were a lot of bars, partying and drinking. We watched that go on for thirty years. There was a lot of violence and spousal abuse, and then the seventies came. The loggers were waning as a group, and the hippies came in and brought the drug years. At first they were growing marijuana, then pretty soon they had cocaine, and the whole feeling was different. We would go over to the bar in town and the people would be acting crazy. You could feel it, and it was scarier than it had been. Then people started pulling guns on one another and fighting over someone being in their marijuana patch.

My nephews were accused of stealing marijuana and the people came to our house and were hollering around out in the yard. Darrell went out on the front porch and they berated him about how his boys had done this theft. They weren't all his boys. Some were my cousin's boys and some were nephews, but they just associated them all with us. Darrell looked at them and said, "Well, if you don't like them doing that, throw them in jail," and walked back in the house. [Laughing] That was his answer to it.

In the 1970s some of the hippie people who moved onto the river asked my aunt Caroline what she smoked to experience an altered reality when she made medicine. She told them native plants, Indian tobacco, and marijuana, but they never asked her how much to use, and she never told them. Medicine people will always tell you something. If you ask a medicine person a question, they have to answer that question.

They asked her where they could find the native plants. She told them that it was a beautiful plant and there was lots of it in a certain field. Then they asked her what part of the plant they could use, and she told them that every part of the plant was toxic: the flowers, the leaves, and the roots. Everything was toxic. So they got some of it and mixed it up with the other ingredients, tobacco and marijuana, and smoked it. They came back later and told her that they had smoked the plants that she had told them about and gone crazy. They had horrible nightmares that bears came to eat with them, and they had eaten like dogs out of bowls on the ground, and one of them thought he turned into a bear and ran off into the woods.

He came back with his clothes ripped up and scratched all over from running through the brush, but he couldn't remember what had happened to him. They ate like dogs and they ran like bears. Auntie looked at them and said, "How much did you take?"

They said, "Well, we smoked all night."

When they had told her this, she said, "Now I know what made you go crazy. You used way too much." That was her only answer. She never did tell them how much to smoke. They didn't ask her how much to smoke, they asked her what to smoke. That's one thing about Indians making medicine, medicine people. They will always answer you. If you ask them a question about their medicine, they will answer you. They will answer your question, but they don't elaborate. Like they asked her what she smoked, and she told them the proportions of what she smoked, but she never told them how much they were supposed to smoke, because they never asked her. You have to ask them every single little question if you want to know something. You have to be precise in what you're asking.

Daypay's Murder

My son Daypay was murdered in 1981 by a paranoid marijuana grower. That is my story; the authorities' story is entirely different. That's when I found that once you're dead, you have no rights. They can say or do anything they want. The detectives who came from the district attorney's office knew what had happened, but because of the laws that protect the criminal, you can't bring up something that would be detrimental against them. So none of that ever got brought up.

The only trouble Daypay had ever been in in his life was when he drove a pickup with a permit but without a licensed driver in the truck with him. He was hauling wood for his father and his father stayed with the rest of the wood. His father didn't ride down the hill with him because he had stayed with the wood, and our son got caught driving the truck. He had a learner's permit but he did not have a licensed driver with him, since Darrell was still hurt pretty bad and did not want to drive in with him with every load of wood.

Daypay was killed after his friend Shawn had walked up on somebody's marijuana patch. When the man shot Daypay he said, "I shot the wrong one," because he had meant to shoot my son's friend, and Daypay just happened to be there and was shot instead. He wasn't the one who knew where the patch was. The grower slipped up on him standing next to the highway in Orleans and shot him five times with a short-barreled Uzi. Daypay was somebody who never raised hell or caused trouble. He was just a happy little kid.

After Daypay was murdered, we had the experience of his coming back to tell us good-bye. One of these times he told Darrell that he couldn't talk to me, because there was some force on the other side that said he couldn't talk to me, because I would keep him on this side. So he talked to Darrell. Darrell said, "I had this dream and I felt like Daypay was touching me, and he felt just like a human being. He was telling me good-bye."

One of our friends said he talked to her and then did something that scared the hell out of her. He said, "It's good over here, and you can just do anything." He said, "Watch," and just splintered into hundreds of thousands of pieces, and all these little pieces were talking, and then he went back together again and laughed and laughed and then was gone.

I told her that people could come back from the spirit world and then leave again. "Since he left so fast, he probably just came back to say good-bye and tell you he was okay."

But when he talked to his sister Beavi he said to her, "Why didn't you take care of Shawn? He was shot and you didn't even take care of him. I was okay."

Beavi said, "You weren't okay. You were dead."

"Well, I'm okay," he said.

About two years after Daypay was killed, Shawn was killed in a motorcycle wreck, and we learned then that he had been carrying a bullet in his chest that no one knew about. He had told us that he jumped behind a tree when the shooting started, but he was actually shot in the chest and never told anyone. I know that he was a quiet, secretive child, but he never even told anyone about being shot. He thought that the man who was trying to kill him shot Daypay because Daypay was in the open, and he had jumped behind a tree when the shooting started. He said Daypay was pleading with the man and had his hands down, talking to him, trying to talk that man out of shooting people. He said, "What are you doing this for?"

I guess the fellow was drunk. The police came and stayed all night, protecting his place and all his marijuana plants and making sure that no one took anything from his place or did anything, because they expected retaliation, like some of us were going to just leave my dying—and then dead—son and run over there and do something to his place or his marijuana plants.

I said, "You're talking about a bunch of kids in this town and one of them had been shot to death. Do you think that they would go back over there?" Actually, two had been shot, though we didn't know it at the time. I said, "You don't think any of them would go back over there now, do you? We're not gangs up here. We're not used to this kind of violence."

I know that the graft from the marijuana growers goes all the way up into the judges. I know, with certainty, that damn judge that was on the case took everything out of the case until you would have thought my son had been shot with somebody's finger. We got a hung jury on a second-degree murder charge. Eleven to one. So with the next trial they took a lot more stuff out of the record and the same judge was on the second case, which is almost unheard of. They usually get another judge for a case that is being retried. Six months later this judge's son got picked up with some guys on a cocaine charge. It was the most cocaine ever found in Humboldt County. Three people were charged and two went to prison and the judge's son was let off.

Most of the Indian people are very careful. After Daypay was shot someone asked me how I was doing and I told them I was living very carefully. They said, "We all do." And even that doesn't work sometimes.

Daypay was so proud that he was going to be seventeen that fall. Darrell had gotten hurt in the woods and Daypay was proud that he had gotten a FEMA job for the summer. He had never had a job before, because Darrell worked all the time and we made too much money to get a public service–type job, and there wasn't much other work available. We didn't make that much money, but too much for him to get a service-type job. We were maybe a hair above what they call the poverty level. He was really proud of having landed this job. Around a year before he died, his sister Carol was growling at him one time and said, "You gotta go to work."

"I'm not going to ever go to work," he told her.

"What do you mean, you're not going to go to work?"

He said, "I'm going to live off my father all my life." He was just dead serious, and that's all he said. His sister was kind of irate at him about that one, but he told the truth. He never had a job and he lived off his father his entire life—but we never realized he was going to be sixteen when he died.

A month or so after Daypay's death, he came to me in a dream. At first we were standing here, by Carol's trailer. The ground was all wet and shiny, like it is in the morning after a hard, hard rain and it isn't really light yet, but there is light coming through the clouds. He said, "They let me come to say good-bye. They wouldn't let me come before, because they said you could keep me, and that you would keep me here, but now I'm going to go across. Clear across." And then all of a sudden we were in the backyard of Zona Ferris, with the same kind of rain and the same kind of morning, and he was still telling me that he's going to go across, and that he's going to take someone with him.

I told him, "Don't take Dale." I don't know how I knew it was Dale Ferris, Zona's son. I didn't just think it was going to be Dale, I knew it. There may have been a hint in my starting out in Carol's yard and then I was in Dale's backyard.

He said, "I'm supposed to take someone with me. I've got to take someone."

I said, "Well, just don't take Dale." And he wouldn't say that he would not take Dale, but he acted like he was going to try not to take him—that he would try to take someone else back with him. So two or three weeks later, Dale is over to town, drinking with Blue Jay Brown from Hoopa, and he gets in the car with Blue Jay, then he gets back out and sits back down on the porch in front of the old store. Then he gets back into the car with him again and rides clear down to Camp Creek, where he changes his mind, and Blue Jay brings him back up to Orleans and lets him back out on the porch again. Then Blue Jay goes on down to Bluff Creek, where he is killed in a wreck. Killed. So I figured he took Blue Jay back with him.

When Daypay finished talking to me, I looked at his eyes—and he had always had these real innocent eyes. It was like a little kid looking at you. He was sixteen years old and he had these little-kid eyes, nothing devious or hidden or adult. Just naive-looking eyes, looking at you.

When he finished talking to me about having to take someone back with him, he looked at me for a little bit and then these kid's eyes changed and became as ancient as the old people's eyes. They were ages old, so he wasn't what I thought he was, not over there. He did not have that young innocent mind anymore. He was as old as the ages.

I've fought really, really hard to get the man who killed him convicted. Really hard—harder than I ever would for my own sake, because I kept having this vision of three children and a yellow car, and the car sitting in Orleans all shot up, and these kids were dead. The vision kept telling me that if nothing was done about Daypay's killing, then this would happen. If a dope dealer can get away with killing one, other kids will be killed over dope too. Someone is going to slaughter these three kids, and their car is going to be all shot up. So I just kept fighting about it, pushing and pushing and marching and doing everything I could think of. Daypay's favorite song was the Buffalo Springfield song about people carrying signs, and that's what we were doing, calling for justice on our picket signs. The man who shot him was tried and got a hung jury on the first trial. With the second trial he was found not guilty. The only thing I couldn't do was make my son white, but I did get two trials.

It was like when Bessie Tripp fought for her son Julius. Julius had been shot by mistake by a bartender who had just had an argument with his brother Hambone. Ham left the bar, and when Julius walked in the bartender just shot him, thinking he was Ham. Julius was a mild-mannered man who never fought with anyone. He drank, but he didn't get rowdy like Ham did when he drank. The Tripp family brought the case to court back in the 1940s, and I remember my grandfather talking about it. It was the first time the killing of an Indian had gotten into court around here. So I had to be satisfied like Bessie. You didn't win your case, but at least you got it to court. You didn't get justice, but at least you got them to look at it and see that there possibly could be the murder of an Indian. The other way was to declare justifiable homicide and boom, that was it. That's what they did every time.

This is one of the ways that I'm connected to Bessie. After Daypay died, she told me how to make medicine in case I wanted revenge for him, and I told her, "You know me. I will never do anything like that." She just laughed. We believe that you can do things, but if you use this power for yourself, for your own vindictiveness for something, then you have to pay, and sometimes you have to pay with the life of one of your children.

Bessie said to me, "You don't smoke, do you?"

I said, "No, I don't like to smoke."

"If you wanted to make medicine about something," she says, "you build a small fire and throw your medicine in it and burn it and wave the smoke toward you. She said, "That way you can smoke it clean, and you don't have to smoke a pipe." When I make medicine I build a little fire, and then when the smoke comes up I wave the smoke onto myself. Otherwise I have a pipe that I fill with one thumbful. The pipe is as big as my thumb and that is the exact amount of the smoking mixture that you need to go into an altered state.

On Being a Medicine Woman

Here's how I look at it. Medicine people have to help people who really have problems. They might not live through these problems if you don't help them to try and muddle their way through. Sometimes you can't help them. Sometimes you can ask them if they need help, but you can't go around as a medicine person and say, "Somebody has problems and I can help them." You can't do that. You can only help people who ask for help. They have to come to you and start telling you what is wrong and interacting with you, and then you can help them, or try to help them, but anyway, do your best to help them.

When we were trained, they told us, "You don't go and offer anyone help. They have to ask for help." They feel something in you that pulls them to you, and that's where you get all these nut cases that come up to you as medicine people. Darrell's complaint in the seventies was that we never got to go to a restaurant in peace, ever. Some nut case would always sit down and start talking to us. I would tell him [laughing], "Yeah, I draw that kind of people."

You do what you can, but a lot of the time you're not going to really help them, because they are addled by drugs or mental illness or genetic conditions that are beyond your control. All you can do is recognize that and be a friend to them and talk to them, but in reality you're not really going to change much of their reality to a different way of life, because due to mental problems, either genetic or drug-induced, they're not going to be able to muddle through. It won't do any good to repel them, even if you don't actually think you can help, because that would just make them feel worse, because they've come to you for something, even if it's just human kindness. As a medicine person, sometimes you do things for people and you don't even know it until they come by years afterwards and say, "If you hadn't talked to me that day, I would have killed myself." Or "I would have left my husband."

I could have moved into one of the tribe's new senior housing homes, but Darrell doesn't like to live around too many people, and he doesn't like too many rules, like you can't drink a beer on your front porch, or you can't have felons over to visit. I don't know who is a felon and who isn't. I know there are people who go to jail, but I don't know if they go for misdemeanors or not. But if you're a medicine person, that's the kind of people who come around you, because they're looking for something, they're seeking something. Now, living here, sort of off by ourselves, we can have all kinds of yahoos come around here to visit. They get all excited when they spot something—like the old tires that I have stacked up to make a fence out of. Boy, that's just what they need for their pickup truck. As long as it doesn't have a hole in it, [laughing] it doesn't matter whether it's the same size as the other tires are not.

I think there are a lot of people in the world who have this ability and these gifts, and their cultures have forgotten how to use them. They think people who do these things are crazy. Nobody ever told me I was crazy, but I thought I was. I thought it was impossible to see things ahead of time. You think about this as a logical person, and start figuring it out, and logically, it does not compute that you can see something ahead of time, or even sense that something is going to happen.

Prayer

It is like Darrell said when his nephew said he had named his grandchild Hope. Darrell turned around and just flatly told his nephew, "There is no hope."

His nephew said, "Sure," in the Yurok women's language. I don't know if it's because the Yurok women are the religious leaders, but they have a language that they speak, and then there is the men's language, which is more for practical things, so the word for hope would be in the women's language. And Darrell was telling him that you didn't hope, you prayed. You asked God for it. He was contradicting his uncle and didn't know what he was talking about, but he used the women's language, because that's what the word hope would be in.

Darrell said, "I tell you again, there is no hope." I know what he meant, and it comes from our belief system. We don't hope. I don't say, "I hope for something...I hope to have a new house...I hope to have what-have-you..." In my Indian religion I would not hope, I would pray. Now, I might say, "I wish I had some deer meat, or I wish I had more fish." These things are your wants—I wanna, wanna, wanna—but there was no concept for hope. I don't hope that my children will be good. I pray that they will. There's good medicine and bad medicine. You invite bad medicine on yourself by doing bad things, and you invite good medicine on yourself by doing good things. I pray that they will be good. I pray that the Creator will take them the way that they need to go.

Sometimes that means you end up in jail or rehab or whatever, but I feel the Creator is answering my prayer. He is taking them the way they need to go to have a better life and be a better person, and if it takes that...then that will be. But I don't believe that anyone really belongs in jail unless they are perverts and have done cruel things to children or beaten people or are truly terrible and killed somebody. In my way of believing, if you stole from somebody, you should pay restitution, not go to jail. You should have to work harder and then work to pay that person back for what you did to them. That is the way my in-laws looked at it. The Creator will give you what you need.

Upriver Indian Devils

They say the spirit of an Indian devil comes up out of the ground near Somes Bar, at Ishi Pishi where a certain woman's house used to be. The house burned down years ago. A ball of fire that looks like a small meteorite comes out of the ground under the Ishi Pishi bridge and flies down the river gorge. It has a fiery tail on it that is sometimes a quarter of a mile long. Millie told me that she had seen it and that it happens when that person's spirit gets up and moves. I asked her what she did when she sees it, because she lived near the bridge where she could look out on that part of the river. She said she covers her eyes and doesn't look, because she doesn't know what it means when the spirit comes out of the ground as a ball of fire, or what that person's spirit is after.

Millie knew a lot about the ceremonies and had been trained in what was supposed to be done, how you're supposed to act and what you're supposed to do, so she knew what to do when she saw something. I figured she was doing the right thing when this spirit appeared, but I never saw it. Two boys I knew were drinking beer up on the bridge and they saw this ball of fire come up the gorge and one of the boys hopped up and ran over and looked over the bridge rail and watched it go down the river. I ask the other boy what he did. He said, "Are you kidding? I was so scared I rolled up on the floor of the car and covered my eyes. I had never seen anything like that. It scared the hell out of me to see a ball of fire come out of the ground with this big tail of fire following it as it went on down the river."

The boy who had run to the bridge rail to watch it was soon in a car wreck and paralyzed. Then other misfortunes happened to him and he died. I don't know if it had anything to do with him running and looking, but nothing happened to the boy who rolled up in a ball and covered himself. So Millie was probably right. You don't look at it. If you saw it, you made sure that you stopped watching as soon as you could. I still don't know where that particular Indian devil's spirit was going or what she was going to do down the river in that fiery form, but I have seen her in action.

I have had experience with one Indian devil. It was just a necklace made of ugly little stones with holes drilled through them and fixed on a cord. Some of the stones were jasper, some were granite. None of them were pretty. We believe that good or evil can be put into rocks through praying over them. Once that has happened and evil has been put into something like a rock, turning it into an Indian devil, you can't bury them, you can't throw them away, and you can't get rid of them. You can't bury them, because fireballs will come out of the ground from where they are buried, and you can't throw them away, because someone will find them. This necklace had passed through several generations from great-grandmother to grandmother to father and finally, when the son went to prison, to his son, who lives near me. This necklace was broken because it kept telling the younger woman who had inherited it to put it on. "Put me on," it called to her.

She said, "The one time I did put it on, it started telling me to do things, and I just jerked it off and broke it, because I wasn't going to use that power. I wasn't going to do that." So then it went to her son, and when he went to prison he left it with his son, who had it in his car when he was going out with a girl. When I learned about this I called the girl's mother and told her, "I don't want her looking in the Pandora's box that is sitting on his car seat. Do me a favor. It is a pale green box with a little gold on it. Pick it up, but don't look in it, whatever you do. Bring it to me and I'll put it away, because it could really harm someone if they got fascinated by it." I felt that this girl could be fascinated by the necklace if she ever looked in the box. The word must not have got through in time, because about a month later she was in a car wreck and never regained consciousness and died. I blame the box. Her mother brought it down to me and told me she had not looked at it. I put it away and then the young man who had inherited it took it back and hid it. I asked him, "What did you do with your Pandora's box?" I told him, "I've been having all kinds of weird dreams. Where is Pandora's box?"

He said, "Oh, it moves around too much, so I put it underneath your bed, because it's quieter when it's underneath you, because you keep it in control better." I didn't ask him what he meant by its moving around too much, I just took him at his word. It wasn't mine and I wasn't going to question him about it.

I said, "Well, thanks. I've been having all kinds of nightmares because that necklace is down there underneath my bed." When the owner had changed into a devil, she became a yellow dog with red eyes. People knew what she looked like when she changed into her devil form.

I would think the fact that looking at an Indian devil terrifies you would be the reason not to look at them. But on the contrary, my mother-in-law said that you walk out there into your yard and tell them to come in and have something to eat. You ask them if they are hungry or if they are cold and invite them on in. When you do that, they have to come in. If they don't come in, you have thwarted their power anyway, because there is no fear for them to feed on. That's what old Gram, Darrell's grandmother Aussie, said. They can hang on to your fear and anger. If you are angry at them for being around, then that is an in for them. If you are afraid of them, that is an in for them. By the time Aussie talked to me about this, she was a Christian. She told me to say, "I believe in God and I believe in Jesus Christ, get thee behind me," and it will go away—and it did, for me.

In the fall of 1964 it was extremely dry when I was deviled by the downriver Indian who had owned the devil's power necklace. Beavi was watching her adopted brother, and I went down the road to get the children who were coming home from school, because I kept hearing a sound like the sound a panther makes when they are thirsty. They make a kind of mewing sound, and I knew that the children were waiting down at the foot of the hill to meet Darrell when he came home from work. I told Beavi I was going to go down and get Long Gone and Carol because it sounded like the panther was getting close. When I walked down to get the children, my dog Mogan was with me, and he wouldn't leave my side. I was almost falling over him. I kept telling him to get out of the way, and he would just stay right next to me, and he usually ran way ahead like dogs do, so I thought maybe he was afraid of the cat.

I got the children and we started walking back up the hill and my neighbor came out of her house and asked what I was doing. I said I had come down to get the children, who were waiting for Darrell but the panther was too close for them to stand by the road. She looked at me for a minute and she said, "That's no panther, Mavis. That's the devil. Be careful."

I said okay, and I walked on up the hill with the two children. I was walking along, and the dog just kept looking up the hill and growling. Where he was looking, there were dried madrone leaves about a foot deep, and he kept walking right in front of me and growling. Then a round rock came flying down the hill and the dog just took off up the hill after something. I lifted my foot to get it out of the way, but the rock hit the bottom of my shoe and went on rolling down the hill. I walked a little ways and then I had this odd feeling, like a nerve sensation, of something going up my leg. I kind of looked at my foot and kicked the dirt a little bit and walked along some more.

The dog was up the hill, chasing something, but you couldn't hear the thing it was chasing. You couldn't hear anything but the dog, even in those dry madrone leaves. I walked on ahead until the children got into the house and then, thinking about it, I kicked my shoes off, because Darrell's grandma Aussie had told me that if anything has been touched by a devil, don't take it into the house with you. Leave it outside. Since it had just hit my shoe I took my shoe off and stepped through the door. Then this cold sensation went up my leg and up my back and the back of my head, and suddenly there were two people inside of me. There was someone else besides me in there, something foreign, something that didn't belong there. It kind of stopped me. It was cold; oh, it was cold, just freezing cold.

Darrell's grandmother Aussie had told me what to do if I was ever deviled. I hadn't been deviled yet, but she knew I was going to be, and when I was deviled I did exactly what she told me to do. She told me not to be afraid, because if I was afraid…and [laughing] I was terrified. I had never had that feeling before, like there's something else inside of you besides yourself. There is another entity in there, another entity inside your head, inside you. You know you're yourself, but when there's something else in there too…this really freaked me out. And then I remembered what she said. She told me, "When you get deviled," and I thought, "Well, I must be deviled. This must be it."

I thought about it for a second and then I thought, "I put my faith in Jesus Christ, and I believe in him, and you have to leave," and it was gone. Darrell's grandmother had told me, "If you ever get deviled, put your faith in Jesus Christ and tell it to leave, and it will leave because there is no fear or meanness in saying that." If you have no animosity toward it, have no fear of it, then it has to leave. It can't do anything to you because there is nothing in you for it to hang on to. If you are afraid, it will hang on to your fear. If you are angry, it will hang on to your anger. She believed in Jesus Christ, so she told me to say that, so I did and it went away.

I went to the hospital the next day because Lena, another Indian Shaker, had had a stroke and was in the hospital. I told her the oddest thing had happened to me. I told her what had happened and she said, "You never did anything to them, so they really can't do anything to you." She said, "That was the downriver devil. It is cold. My mother got deviled by her when she took that devil's man away from her." Lena's mother had a baby by the husband of this woman. She said, "She deviled my mother just like that. But my mother had done something, so it had more effect on her. But you've never really done anything. They're mad at you, but you're not doing anything to them that they should be angry at you about, and it should just go away." I was told that she was angry with me because Darrell and I were having a good effect on one of her descendants, and we would ruin him for being an Indian devil. He would not become one. So that was my own experience of being deviled.

At one point, after having this power left with him, the young man who had been given the necklace became angry with an Indian woman who was friends with us. She was talking about him, saying he had done Indian devil things, when he hadn't really done anything other than being a young smart-ass kid like smart-ass kids are when they are in their teens. He got mad at her because she kept saying things about him and he said, "I'm not doing the stuff that she keeps saying about me."

She had a really nice older car, made in the 1970s, and this was the late seventies or early eighties. This youngster with the Indian devil ancestor said that he wished something would happen to her car. That would teach her to talk about him. He said, "I just thought it. I never even said it out loud. I was just feeling mean and thinking that." He was friends with her sons, and her sons were driving down the road in that car, and in the widest place in that road, a place with a big turnout, that car went out of control and went over the bank. The boys didn't know how it went out of control. It just happened. The boys didn't get hurt badly, but the young man said he knew what it was, that he had done that by thinking mean. He said, "I almost killed my friends by being mean, and I'll never think that way again."

I told him, "Yes, you have to be careful because you do have that power from the dark side." I said, "That power was ruined for you by your mother giving you to medicine people to raise who would steer you away from the dark side. That is why your great-grandmother didn't want you to be raised by the people your mother gave you to. When your mother gave you to that couple to raise, she knew that you would never be a devil. You may have that devil's power, but you would never be one, because they would raise you differently and you would think and feel differently."

Another time, a young couple living together up the hill from me, here in Orleans, got into an argument and they both came from powerful Indian devil families. One day my daughter Carol and I were sitting in the living room and I said to Carol, "What in the hell is that?" She asked me, "What?" I told her to look out the window for a minute and she saw what I had been seeing: big balls of fire were dropping down in front of the window, basketball-sized balls of fire. I said, "Is the house on fire?"

She said, "Mom, we don't have a fire. It's May."

I said, "What in the hell is going on?"

She said, "I don't know, but I see balls of fire falling down in front of the window!"

I said, "Well, I'm going outside."

"I wouldn't go outside, Mom. You don't know what it is. It might be Indian devils."

I said, "Well, I am going out on the porch anyway." I stepped out onto the porch and sure enough, these balls of fire were coming down, rolling off the roof and just sinking down into the ground.

Then all at once I felt an ice-cold chill coming. I told Carol, "That couple is fighting again."

She said, "How do you know that?"

I said, "I can feel that other woman. That cold coming across the porch here is from his great-grandmother, and those fireballs are from her great-grandmother. They came out to protect their grandchildren. That is what's going on." I turned around and told the spirit of his great-grandmother, "Just go home. Your grandson is okay, he'll take care of himself. It is just an argument between two young people. It's no big thing." The cold kind of stood there, kind of paused for a little bit. It was sort of like you had a snake in front of you, but it was a cold feeling in front of you, and then it was just kind of gone. Then I turned around and looked at the fire and said, "You can go home too. She left." And it just quit. The balls of fire quit falling off the roof and I went back in the house and sat down. I did not invite these Indian devils in to eat, but I did go outside to talk to them.

The next time I saw him, I told the young man, "Your great-grandmother was here. You guys have to quit fighting and arguing with each other. You had both of your grandmothers out. They don't have to come out because of you guys's stupid arguments. Don't argue with her, you bring out powers you don't need around." ["Great-" is not usually included in spoken references to distinguish between generations.]

I had two medicine rocks that were given to me by the powers when I was at Doctor Rock. They were both perfectly round limestone rocks, one was heavy and one was light, so that I had a balance of medicine rocks. The powers that gave them to me said that I needed them. We did not find them after my house burned, so I figured I didn't need them anymore. If I needed them they would come back.

My aunt Caroline had a little green jasper-jade rock and Long Gone said that when he was young, every time something adverse was going to happen to him, this rock would show up on his dresser. At first, when he was a child, he would touch it and pick it up and look at it and think, "That's Auntie's rock," and put it back down. But when he came to be older he realized that when that rock appeared, something bad was about to happen to him. Like when he broke his arm on a bicycle as a child, or later, when he was shot in the lung. Finally he realized that if something was going to happen to him, that rock would show up to warn and protect him. Then after it had happened, the rock would be around for a while and then it would be gone again. He hasn't seen it since the house burned down.

A lot of young Karuk people today don't know these things. Duane Allen, who is about my age, and I were sitting around at Tishaniik one day, just gossiping about all this medicine stuff and Indian doctoring. We were just kind of visiting, and somehow Duane started talking about Indian devils, so I told him about my experience with the Indian devil down the river. Then he said, "They found that jawbone."

I said, "Which jawbone?"

"The one that one of the families had their devil power in. They found it way out past Red Cap. Remember, when the man died, they buried the devil with him and fireballs came out of the earth?"

I said, "I remember Forest Service people complaining that fire was coming out of the ground, and the Karuk people had to take something out of the grave because the Forest Service was complaining that they did not like to have fireballs coming up out of the ground [laughing]. So the family took the jawbone out of the grave and took it off into the mountains where it wouldn't bother people."

Darrell knows way more about this stuff than I do, but he won't talk about it. He says those days are gone forever.

Upsancutta

There was no village at Dillon Creek. There was a big creek there and a flat place and plenty of room for a village, but there was never a village there. The next village was about three or four miles downriver, across the river and up the river a little ways from Ti Bar village. There was no village at Dillon Creek because Upsancutta was supposed to have laid her eggs in that big pool where Dillon Creek comes in. She was supposed to be a sea serpent that came up from the ocean to lay her eggs, like the salmon, steelhead, sturgeon, eels, and shad do. We had always been told that Upsancutta goes downriver and back to the ocean with the big high water.

Then when I married and moved downriver to Yurok country, Darrell's aunt Lillian said they saw Upsancutta in a deep part of the river about a mile upriver from where Darrell's village was at Notchko Hiko. It was lying up along what they called Bare Rock or Snake Rock, and it had two heads with an eye in each head, and it was looking at them with these huge, plate-sized eyes. She said it was huge, probably three or four feet in diameter. She kept pulling at her sister to get her to leave, but her sister kept staring at Upsancutta and did not live long after that. She just died. They didn't know what she died of. So Lillian always thought her sister had died of being charmed by that snake. Lillian was a very practical, hard-working woman who wasn't known to tell stories or make things up to get attention. She was kind of reticent and didn't talk much. When she did talk, she talked about commonsense things—that kind of person. So I believe what she said when she said she saw that snake. So I don't know, but maybe it does lay its eggs at Dillon Creek and go back downriver with the high water. Maybe the water is getting too polluted and it doesn't want to come up the river anymore.[16]

Vision of a Murder

In 1989, eight years after Daypay was murdered, I was in Eureka studying really hard to become a nurse, and I thought I had kind of buried his death behind and was getting over it, because I was getting older and didn't get as many visions and as many calls as I had before. I thought I was going to go into my "golden years" and I wouldn't have to deal with this anymore. Then I had a vision of a pickup truck that looked just like Long Gone's 1977 Chevy. In the vision it was parked and had been shot up. I thought, "What happened to Long Gone's pickup? Who would be shooting at him?"

Well, it turned out to be someone else's pickup that looked exactly like Long Gone's. The truck had been shot up and three young people were missing. No one knew where they were, but there were bullet holes and blood in the car and it was parked right where it had been in my vision. At first I didn't know who the vision was referring to, but then I mentioned to Carol that I had seen Long Gone's truck in a vision and it was full of bullet holes. She told me that she had learned that a truck that looked like Long Gone's had been shot up. Eventually a man who lived up on Onion Mountain was blamed for the shootings and he was then found dead, supposedly of suicide, about a year later.

When they couldn't find the bodies of the three missing people, a medicine man was called in who told them places to dig on Onion Mountain, but when the diggers could not find the bodies, the medicine man would get another inkling of where they were and the diggers would go out again and still not find any bodies. People were just combing the mountains looking for the bodies of those kids, who would have to be dead, because there was so much blood in the truck. Then one day they finally found all three of them in one sleeping bag in a place where people said they had searched at least a dozen times, so it seems like the bodies were being moved around and rehidden.

I had had nightmares about these killings that were so terrible I didn't even want to see them. This was just after I got my power. I kept seeing severed heads and a little two-bedroom cabin with a loft and front porch. I never saw anyone around the place other than someone who was burying people. I felt that it wasn't anyplace that was close to here, like Hoopa or Weitchpec or Orleans or up the Salmon River. The ground was flat, and I thought that it might be in Happy Camp or Yreka, and I wondered why I would be dreaming about those places.

In the dreams I saw someone burying people and putting balls in the back of a car. I thought this was so bizarre that it must just be a nightmare and not a vision. Then I had a dream again and it was not balls he was putting into the back of the car, it was heads. I got the feeling that I had better get Josephine Peters to help me with this. I could tell by now that this was real and serious, and that I needed to get someone else to help me pray. Well, something was going on that kept me busy for a while, and I didn't get over to Hoopa to see Josephine. Pretty soon they caught a man up in Oregon with human heads in the trunk of his car. Martina Reed was a woman I had known when she was a little girl, and she had been living with this man who had been picked up for the murders, and now she was missing. I guess that was the connection that led to my visions, because I used to live next door to her. Later on Josephine told me that the medicine women in Hoopa had been praying about it too, because they were getting the same horrible vision.

Medicine Stories

Someplace in my training I had been told, "When you see the light, don't look into it. Close your eyes and look through your eyelashes." Daisy and the other women used to talk more to me in the training than my aunt Caroline, who did most of her training of me telepathically. She just talked inside my mind. I don't know who told me not to look into the light—it could have been just one of those voices that come into my mind—and I forgot about it for years and years and never saw the light, ever. Then, around 1968, I was in a wreck and was rear-ended in Eureka. I was about three months pregnant. And the wreck threw me against the steering wheel and injured my breast. I couldn't raise my arms for two or three weeks because I had hit the steering wheel so hard. I lost the baby because I was wearing a seatbelt. The doctors were pleased that I had lost the baby because I was already getting very sick from the pregnancy.

Years later, around 1995, I had to have breast surgery to remove what the doctor thought were probably cancerous cells, and the surgery was scheduled for a week or two in the future. One night

I was asleep at home and I kind of woke up and saw a bluish white light that was more blue than white. When I saw that light I started to open my eyes to look at it, but I remembered being told not to look at the light. "If you see the light, don't look at it." So I kind of looked through my eyelashes and there was a light going down along my bed and over to the wall and then back up past my head and then back down. The light did that about three times. I wouldn't open my eyes all the way and look at it but I could see the light because it was really bright. I would compare it with the light from arc welding. Even with my eyes mostly closed, it was painfully bright.

I wondered what the light was, and what it was doing. I never really found out, but a couple of weeks later I went for the surgery, and when the doctor scraped the cells out they were not cancerous. They were different from the other cells around them, but they were not cancerous. I mentioned that to some other Natives, and the mother of one of them had also had that experience. She had been in a wreck and was unconscious, and someone who was there could see a bright blue light all around her in the car. She had had a concussion but got well, and the concussion was not as serious as it had looked. Her mother always credited her recovery to the blue light, which she said had come from God and cured her. Her daughter asked me if I felt the light had cured me. I said, "I don't know what it was, but the surgeon thought it looked like I had cancer, based on what he saw on my X-rays, but when they operated, the cells were not cancerous. The only thing that happened was that the light had gone around me two or three times for about fifteen minutes. Then the cancer cells weren't there, so perhaps it was a divine light that cured me. I don't know."

When Darrell was hit by the log loader and was calling me, it was the same feeling as when the Fatawanun calls me. I knew who it was. Another time I felt that call was when Millie had a stroke and a heart attack and had been taken to San Francisco. I sent her whatever I could. I can't explain what the sending is. It is physical. It feels like you pull something out of your solar plexus and you pull the strength up to your forehead, and then it is like an impulse goes out. I equate it with sending whatever strength or power you have available at the time to someone who needs it. Where you are when you send the power doesn't matter, and it is entirely different from what happens when I appear to the Fatawanun on the trail.

My first experience of doing that was after Auntie had died and my nephew Cart was calling me from the hospital, where he was sick. I think this power was one of the gifts that were in the basket that my aunt threw to me in a vision. It wasn't one of my own powers. It was something that was dropped on me. This is not something that I was trained for; it was an ability that my aunt passed to me. Before she gave me the basket of gifts I had not been trained to project power in that way and I had not done it.

This is something that an Indian doctor would be able to do, but it is not part of my set of skills, so I was very surprised when I was called to do this and it happened. At a certain point I realized that I could project out my powers in response to a call for help from someone, but it is not something that I could do in the beginning. I knew that as a spiritual medicine woman I had minor telepathic powers and could respond to a call for help from a Fatawanun, but the ability to respond to someone's else's telepathic call for help wasn't something intrinsic to being a spiritual medicine woman; it was a power that belonged to an Indian doctor, and I wasn't a doctor. When Auntie gave me that basket of gifts and powers, these were things that I could carry and use, but they weren't really mine. In the thirty years since Auntie died, I have used that particular gift of response to a telepathic call several times for different people.

Projecting power into someone in this way is different from making medicine. If I was making medicine for a person, I would be praying and going to the power spots, talking to the four winds, talking to God, and that is making medicine for someone. I know there was a power spot over where Georgia Henry lived, and I'm pretty sure there was another one where Daisy was, and it only takes seconds to go from one place to the next. If you are in one power place and you are using the power, it doesn't take long to get from one place to the other.

I feel the surge of power leaving me that I'm throwing out, back to where the call came from, and with some people I could feel them thinking back. Then I send out more power—I send an answer back. In one case, I was easing a medicine person across to death who had been fighting really hard against dying. If she came back, there would be none of her power left and very little of her mind left, and probably no mobility. She had always trusted me, and I persuaded her telepathically that she could do more if she went across. If she wanted to, she could come back and do more for people than she could trying to stay as an invalid. Finally she agreed with me and I could feel her just letting go. But how it happens, or what, why, or anything else, I have no idea. But it is one of those gifts that Aunt Caroline left with me when she gave me her various gifts of power. That is one of her gifts that I have used, but many of them were beyond my capabilities. I didn't know how to use them. Several of the things that she could do just as easily as another person could walk or talk are beyond me. I don't necessarily know what these gifts are, I could just tell that they are there and I am incapable of using them—like I can't pray for someone and put my hands on them and make them well and make the pain come out, but I can reach in mentally and take their pain if they let it go. But then I have it. I don't know how to take the pain and then brush my hands and throw it away. When I have tried that, it doesn't go away from me.

But this power to respond to telepathic calls is what Indian doctors do and is not within the realm of my training. Mostly I've been trained to see things and to make the world around me a happy place. I can make you feel better about where you're at in this world and in this life, but I can't change where you're at. Not me, not my gifts. I can only make you feel better about it. I can give you a different attitude, but I can't change your life.

With this other set of powers, I'm changing something. I pull this power together and then throw it out and it changes things. I could slow down things and change a sequence of events in time, but before my aunt's gifts in the burden basket, I could not give a person power so that they would survive. The other thing I could always do was if a person was hurting—say they had a toothache or a backache—if they could give it to me I could relieve them of that pain. I could only do that if the person could let go of the pain, and most people aren't taught to let go of pain. Instead of turning loose of the pain, they hang on to it, and I can feel them just pulling it into themselves. When they do let go, I feel the pain for a few minutes and sometimes I'll feel twinges of it off and on. One woman came to me who had something wrong with her breasts, and after that when she had pain I would feel it too. I can't get rid of my own pain, but I can deal with someone else's pain.

When we feel the Creator is speaking to us and telling us to do something and we really don't want to do it—we have a mind-set against it or for some reason we just don't want to do that task—whatever it is that the powers are telling you that they want you to do, you don't really win the argument. You feel like you are arguing with the power, but you really don't win the argument, because if you really have a mind-set against this guidance that they are trying to give you, then the power just drops it off and doesn't force you to do it. I believe that you would have to do it if the power didn't just back off. The reason it backs off is probably that it sees that you have such a mind-set against this task that if you did go do it, you would do it in a manner that wouldn't suffice or fit.

The Fire

In 1998 my house burned down. Darrell was the only one home at the time, and the house burned so fast that he walked right by the chainsaw sitting on the porch and [laughing] threw the plastic chairs off into the yard. Although I had quite a few warnings that it was going to happen, for some reason, even though these hints were coming to me, it was like I was in a daze and didn't really connect the dots that were telling me that the house was supposed to be gone. I was told, but I guess I was in denial. I was getting messages that

Grandpa was taking the house back, that I didn't need it. This came to me in dreams, but also, when I was awake I would get a message that told me the same thing. I would see a big flame just swirling and curling out.

The first time I had this vision, I thought it was someone else's house. Then when Zona's house burned I thought that maybe that was the house in the messages, because it had been my house at one time. But then the message came to me again and again, and finally a voice told me that Grandpa was taking the house back. "You don't need it anymore. You don't need this, and so he's going to take it." According to our beliefs, anything that is in this world that belonged to someone on the other side can go back to them in smoke. That's why you don't keep any of their stuff over here on this side. You burn their clothes and their belongings. That way you send it to the other side right after them, and they can have whatever is theirs. So it went back to him in smoke and he got it all back. It was all his, it wasn't mine. I just got to use it for a long time.

When my house burned, I had everything I needed and probably three of everything I needed. I really had way more than I needed, and the Creator took it away from me. It was sad to lose these things, but they went over to the other world to the people that really owned them. When things burn that had belonged to people who have died, these things go back in smoke to the other world, and then the people over there have their things back again. Some of the things that burned were mine, but many things had been my grandfather's or my aunt Caroline's, so they got back these things that I had had for a few years.

Once when I was in school studying to be a nurse, a girl asked me what it would be like for me if I was homeless and had lost everything. I told her, "I'll never be homeless."

She said, "You could lose everything."

I said, "Yes, I could lose everything, but someone will be there who will take me in, and I'll have a place to stay and something to eat."

She asked me why I said that and I said, "Because over my

lifetime I've taken in many people who had no place to go, and they stayed with me for a while, and then they left and went on with their lives, so that's what would happen to me. Someone will take me in and I won't need anything from the Red Cross. I won't have to get in a soup line. None of these things. If something happened, people would take me in and keep me, and then when I got on my feet I would go on with my life."

She didn't believe me, but when my house burned, the Seventh Day Adventist church people came over that same afternoon and brought me blankets and towels and a nightgown. They were already gathering up what I had to have while the house was still burning, and they wanted to know if I needed a room at the motel, but a friend who was here with me said that we could come up and stay with her until we got someplace set up. Even when the house was still burning, a lady who I didn't know came over and brought me a blanket, a little pillow, and a teddy bear. After about a month we had a little trailer with the room that we added to it so we could kind of camp out there.

We tried hard to get another house built, but we couldn't do it. This year, about seven years after the fire, we finally got this house with the help of the tribe, who hung in there arguing with the county officials for about eight months. When I was young I had jewelry, way more than I needed. Now I'm old and I don't think I need jewelry. I don't need frivolous things like that, but I do need a house to live in. I could have lived in that little trailer the rest of my life if the county would have let me fix the bathroom and make the living room and kitchen bigger, but the county wouldn't let me do that, so it is better that I got another house that has a good bathroom and a big kitchen and living room where I can live comfortably. I am perfectly happy with it. I didn't need a five-bedroom, two-and-a-half-story home now that my family is raised.

So now I live in a nice comfortable house and it doesn't matter if it's a modular structure that is only going to last probably fifteen or twenty years. I probably won't last that long, so it is just perfect for me.

Medicine Woman for the Brush Dance

In 2001 we learned that the downriver Karuk family who had been giving the Brush Dance in Orleans wasn't going to be available on the weekend that the ceremonial leaders up here wanted to have the dance take place. They decided to get me to be medicine woman for the dance so they could hold it when they wanted to. It was controversial because the family who had been giving the dance didn't want us to give it, but the tribe wanted to go on with it. Grant Hillman approached me first about this, and after that the medicine man asked me if I would be medicine woman, if I could do that.

The way I look at it, to be the medicine woman for the Fatawa-nun, to be the Fatawanun's woman, all you have to do is be. You don't have to do anything else, other than being in this totally happy state of mind in order to have the right effect on the world, because we're making medicine for the world, and I'm to make it a happy world, a balanced, happy world that doesn't have negative thoughts in it. It is hard to reach that view and keep it—a kind of Pollyannaish view—because the world is not a Pollyanna place, but that's what I was trained to do. I also had the power to be the Brush Dance woman and could do it, even though that wasn't specifically part of my training.

Years before, Daisy Jones had told me that if I was ever called to do a Brush Dance at some time in my life, I should do it for them, because I had the power to do that. It wasn't my calling but I could do it. I guess you could say that wasn't my optimum job. "The Creator will give you the power and you can go ahead and do that, even though it isn't your job in life," she told me.

Daisy told me that if I went to be the medicine woman for the Brush Dance, I wasn't to ask anyone what to do. I was supposed to go up to the valley to get what I would call divine guidance, because there wouldn't be anyone to tell me what to do. She evidently knew that there wouldn't be any more Fatawanun's women here to instruct me, because no one started that training after me. Even though there might be girls being trained downriver to be the Fatawanun's woman, their dances are different from ours. They weren't exactly the same, tribe to tribe. The Yurok dance their Jump Dance in a pit and we dance our Jump Dance on the ground, with kind of a rock wall behind, in some places. In the other places there is just the mountain behind the dancers.

My job in life, my training as the Fatawanun's woman, is to make this little world of ours here on the river a happy world, and to make this a happy place. I don't really think I can do that, but that is our belief, and that is the focus of my life. I am not to judge people. I am to make them feel better about themselves. Whatever situation is in this world, I should make them feel content with that. That's what I'm supposed to do.

This Brush Dance was controversial because the family that had been giving the dance had continued to say that they were going to do so, when the time was right for them. I told the medicine man that I could be the medicine woman for this Brush Dance but that I didn't want to argue or fight about it. If the family who had been giving the ceremony didn't like me being medicine woman, I did not want to have to say anything or do anything about it. The tribe would have to do all the political stuff that had to do with giving that dance. If there was too much controversy I couldn't do it, because I'm not here to fight with people. I'm here to make it a happier place, not to go fighting with people about things. I don't like to argue and fight about anything.

When it was decided that I would be the medicine woman for this dance, I went to Elk Valley to make medicine for the ceremony with my granddaughter Bianca, who would be my helper, my grandson Cogie, who would help me on the trail, and a small crew, who would help out in other ways. You don't take many people with you when you go to Elk Valley, because it takes a lot of strength to pull them together. On this trip Sonny Buck was there to cook for the crew and Long Gone was with us to help out.

The first day, I ate acorn soup to get ready for my fast. The next day, Saturday, I had a cup of water with about a spoonful of acorn soup in it for my three meals. Then on Sunday I had two meals like that. On Monday I went up the mountain and stayed overnight, and my granddaughter Bianca, who was my female helper, and I danced and sang, with my grandson Cogie, my male helper, camped below us. Every so often he would come up and put wood on the fire, and he danced and sang down below. I knew I was supposed to start singing and dancing just at sunset, and the sun was not completely down yet but the sky was getting kind of gray-looking. Cogie thought he heard us singing, so he started, and when we heard him we had to start whether we were ready or not. We started, and we sang and danced all night long—I still had a clear mind—and then I bathed in the lake on Tuesday morning. Then I went down the hill and continued to fast, just having two cups of acorn water every day. The acorn water had to be in a glass with a glass lid on it. One of the rules was that if the acorn water wasn't held in a glass it would have to be in a waterproof basket, and it couldn't touch metal. A metal pot could not be used. They used to use agate pots or pots with a porcelain finish. I don't know why that is the rule, but you have to go by the rules. Around this time, on the second day, I started getting an altered state of mind. On the third day all the impurities in your system come out. You will throw up yellow bile from your liver. Sometimes it is black because you have so many poisons in you; your whole system becomes thoroughly cleaned out. Fasting is an important part of preparing for and taking part in ceremonies. Fasting alters the state of your mind and cleans out your whole system.

When you go up to Elk Valley just to clean up or to stay a few nights, you stay at the first camp, near the opening of the valley where the road comes down into the valley. There's water and everything you need there at this camp. When you're making medicine for the Brush Dance or some other reason, like I was, you stay at the other end of the valley, higher up. I don't know what the differences are, but when you stay down at the first camp nothing happens. The voices don't talk to you. You have good feelings, but the voices don't talk and the valley doesn't talk to you. But if you leave the valley floor and start going up toward Chimney Rock or Doctor Rock, they really start talking loud to you.

When you're there making medicine, picking up power for some purpose—for a dance, for a healing, for a reason—you go to the last camp, up high in the valley, and listen to the voices, but if you're not going to do something with the power, it's not good for you to have it.

When I was a six-year-old child and went up with Auntie and the other women for the first time, we weren't preparing for a dance, so all of us except my aunt stayed at the first camp, where the trail just starts to go up out of the valley. Since Auntie was purifying herself, she went up the hill and bathed and cleansed herself and did her thing. She stayed up there all day and then came down in the evening.

Every time I've been to Elk Valley, the power starts talking, and it talks until you close your mind to it, and then the voices will stop. Unless you're going to do something like be in a ceremony, you don't listen to the voices. When you go there to pray or purify yourself or just to be there, you don't listen. You're not picking up any power; you're just kind of renewing yourself if you have a burden on your soul.

In one case you go up for your soul's sake, and in the other you are there to pick up power to give out to the people so they will feel good, and you have to give all that power away. If you hang on to any little piece of it, you suffer for it. If you pick up power and keep it for yourself rather than giving it to the people, you will suffer for that. It's not a place to mess around with. It sounds crazy. There's just this quiet valley with a little breeze blowing and not a thing in it, [laughing] nothing you can see.

The medicine people I grew up with talked about the little-people trails and their nests. These were the little people who come and torment you before you die, who can drive you crazy if you go to their place and start talking to them. Whenever you go out to make medicine, you always have someone along that you can call out to in case anything goes wrong. I always feel that they are there to watch your back for the little people, and to keep the little people away from you while you are open and unprotected, the way you are when you are making medicine. If the little people get to you, you could go crazy. Or they might steal you away and take you back with them. Or they might take away the medicine that you're making, for themselves, instead of letting you have it for the people. I don't know what they really do, but you watch out for them. They like tobacco, so you leave tobacco for them as a gift. Then they are supposed to leave you alone, even though you are in their territory.

When you go up the medicine trails, you stop at places on the trail as you are walking along and leave a little tobacco here and a little tobacco there and you burn a little bit for the little people and make a little medicine each time to feed the little people so that they don't torment you or follow you up the trail. You just stop at places as you're walking along. "This looks like a good little place to leave something for them. This looks like a good place for them." If it feels like a good place, you throw out some tobacco there for them. When Long Gone was working as a surveyor he would tear up his cigarettes and leave tobacco for those little people when he got into the high country where the little people live. Pay them, say, "I have some things for you…" If you get too high into the mountains and the feeling gets too strong, take a few little shells with you to leave too, because it might not just be the little people, there might be the big spirits up there.

When the Creator talks to you, there is an awesome feeling, like looking into the Grand Canyon.

Even though you can't see them, there are powers in Elk Valley. The medicine man said he went up once to help out with a cleansing for someone who had been reburying bodies that had washed out of the ground during a flood. The medicine man and his family camped next to him, and it snowed on them, and there were things going around the medicine man's tent and shaking it and making noises, scaring him, and when he looked outside the tent there was nothing there. Nothing at all. Finally he and his children and wife got in their car and drove home in the middle of the night. The person who was there to cleanse himself and his wife were asleep in their tent and didn't even hear the medicine man and his family get up to leave.

When the medicine man came back the next day, his tent had been crushed by a big limb that fell off a tree. He said he knew something was trying to chase them away. He figured this happened because the person burying bodies had a reason to be in that camp, which is a medicine camp, and he and his family had no reason to be in that camp, because he wasn't doing anything. Only the people who are making medicine stay in that camp. The helpers stay in lower camps.

My granddaughter Bianca was my helper and fixed the acorn soup for me. The helper doesn't have to fast like I do. She fasts for maybe twenty-four or seventy-two hours, and then she will fast for three more days when we're down the hill and going in and out of the Brush Dance pit. She helps me there, but she doesn't fast all the time. She only fasts when she's in the mountains purifying herself. Then she stays up all night, dancing and singing. There are other places you can go to make this medicine, but the place I was told to go as a child was Elk Valley.

We were going to Chimney Rock rather than Doctor Rock, because I wouldn't go to Doctor Rock unless I was going to pick up the medicine and become a doctor, and I have no call for that. The medicine man says I have a calling for it, but I have ignored him. That's his statement, mine is that I have no calling for it. But I had to go to Elk Valley to purify myself for the Brush Dance. It had been a long time since I had been there to go through the purification process, because I had not done a ceremony like the Brush Dance.

It takes a lot of spirituality, or whatever they call it, to pull together picking up power anyway, and my grandson Cogie and my granddaughter Bianca were helping me make the medicine. I didn't quite do it right, but it was okay. Bianca was ahead of me a lot of the time, and I'm supposed to be in the lead so that the powers know who to focus on. Bianca being out in front of me kind of threw it off, but Cogie stayed behind all the time because he was there to protect my back on the trail.

We went on up the trail and Cogie made his place to stay where he could hear us, even though he was quite a ways down the trail from us. Bianca and I went further up the trail and stopped by the second lake. We were supposed to stay by the first lake, but there wasn't a good campsite there and it didn't really matter, so we just went a little higher on the mountain, to the second lake. I looked to the west because I was making good medicine and Bianca looked to the east. When we got to the second lake we danced in all directions and sang. The valley is kind of like an amphitheater, so people all the way at the end of the valley could hear us singing from our camp.

There was a bear, off the trail, close to us. We could see his signs all the way up the trail and we could hear him—"Snuff, snuffle, snuffle," you know—snuffling around over there, and then he would walk away and then snort again, kind of like a hog. Bianca got scared and hollered. I told her, "Bianca, you're not supposed to be afraid of anything." I said, "He's coming to give us power. I don't care what you see, don't get afraid of anything, and whatever you do, don't go to sleep. Never go to sleep."

When Bianca and I would start singing and dancing and praying, Cogie would hear us down the hill and start singing and praying too. The helper who goes with the woman who is making medicine is always a medicine man who is a relative to her. He is there to help by bringing wood for the fire and to protect the medicine woman in case a bear comes or something like that happens. But actually, nothing really bothers you when you're making medicine.

We were dancing and singing and making medicine, putting tobacco in the fire and singing, and got tired. It didn't take me long to get tired kick dancing. You kick one leg past the other when you are kick dancing. You hang onto each other and kick your leg back and forth. That's what women do. We were singing, and I don't sing very good, so I let Bianca do most of the singing and I kind of mumbled along, about like if you are going around the house humming to yourself. So she and Cogie were doing the majority of the singing and I was just kind of mumbling along, but I was kick dancing as hard as she was. I lasted about twenty minutes before I got tired and sat on a rock to rest. Down the hill, Cogie could hear that we had stopped singing, so he quit too. Then we got up and did it again, and I could hear him start down the hill. Then I sat down again and we were quiet for a while. Then the wind started coming up and Cogie came up the hill and built up our fire, put more wood on it. Bianca had been putting a little wood on it, but he built it way up because it was getting cold. He brought some more wood in and then went back down the hill to his place.

We danced some more and pretty soon Bianca was getting tired and sleepy. I told her, "Don't go to sleep!" It is hard to stay awake [laughing], because you haven't had any caffeine for days and days. We kept trying to talk about anything and everything, just trying to keep awake, and pretty soon she dozed off. I looked at her, and I don't see very well anyway, and it was just firelight and dark, and then she had turned into a troll! She shrank that much and just looked like a little old man a couple of feet tall. I said, "Bianca, are you awake?"

"I think I was going to sleep," she said, and she's not a man anymore, she has turned back into this five-foot-tall woman. I said, "Now I know why we're not supposed to go to sleep. You turned into a little troll. Evidently we change into something else when we go to sleep making medicine! When she started to doze off again, probably about three or four in the morning, I said to her, "Are you sleeping?"

She said, "Gee, I'm getting awfully sleepy. How did you know that?"

I said, "Because your face started to change into that man's face again. You hadn't shrunk this time, but you were getting the troll face again."

Then we danced on, and early morning at first light—it must've been around five o'clock and there was no sun up yet—Cogie comes up and asks if we are ready to go down the trail. We told him no, that we still had to bathe. So we got in the lake and Cogie swam across to the other side and back. Bianca did not have a good time, because she did not want to get into the water. It was cold. I told her, "The water isn't cold, Bianca. Just get in!" I had on a robe because you have to wear a dress when you go into the lake and you don't want to have to pack anything extra, because you don't get to eat. You're starving. Since you don't want to pack anything extra, I just wore a sweatshirt robe I had that is like a long dress, and with the fire I was fairly comfortable. It was June and still cold in Elk Valley, at 7,000 feet. It was really cold early in the morning, but when you got into the water it was warm, with steam coming up from the surface of the lake. When we dove in the water all these water dogs are there. They are really big salamanders with little round eyes. They were looking at me. I do not like water dogs! They always give me the heebie-jeebies. My aunt always said to me when I was about fourteen years old, "When you go and make this medicine, they will come and kiss you."

I told her that I didn't want to go to Elk Valley and have that happen, and she said, "Why, you don't want them rubbing your belly and kissing you?"

I told her, "I don't want to even get near a water dog, let alone have one kissing me! Of all the things in the world I do not want to do, [laughing] one is be kissed by water dogs." When you're swimming, the big orange ones roll up against you and swim across your belly. Cogie just loved it! They would swim up from the bottom and bump against him. He thought that was just great. When they touched me it was kind of grin-and-bear-it time—"this has to be done."

They were a little bit leery of me because I had a cane that I needed, to get down into the water, so they kind of backed away from me a little bit. I thought, "If they don't come, it isn't any good. They have to come to me," so I put the cane down in the water and swam along a little bit and held the cane down. Then they came swimming up and started bumping against me, but they didn't like that stick. Then I swam across, and Bianca got into the lake. She didn't like the water dogs either. I said, "They have to come to you, period. If they don't come to you, the medicine didn't work and you're not pure." They swam up to her and she was making all kinds of faces, but she didn't say anything. Then she got right out. She said, "I don't have to swim clear across, do I?"

I said, "No, you don't have to get bumped by the water dogs like Cogie and me." I had to swim over some deep parts of the pond, but I didn't swim clear across because of my diabetes, and I didn't want to expend too much energy. Our fires burned out while we were swimming, so we stamped them out some more and made sure no coals were left, and then Cogie put water on the ashes and made sure they were totally out.

I had a mile and a quarter to go back down the trail, and I wasn't going to get to eat, because you're not supposed to eat on the quest. Darrell couldn't figure out why you don't go to the bathroom when you are making this medicine. You can't go when you are on the trail. But you are dehydrated, so you don't have to go to the bathroom the whole time you're up there. From the afternoon, all night long, until you come down in the morning, you haven't been to the bathroom.

You don't eat or drink when you go to purify yourself. The day before you go up the trail, you don't even get acorn water to drink. You don't get anything. When I came back down the trail I got to drink some acorn water, but I had been twenty-four hours without eating or drinking and they had been twenty-four hours without drinking. Bianca says, "I only had to go a day, didn't I? Can I eat?"

I said, "I think you can eat at midnight, when the day is over."

She says, "I never knew it was so hard to go without eating."

I had been drinking acorn water for three days before we started and then had gone twenty-four hours without eating or drinking anything: I went up to Elk Valley a day or two early to acclimatize myself because I figured that I have these disabilities of diabetes and heart disease and I have to work around that to get up there into the thin air of the high country before I start making medicine, walking up the trails, and doing all the other things that you have to do when you're making medicine. So at midnight Sonny Buck made a big stew for the helpers. Cogie hadn't been asking when he could eat. He just went without eating. And I thought he would be the one to be starved, because he has diabetes and is always eating, but it didn't bother him. He just went without food and water for twenty-four hours like it was nothing.

The next day I walked down into the valley and walked back up, and then the voices started talking to me and told me I was going to have to go up and purify myself. I had never done that before, because I had never been the medicine woman at a dance, and I had to do what it told me to do. I walked the trail through one creek and put water in my mouth, swirled it around and spit it back out into the water and walked on up to another creek, took some water into my mouth, swirled it around and spat it back into the creek. When you come back down the trail you do the same thing. Nobody ever told me why you do that, I just know it's what you are supposed to do. Like Auntie said, "When they tell you to do something, you do it. You don't ask them why. If you need to know why, they won't have you. The voices will try to chase you out of the valley." When you get to just about where you're going to go, it starts trying to push you back and change your mind, trying to scare you. This power is pushing at you to go back, but if you persevere and keep going up that trail, then it will start helping you. But at first it's like it's trying to tell you, "Stay out, stay out. Go away, we don't want you." You have to be determined that you are going to go up that trail.

When you start out at the bottom of the valley, it's nice and easy, and then when you just start to climb up the trail a little bit it feels like you can't breathe, and you're tired, and something is trying to chase you back. By the time you get to the prayer rock—which is only about two hundred yards from the bottom of the trail—and you sit on this little rock, then it starts talking to you, and from there on up it isn't hard at all. It's a struggle for me because I have heart disease and I'm too fat and diabetic, and everything else is wrong with me.

So they never told me why, and I never asked them why, and

now it's too late to ask, and I'll never know why. I have no idea why you go up that particular trail toward Chimney Rock and don't take some other trail. I just know that that is the trail to take. When I made this medicine it was physically very hard, because the trail was steep and the rocks were sliding. I was using two canes because my back is bad, and in places Cogie had to get behind and push me when the trail got too steep.

Before leaving the valley, I made medicine and blessed some *kishwuf* Long Gone had wanted blessed.[17] While I was doing that a group of about twenty people from the city came by. They were going on a camping trip at the other end of the valley and then planned to drop down the other side of the valley into Smith River country. Sonny Buck and Long Gone told them they couldn't come up the valley or stay there because I was there making medicine for a ceremony, so they walked all the way around the valley to where they were going to go. We could feel as well as hear them coming.

Since I had finished making the medicine, I could sleep that night. When I went to sleep, instead of having my usual dreams, I had dreams of people racing cars on a city street. I kind of woke up and thought, "What the hell? Where did that come from?" Then I fell back to sleep and started dreaming about something really bad happening in a city, some kind of confrontation, with a gun going off. I didn't see what really happened, but I felt the ominous influence of it. I thought, "Go back to where you belong and get out of my mind," and then it went away. After that, I started having the more traditional dreams that I had expected to have, so I figured that the influence of those people from the city had been getting into my mind. I wondered what I was putting into their minds, because if I was getting their thoughts, they must be getting mine. It's a two-way street. I was probably freaking out some city person, because when my dream came to me [laughing], I was shape-changing on a cliff someplace.

When you go to Elk Valley or to other spiritual places to make medicine, whatever that power is starts talking to you, but you don't know what it's saying. You want to know what it is saying to you, so you fast and starve yourself and go without water. You pray and go into a trance. Then you will understand what has been said to you. I don't know if people hear the same things or not, because in the high country there is no comprehension of the language they are speaking. To me it sounds like the language of speaking in tongues among Christians. But then after it talked to me for a long time, the voice would stop and then I would feel tired and lie down and rest. When I woke up from that rest I would know what had been said to me. During the rest it was interpreted for me, because I guess it knew [laughing] that I was incredibly stupid. Anyway, it took the time to be interpreted for me. So it's similar to the Christian experience of someone talking in tongues and someone else interprets what they said, but in this case the interpretation takes place in my mind while I'm resting. I don't know if I'm in a trance, if I'm asleep, or if I'm just resting. My helpers who saw me at that time thought I was napping. My grandson Cogie was my male helper because he has gifts too.

For the past four or five days I just had a little bit of acorn water, about a half a cupful, a couple of times a day, but my helpers only fasted before they were going to help me with something, like going up the trail or whatever I needed to do. Cogie wanted to know if he could eat and I told him that I didn't have the slightest idea if my helpers could eat yet or not. We had come down from the mountain, and they had not eaten since the day before. Cogie said that he was hungry, and the cook had made stew for my helpers, and for the others who were there, helping my helpers. I had quite an entourage with me. You can take five or six people with you, or you can just take one or two people. There are always at least two people helping. My helpers wanted to eat. They just couldn't stand to go without eating. I told my granddaughter that it would be the end of the day at midnight, and they would have gone all day without eating, but that I didn't know for sure what they could do about eating. My grandson said, "Go to sleep, Grandma. Go to sleep and then come back and tell us what we can do." [Laughing] He said that because he knew each time I went to sleep I would come back and know what I was supposed to be doing. This was all new to me, because I had not been trained to be the medicine woman for the Brush Dance.

It feels like you went for a nap but you don't feel like you took a nap when you wake up and come out of this whatever it is…say nap, just to make it understandable. But when you come out of the trance, you know what it said. This time it told me, "Go home. You have all the power you need for that dance." Sonny Buck was with me, helping out, and I told him, "I'm going home."

He said, "Oh, those people scared you off, so you're going home early."

He still thought I was just afraid of those people, so I told him that it was late anyway, and we would just go home tomorrow, but he said he was going to stay out there until Wednesday.

I said, "No, it told me to go home. That thing out here told me to go home." He just kind of laughed at me. I said, "I'm supposed to go home tonight. They never scared me off, Sonny. I'm through. It's made. It's done. I've got everything I need. I don't need anything more. You can stay out here as long as you want to—I don't own the valley—but I'm going home."

He had seen a big elk track and wanted to go hunting.

I said, "You can't go hunting." But animals were just coming to us, like a black deer came down, animals you would never see ordinarily. I said, "You can't do that when we are out here making medicine. You can't kill anything. I'm out here picking up power for the dance, and you can't go hunting."

He said, "No, I can do what I want to do."

I said, "Okay, I'm just telling you; you can't do that." He went to sleep that night and dreamed he was going to get an elk, and all at once he looked up and there were elk all around him. They all raised up and started walking toward him.

The next morning he got up and he never said anything about staying. He just said, "We have to go home today" and started breaking camp, so I knew that it had told him to go home too. We were through. It was time to go home. [Laughing] And he had wanted to go hunting.

I said, "See, I don't really have to tell you anything, the powers here will let you know what you can do and can't do. Didn't I tell you that you can't kill anything?" Their walking toward him was a sign they couldn't be killed. You couldn't do it. Might not be logical, but…it happens.

The two types of voices that I hear are completely different. In the case of Auntie speaking to me telepathically, that voice just talks directly into your mind. You think someone's talking to you. It is just a voice in English in your mind, and you can comprehend it. I don't like to say that it's a voice in your mind, because that makes you sound like you're nuts, but it's a voice that comes to you from inside your mind. The voice tells you the damnedest things sometimes.

The voices that I hear in the high country sound like talking in tongues, and in order to understand what has been said to me, I go into a trance, and when I come out of it I know things that I hadn't known before.

People who are not medicine people cannot hear these voices. They go to the medicine site near here and want to build a house there. They will say, "This is the prettiest place in the world." Darrell always wanted to build a house there, and it was about four feet from the crossroads. [Laughing] It just feels good there. People get there and they start saying what a nice place it is. It is a good-feeling spot. That's like the Druids' ceremonial places, where they said they felt good, and I'll be damned if the Christians didn't come and build churches on them. They didn't know that those were the Druid places for sure, but they put a church there, right where the Druids thought was spiritual. And here they would try to put a house at those places.

There's nothing that stops people from building houses on spiritual places here, but if they do, or they build it too close to the spiritual place, they feel that there are ghosts walking in their house. Even that small trailer on this place is too close to the crossroads. It wasn't too close for me, but it was too close for other people.

It is better to take as few people as possible with you to Elk Valley, because when you go out there, the people who are with you get euphoric and you, the medicine person, feel euphoric too, but it seems like you have a little more control because the power is focusing on you. But people with you are always dancing in the daisies or something. You just wonder [laughing], "What in the hell are they going to do next?"

Sonny had been euphoric, and the dream of elk approaching him brought him back to reality. Because he was a hunter, he became euphoric about hunting possibilities. When Long Gone went to the valley, he became euphoric about getting gambling power, because he was a gambler. Bianca became euphoric and she was going to look for love, and Cogie actually was more stable than he is here at home. He was a lot more stable there in the valley, and more down to business in keeping his mind on what we were doing than he is when he's home. He was down to business; he just tended to business when he was in Elk Valley.

When we got back to Orleans we stopped at the dance pit to leave off the medicine we had made, because I wasn't going to pack it around with me for the next two or three days until the dance was made. Even though the medicine is not a physical thing, we placed it in the pit as if it was an actual object. I just threw in the medicine that I had made. Then Cogie stepped up and said, "I'm going to do mine dramatically." He stamped his foot and he threw his medicine down like he was throwing down a lightning bolt. Then Bianca just put her medicine down like I had, just put it there, like you threw a little bundle down. And then, even though it didn't make any sense to him, Sonny threw his medicine in too.

I told him, "Whatever medicine you picked up there, you have to give it to the dance. It belongs here, it doesn't go with us." I said, "If you take it with you, Sonny, you'll pay for it. If you keep anything for yourself, you pay for it. You have to give it all back to the dance. That's what you are doing when you throw your medicine into the dance pit. You are getting the medicine for the people, and you give it to the people."

When we came down from Elk Valley we learned that the girl who was supposed to be the medicine girl had gotten into an argument with a medicine man and never came out, and we learned that other people had not done anything to prepare for the dance, with Sonny gone. It was a great big muddle. I thought, "Well, if it is going to work it will, and if it's not going to work it won't. I'm ready for it, I don't care what."

Darrell insisted on coming out to the valley every single day, because he didn't want me to make a mistake. I told him I wouldn't make a mistake, but he was afraid I would, and to make a mistake means death for someone in your family. It's like God has given you a little recipe, and you do what they tell you to do, step by step, and you end up with a cake. Everything with the dance worked out all right and then the next day I rested and could have a little acorn water. Then I fasted again from Friday night until Sunday morning. No water, no acorn water, no food, no nothing.

On Saturday I went out again and picked medicine plants and made medicine. When I made medicine on this side of the river, the bird who was guiding me took me along and landed in a place on a landslide where I couldn't go, so I just went up the hill a little ways, to a place where I could make the medicine. The bird kept showing me a place to go where I couldn't go in this form. A few days before, when I had gone up the hill to make my medicine for the Brush Dance, a little bird flew right at the truck. It didn't come when I had gone to Elk Valley just for myself, to cleanse my soul. He flew down and hopped and flew and hopped along the road ahead of us all the way into the valley, like he led us into the valley. I don't even remember what kind of bird it was, but it was grayish with white on it.

Then, when I made medicine on this side of the river, the bird went out and just hung in the air over where the slide dropped into the river. Evidently there had been land there at one time, but it had slid away. I didn't know if I was supposed to go out into the edge of the slide, out over the river, and that confused me a little, so I just went up the hill to where I was out of sight and made the medicine there. No one told me that that bird was going to guide me to the place to make medicine. I just knew that. What the bird was doing was divine guidance, letting me know what I was supposed to do, but there was no place to go. I looked and the bird was just hanging out over the water about twenty feet from the bank—and I was no bird! So I made do and [laughing] made the medicine a little farther back from the river.

After the medicine was made and placed in the pit, I got to stay in my house during the day. But at night I had to go out and sleep in the pickup truck because I couldn't stay in the same house with my husband. A friend came over and said that she had not seen me and I told her I was in seclusion because once you make your medicine, you're not supposed to be out in public. People can come and see you at home, but not many, because you have withdrawn from people. That way you don't give any of the power of the dance away to someone. If someone came and had a great need, you might give some of it up. That is my thought on it. Then the dance started and I quit eating. The medicine man said I could eat, but I didn't eat anything. I had just had about a pint of acorn water on Wednesday morning.

Then I went out and gathered the medicine plants and made medicine for the little girl who was going to be my medicine girl. What herbal medicines you collect depends on what you're doctoring the child for in the Brush Dance. You're not going to use the same medicines for a child whose parents feel it needs protecting as you would for a child who is sick all the time. The voices told me to go to Le Perron Flat to gather the plants I needed. Everything was there except the dandelion, and it was dried up, so the medicine man brought me some fresh dandelion from his yard. When I'd gotten all the plants I made my medicine, praying and burning these plants in a little fire. Different people burn different plants for different purposes. I was doing a Brush Dance, so I gathered and burned Brush Dance plants. I made my medicine, said my prayers, talked to the Creator, and then went down and did the dance.

The first night of the ceremony, everyone had gathered when someone drove up and said that Karuk people living downriver were coming up to take over the ceremony. This rumor really upset people, because it was hard to tell what might happen, and the last thing you want to take place at a ceremony is any sort of violence. When I saw how upset everyone was, I told them about a vision that I had. In this vision people had come to the dance from downriver bringing their ceremonial regalia with them. They set the regalia down on the ground and walked away from it, and when they did, a torrent of green water that looked like the water in Camp Creek burst out of the ground, separating them from their regalia. The vision ended with them crying and carrying on because they could not get back to their regalia. That meant that they were not going to interfere with the ceremony, that nothing was going to happen along those lines, and nothing did happen. After the people who were there for the ceremony heard this vision, everyone relaxed and we were able to go on with the dance.

At the Brush Dance the Karuk men have a medicine fire, and if the Yurok are taking part in the dance, the Yurok dancers who have come for the ceremony have their own camp and their own medicine fire, and there is a third camp for the girls who take part in the dance. First the medicine man comes over and brings me fire from the Karuk men's camp and puts it in the dance pit where I am sitting, and it starts my fire, and then the leader from the other camp brings his fire over and puts it in my medicine fire, and I stir the fire up a little bit. Then the Karuk men who are dancing come up to the dance pit in a line, and as they pass by the girls' camp, a girl steps into line with a Karuk man on either side of her. Then they all file into the pit and the dance begins.

In a way I was not being traditional, because I did not sleep in the Brush Dance pit. I slept by the pit, but I didn't sleep in it. Whichever way it might be done, there's no judging. Medicine people do the best they can in every ceremony. They go without eating and do the rituals, and the more the medicine person sacrifices, the more power the powers will give you. That's also true when the Brush Dance medicine woman goes out to pick up her medicine. The more she sacrifices of herself, and the harder it is, and the greater the struggle, the more gifts of power will be given to you for your dance.

At the dance I made medicine for the child that the dance focused on. I put medicine on the child and prayed for it. I didn't sing very much, because I'm not a very good singer, not loud enough, and the people at the dance couldn't hear me, and I didn't do a good show, according to one of my constituents. I told him, "I made good medicine."

"Yeah, you made good medicine."

"But your complaint [laughing] is that I didn't make a good enough show of it?"

One of the complaints was that I was too serious. Even when I was growing up, some of the children said that I was too serious. I think I was so serious being the Brush Dance woman because I had never done it before, and I had to keep listening and watching and paying attention to what the powers were telling me to do. I was trying to do all the tasks, and focusing on these tasks. At the end they said it was a real good dance and made everyone feel good. There was a lot of power there, and there were a lot of blessings from it, so that part I did was all right. I made good medicine, I was just was too serious about how to dispense the medicine.

Darrell asked how it was, being the medicine woman for a Brush Dance, and I got facetious. I told him, "You know what, Darrell?"

He says, "What?"

[Laughing] "I got to see the dancers the best I ever had in my whole life." That was one of my blessings for being the medicine woman.

They say the animals come to see the medicine woman, and before the dance, while I was making medicine in Elk Valley, a skinny black doe that looked like it was starving to death, poor thing, came right into camp and looked straight at me. She was pure black and she was so thin that I expect she was feeding twins. I had never seen a black deer in my life, and both black and white deer are sacred.

I had been complaining for quite a while that I never see any more orioles or butterflies, and when I was in the valley waiting to go up the mountain to make medicine, there was a huge oriole sitting in a pear tree and singing for maybe an hour. Then I saw an eagle while I was out making medicine, and other animals all the time. But that's what they say—when you're full of the gifts of power, the animals will come to you. The Fatawanun claim that when they're on the trail the animals just come to them and they see all kinds of animals. They come there to bless you.

After the dance was over, I went back to work too quickly. You are supposed to wait about three days before you go back to being around people, but I had this work to do, and I needed to get back to work, so I only stayed at the dance ground one day before I went home. I couldn't go swimming, and you're supposed to swim in the river, but I couldn't swim in the river because I couldn't get to the river. The duck grass was so thick below the sweathouse that I couldn't get down to the river, so I had to go home and shower. I went back to work in the kitchen at the tribal council building, and a monarch butterfly came flying into the kitchen. I turned and looked at it and turned back and was fixing things on the counter, and the butterfly flew clear around me and fluttered back and forth right in front of me. There he was, all golden brown with great big eyes on the tops and bottoms of its wings, and then it went back out. I was working with Lorraine Hillman and she said she had never seen a butterfly act like that before. I told her I had been complaining that I have not seen a butterfly lately, and it wanted to make sure I saw it, so that must be my last blessing for giving the dance.

Some of the people running the Humboldt County senior program who weren't Indians had a little trouble understanding why, when I was medicine woman for a dance that lasted three days, I needed to have two weeks off in order to go out to Elk Valley and prepare my state of mind.

A Change for the Better

In January of 2002 I had corrective eye surgery and my vision improved enough that I thought I should get my driver's license reinstated. They took my picture and I saw that I just looked terrible. My complexion was gray and I had black shadows beneath my eyes clear down to my cheekbones. I knew I wasn't feeling well. I was tired all the time. It got so bad that they flew me over to Redding to have my heart checked, but there were a couple of other emergencies in front of me, and I got to feeling so bad, sitting there waiting, that I told them that if they couldn't see me right away I thought I would just go home and go to bed and forget about seeing them, because I was too tired to wait around anymore. So then they took my oxygen stats and it was down to 90, which is about what it reads when you aren't doing well.

At this point they checked my heart, using a catheter, and saw that the small blood vessels were clogging up, mostly because of diabetes. Then for a couple of weeks they had me on a therapy which involved increasing the pressure to the heart with the goal of growing new blood vessels. After a couple of weeks of this I was much better and could get out and walk around normally. It just turned me right around. In a matter of weeks I was doing things again. That was almost four years ago and my heart is still working normally.

White Deerskin Dance, 2002

In 2002, the year Cogie was the medicine man at Tishaniik, it had been raining for a week or so and I woke up and there was a pretty, pink, rosy light, and I thought, "Oh, the sun is up this morning." I got up and walked into the kitchen and there was a beautiful light shining in, but then I could hear rain. I opened the door and it was raining by Cogie's room, but when I looked down the outside of the trailer, past my room, there was a pink, rosy glow around the trailer and clear down to the living room door, and it was raining. I didn't know what in the world this pretty pink light was. I talked to the medicine man about it and he said he thought I was being called to be a doctor and that the light was blessing me. I told them there was no way I was going to go through that hell and dance for three days straight. I had a hard time dancing one night without food or water.

The medicine man said that he was just telling me that that's what he thought the light was; he was not telling me that he thought I had to do it, but he thought that that was what I was supposed to be. I told him no, that I just thought I would stay the way I am and be the way I am. I know what this is. I am too old and too tired. If I were younger, maybe, but I was so busy all my life raising children and working...Thanks, but no thanks.

Toward the end of the White Deerskin ceremonies, when the Fatawanun is standing on a small rounded rock just up from the dancers, he throws his medicine to Offield Mountain and I have to break it so that some of the medicine will fall down on the people and the rest will go to the mountain. That was my job. That's what I was trained to do. Don't ask me how I break it; don't ask me how I know its coming. It's like a shock wave, and I just look at it and break it, and it looks to me like fireworks dropping down on the people. I see this but I don't think other people do.

The medicine people in charge of the dance placed me kind of off to the side, where I couldn't see what the medicine man was doing. That's why I say being the Fatawanun's woman is easy, because all I have to do is break the medicine when the medicine man throws it and make the dance a happy place. Sometimes when the Fatawanun throws his power it almost knocks you over. Other times it's like somebody skipped a rock across a pond, so I guess it depends on how much power a person has picked up or how much natural ability they have.

When Cogie threw his medicine toward Offield Mountain he did not see me shatter off a piece. He said he feels the medicine going down his arm like a shock wave when he throws it, like a gun kicking back at you. I told him that it feels like a shock to me to break a piece of it off. I just look at the medicine when he throws it and a piece of it comes off and it looks like fireworks falling and sprinkling down on the dancers. When you see the fireworks break off the medicine when the medicine man has thrown it, then you know you have done it; you've taken a piece of the medicine.

According to Millie, there are people who live in this world who can see what you're doing when you do these medicine things. She said most people can't see you are doing anything, but there are other people who can stand back and see what you're doing. She didn't know if these people could pick it up and do it too, after watching you make medicine. She said that to most people, it won't look like you're doing anything except making a little fire, and they can't see what's going on, but there are these other people who can see the medicine being made and how it happens.

That's why the medicine people are always so careful not to do something in front of anyone unless it's one of those times when you are supposed to do it in front of people, like when I break the medicine at the White Deerskin Dance.

I told her that they were doing better than me, because [laughing] I don't know how it happens.

Cogie did really well at being the medicine man, but it kind of knocked him off-center mentally for some reason, I don't know why. I think maybe because his wife had left him and taken the children, and he wasn't stable enough to go through that demanding ritual. He did well at being a Fatawanun, but there's no standard. You just have to be from one of the medicine families, and how far you go with being a Fatawanun and how deeply you are enmeshed with the power of the Creator depends on the person. You can just kind of skim along with the medicine or you can go very deeply into it. He did really well at actually making the medicine but it knocked him off-balance. His psyche was too fragile to put that much out.

I told Cogie that he didn't have to be a Fatawanun to become a medicine man. "All you have to do is get your thoughts together and go up the mountain. Take one of your relatives with you and make that commitment and dance on Doctor Rock and stay up there in Elk Valley for a couple of weeks, and stay on Doctor Rock for three days. That's all you have to do and you will be a full-fledged Indian doctor. Nobody can stop you from doing that, because you have that gift and you come from a medicine family. No one can tell you that you can't do that. Then you can do personally whatever you want to do with that power of being an Indian doctor. But you will pay for everything you do with that power, so you have to be very careful that you don't use too much of it for yourself or your family. You have to spread your power and your gifts and your healing around." So now the ball is in Cogie's court, and what he does with it is up to him. The choice is always yours, but if you don't pick up your medicine and powers, you pay for it.

When Cogie was the Fatawanun for the White Deerskin Dance, his mother, Beavi, was his cook, and Summer, the medicine man's little girl, was Beavi's helper and cooked for her. Summer fed Beavi and made sure her meals were ready so that too many people were not touching her food. She told Beavi, "I can do it for you." She had heard Beavi say that she had to find someone clean to do this. I had told Beavi that I couldn't do it because I had promised to help with the cooking. Little Summer was standing there listening to what we were saying, and she was about seven years old. She brushed her hands off on her clothes and said, "My hands are clean."

I laughed and told Beavi that you couldn't find anyone cleaner than that. Not only clean, but innocent. So Summer helped Beavi, and she was very good about it. She was there for Beavi every instant, making sure that she was fed and that nobody touched her plate. When Summer had to leave early she had the plate all made up and covered up and had made sure that someone would give it to Beavi when the time came.

Cogie said that when he was on the trail, it was getting kind of late and he kept hearing me talking to him, saying, "You better hurry along now. You better come out of there. You better hurry along. It's going to be late, come on along now." He said because of hearing my voice he got down the hill by two-thirty in the afternoon, and he would have had plenty of time to make medicine for the fish before it got dark. He said he could hear me the whole time, like I was standing there talking to him, or like there was a little radio in his head saying, "Come on, now. Hurry along."

I think that if you are going to be a medicine person or an Indian doctor, sometime before you are forty years old you should have gone out and made your statement and made your adjustment to life that you have to make. That means you have to start living so that people will believe in you. You have to live an exemplary life. You have to live conservatively. You don't have to really live with one person, but if you do it's better—if you can find someone who is stable enough that they can put up with your disappearances. You just disappear. You're not here and they can feel you're not here. If they are close enough to you, they can feel that you are not on this earth: even though your body is still here, you're not. I think the body is still here. If it is with me, it isn't me. It doesn't look like me. I know that much. If a person is close enough to you, they will realize that you're not here. You're gone. I always tell people [laughing] that I must've been to St. Elsewhere.

Beavi's Illness

In January of 2003 Beavi's abdomen began to swell and she pretty much stopped eating, because whatever she ate made her sick. I told her I thought she should see a doctor because she was only fifty years old and had all these things wrong with her. That wasn't normal, she shouldn't be sick at all at that age. When her blood was tested, we learned that she had hepatitis C. Then a couple of weeks later, she lost her mind and was wandering around the house all night. She didn't know who she was, didn't know who we were, and was incapable of talking. In two weeks she had gone from being sick to dying.

By May I didn't know if she was going to make it or not. In July she rallied, and her health held until January of 2004, when she started failing again. She would rally, and then she'd fail. And we just went from week to week and day to day trying to get her to eat something, trying to find something that she could keep down. We had to make sure that she took all her medication, because she would forget to take it.

When we thought Beavi was dying, our family went to Elk Valley to make medicine for her and to soothe our souls, because it was hard. Darrell and I weren't there to make medicine, so we stayed in the first camp and we didn't do anything. Long Gone stayed at a higher camp because he had come there to pray for Beavi, to make himself feel better and to make us feel better about Beavi dying, whether she died or whether God was going to let her stay. But we weren't picking up power.

We didn't know if she was going to live or die. Beavi commented that I didn't get scared about her dying, like Darrell and Long Gone did. I told her, "Well, Beavi, maybe it doesn't scare me. To die may not be a bad thing" [laughing].

The doctors kept wanting me to give up on Beavi because "You know she is dying, and she is suffering..." They were just rude. I told them, "It has nothing to do with me. It's her choice if she wants to live. It's a matter of how badly you want to live. If you want to suffer everything to live and you don't want to give up, you want to live that bad, then that is your choice. It isn't my choice to tell her she has to live or to tell you to turn off the machine and let her die. I just support what a person feels they need to do."

Long Gone also has hepatitis, and he says that he is going to eat healthy, and try and not drink, and stay away from drugs, and try to live a better life, and when the time comes, he will just die. He will just go to the Creator. Beavi is pushing him to give up everything and just want to live, but he says he doesn't want to do that. So that is his choice. He will do the best he can to stay healthy and live as long as he can and then die. That is the way he looks at it, so that's his choice, and I have to support that choice. Beavi's attitude is that you have to do this, you have to do that, and if you don't, you're going to die. Long Gone may not think it's such a bad thing to go on. He may be more like I am. When the time comes, I'm ready. I'm as ready as I'll ever be. I don't say I'm that healthy or that good. I'm just ready.

Beavi's health failed to the point that she was scheduled for a liver transplant and was spending months at a time in San Francisco, with somebody from the family staying with her, while she waited for the transplant. At one point, she got a little better and came home. But two days later, she was back in the hospital. About this time, Darrell broke his hip and I was staying in the hospital with him in Eureka, and Beavi was in the hospital in Mad River. I was sleeping in my bedroom in the trailer here in Orleans and I felt someone come into my room. I woke up and looked around and Beavi was standing there. I asked her what she was doing here, and she said, "Mom, I'm scared. I don't think I'm going to make it."

This was in September, around the time of Pikiawish, and I told her, "I don't know how much power I have left, but I'll give you what I have." I pulled up all the power that I had and I just gave it to her. I told her, "That's all I can do, because I don't think I have anything more that I can give you."

"Okay," she said, and then she left. When I saw her in the hospital, I asked her if she had gone to anyone else for help and she said no. So I must have had some power left, and she lived through that episode. She said that she had been really afraid when she came to me that time in the spirit form. It startled me, because I hadn't expected to see someone in my room. Then they flew her to San Francisco for the transplant and I went down to stay with her for the next month. It was kind of touch-and-go at that point because her kidneys had begun to fail as well.

Beavi's children found it hard to take that their mother might be dying. It was hard for me, and I'm one of those that is blessed. So it must have been even harder for them. Hepatitis C has become an epidemic and I knew it was coming back in the early nineties, but I didn't know that it was going to affect my daughter, the one who didn't do IV drugs. We need to start a group where people can get information on this disease. We don't want to be preaching and changing their lives, but we want them to have all the information available so that they can do the best that they can do for themselves.

Every time Beavi would come back from one of the hospitals, she would be a little sicker and a little weaker and wouldn't rally the way she had before. I didn't know if they would get a transplant for her in time or not. She not only got one transplant, she got two: a liver and kidney. I told her it was a miracle. One day she's dying, and the next day she has two transplants and is getting well. Now she has to pay back for that by helping to organize the classes for other people with hepatitis C, so they may not have to go through what she has gone through. I told her paybacks are a bitch. You gotta pay back, though. Every time God gives you a blessing, you have to pay for it with service, time, and energy—probably put all that energy and medicine into someone who doesn't even mean that much to you, who is just another human being, and you have to try to save them. If you can't save their lives, you have to try to save their soul.

For the last couple of years I've been expending most of my power on my immediate family, and I will probably have to pay for it. That's probably what my leg going dead is a manifestation of, because I have been using my power to keep Beavi alive and to heal my husband. That is not what the Creator gave me this power for. I'm supposed to give it to the people, not just my people.

When I was young, really still a child, Daisy Jones had prophesized that I would have children and they would live long enough to have children. She said she couldn't save all of them and that I would lose some along the way. Daypay lived to be sixteen years old and was murdered, but before he died he had a child, one boy; my daughter Carol had a boy before she was killed in a wreck, when she was thirty-six; and my adopted son, Chucker, has nine children. Beavi and Long Gone are still alive and they have had children, so Daisy Jones's prophecy was true, and I had the four children I wanted. By hook or by crook, I had the four children and my adopted son has nine children. Between my other four children I have had nine grandchildren and lost two of them to crib death when they were tiny babies.

Medicine people have a vision of their death. It may not be exact, it is just an inkling. What I see is that I am supposed to be leaving, and I am supposed to be picking up souls to take across with me. In this vision I have to fight to leave this life, because there are people trying to keep me here with those souls. I don't know if these are people from that side or from this side. I just know that there is a fight when I go, and people have come forward and said they will defend my back. And some of them are already dead, but they will defend my back, whatever that means [laughing]. I think that means that when I'm trying to go over and other people are trying to stop me, they will step in and help me go across to the other side. According to this vision, these souls that I am to take with me will be coming back, but I will not be back. I will leave this world and go to the spirit world, but those other people who are going to the spirit world with me will come back. The vision does not show me how these souls will come back, but the Hopis have a legend that they take the living into the other world, and when the world turns and ends, then later these souls will come back as people again. Now, I don't know if my vision is part of that or not, because I can't find that out from my Karuk people, but the Hopis have that belief and they say they've been here five times.

There are all kinds of medicine people, and we all do different things, cover different areas. Nobody is just all-powerful. A friend of mine would say, "I don't know what good being medicine people does you or Millie. Neither one of you are rich, you are both poor. You have no money, and it doesn't seem to make either of you any happier. It looks like you worry about people more than you should. You're always worrying that something is going to happen to this one or that one. And you have to help them out, because something is going to happen. You are always worrying about somebody else, and having this power doesn't seem to do you folks any good."

I said, "Well, they never told me it would make me rich, and none of the people who taught me were rich. And they never promised me I would be happy. They said I would have my happiness. And I figure I had that when I lived down the river and just lived for my little family. That was my happy time. When I came back up here to Orleans, then the demands of being a spiritual person started up again and the calls started coming. The powers had things that I needed to help them with.

When some people get their medicine, they get so full of themselves and their powers that they think they can do all kinds of things. I say you can't do anything, you just have an affinity to be able to flow the Creator's power through you to something else. That's what I feel it is; someone else may have a different idea, but my figuring and thinking and mulling on it has led me to think that that is how it is.

EPILOGUE: DARRELL'S DEATH

I ALWAYS HAD A BARGAIN WITH DARRELL that I would get to go first when the time came, since I had lost my parents early and so many in my family had passed over. I asked him if he would promise that I would get to go first and he said, "Yeah, if that's what you want, I'll let you go first." Then last September he said to me, "Mavis, I don't want you to die or anything, but you know about your going first? If you are going to go first, you had better hurry up." We went to the doctor about that time and he told Darrell that his lungs and kidneys were getting old. After we walked out the door Darrell said to me, "I've got news for him. All of me is getting old" [laughing]. Later he told me he was getting tired, and that he had been hurting and not feeling really well since he was run over by a log loader in 1981. He did not feel sick, he just hurt all the time and was getting tired of hurting. He told me he was tired of getting tired, tired of living. He didn't like not being able to take care of himself. He couldn't take his socks off and couldn't put his shoes on, or if he did, it was a big struggle. I told him that I would do anything for him and he looked at me for a second and said, "Maybe I don't want you to."

It's like the time I told Aussie about a dream and she told me to remember that the person in the dream is not going to be the person that it will really happen to. So when I had a dream last spring that Long Gone was going to die before me, it just tore me apart. But it wasn't Long Gone; the dream was telling me that Darrell was going ahead of me. I should have known from the depth of my feelings that it wasn't my son the dream was referring to, but I didn't want to know that it was Darrell. So the dream was protecting me and I was protecting myself. I wouldn't look at it too closely. The earlier vision, when Long Gone was shot and supposed to die, bothered me. Three people were supposed to die, but they wouldn't show me a face on any of them. The vision just showed me three people who were going to die in the Ishi Pishi Club, and the bar would close after the shooting and not open again. I prayed to change the face of the dream. You can't say something won't happen, "Don't let this happen." If this thing has to happen for some reason—the Creator obviously wanted to have that bar-room closed—if this has to happen, then don't let anyone die. That was my prayer. I also pulled him back in another way, when I told him I would see him in Eureka and he thought that meant he would not die, and then he did not die.

Then Darrell developed pneumonia and was in the hospital. At one point he said to me, "Slow down, don't go so fast." He thought he was headed down to the river, with me driving. The next day he thought there was a tree in the way. "I can see the river but I can't get down there." Then, the last day of his life, he kept saying the river was coming to him and was right outside. Then he saw someone coming with thin legs, wearing a deerskin wrapped around their waist and with an old-fashioned bowl haircut, the way we cut our hair a hundred years ago or better, and I could see him too. Darrell asked me if I could see their face. Then he glanced at me and said, "Oh, you can't see." I told him I couldn't see their face, and besides, it wasn't out there anyway, it was a vision because he was in the hospital. So when the nurse came in he told her he was in the hospital. The nurse said, "Who told you that?" He said, "She did!" [laughing]. The vision was of someone coming to pick him up to take him over to the other side, and I held him back three times. The last time, it didn't give me a chance, or there was not enough left of Darrell for me to hold on to. I have no idea how I do that. I just know that I can do it. I don't know if that's one of the powers Auntie left me, but I don't remember being able to do that before she died.

When Daypay was shot, he died immediately. He just left. His heart was still beating, but he was gone. I could feel he was gone. When he came back he got to see Darrell and Carol. Beavi came over from Redding and he got to see her. I could hear them in the living room, and he wanted to see me, and I never saw what was with him. I just heard them say that he couldn't see me, because I would keep him there. Darrell said that he had always thought a spirit was like fog, but when Daypay told him good-bye and grabbed hold of his shoulder, it was just like a human being had grabbed his shoulder. Each person in the family had their own personal experience of saying good-bye to him. Carol never came back after she died.

I told Darrell, "Well, just remember, I'll keep you here. Even if you are a zombie, I'll keep you here."

He said, "If it comes to dying, I want you to let me go." I told him I didn't know if I could do that either, but it was taken out of my hands at the end, when he went so quickly.

On Tuesday I got to the hospital to stay with him after he had gotten out of the intensive care unit. When they moved him into another unit they put in a little cot for me that was about four inches off the floor. The last night I stayed with him he would say, "Mavis," with a question in his voice, and I would say, "Yes," and he would say, with relief, "Oh, you're here."

The next morning they cleaned him up and did all the things they do in the morning, like take their temperature and blood pressure. After they did that I went to the cafeteria and had a little breakfast because it would be a long day living on junk food, and the cafeteria was only open for a short time. When I came back he asked me what I had for breakfast and I told him. And sometime later, he got up to go to the bathroom and took two steps and collapsed. I knew by his eyes that he was gone. He breathed for another forty-five minutes, and the nurse gave him a shot to speed his heart up, but it didn't pick up, and then he was just gone. We called around and the whole family started coming in to the hospital to see him before they moved his body to the mortuary.

Darrell used to tease me and tell me that if anything happened to him, the next day I would have a new husband. I told him that I wouldn't, and that I was only going to have one husband in my life; I loved him, and I was going to love him all my life, and I would never have another person. He would just laugh at me and say no I wasn't, I was going to find somebody the next day. So after he passed away, and the kids were all upset, and we were getting ready to go out to town to make the funeral arrangements the next morning, they were saying that it was going to be a hard day. And I said, "You think it's going to be a hard day for you?" They looked at me and I said, "I'm going to make funeral arrangements out there today, and [laughing] Darrell told me I was supposed to have a new husband today, too!"

Traditionally, since the Yurok people have started to take bodies to mortuaries, they would bring the body up to Klamath and then bring the body the rest of the way upriver in a boat to the burial and service. Long Gone took his father down to see the ocean in a boat and then came on up the river with him to Notchko, and then turned around and took him back down to Johnson's. When you're coming up the river with the body, their head is facing toward the ocean, and when they get to Blue Creek they turn the casket around and their feet face the ocean. Then they go on up to the burial place, and when they are buried their feet face the ocean, so they are facing west, just the opposite of a Christian burial. His seven grandsons were his pallbearers.

Joe Boy was standing over by the Shaker church to make sure they had everything ready, because they don't have Shaker services every week anymore. Darrell wanted a Shaker funeral, but there weren't many people to get hold of who are Shakers any longer, so there was just two women and one man who were Shakers at the service. He said he looked down and the sun was just hitting the river when Darrell came by. Then the boys put Darrell's body in a Yurok Tribe pickup truck and hauled him up to the church, and the boys packed him in. There were about three hundred people at the service. In this country we don't have gravediggers, the family just gets together and digs the grave when somebody needs one. To have a burial is a big group and family effort. Everything has to be coordinated. The family has to get hold of people and ask them to do this and to do that and bring food and make sure there is enough food.

Then I did something I didn't know I was not supposed to do, after fifty-six years in a Yurok family. I cooked deer meat the night before, because a friend from Hoopa brought it over to feed people with, just to help out, and I cooked that until about two in the morning, just to make sure there would be enough food. I wasn't sleepy anyway, but I forgot to put salt and pepper on it. My mind just wasn't working right [laughing]. Then I learned that you aren't supposed to serve meat at a Yurok funeral. One of the Yurok elders told Long Gone. Of all the funerals I've been to downriver and up here, I have served ham so many times, and no one ever told me we don't have meat at funerals—they just served it. I'm sure Darrell knew that rule, but he never said anything. I would tell him I was going to bring this or that to a funeral and he would just say, "Whatever you want." Well, next time I'll know not to bring meat, but it got eaten up anyway.

After Darrell's death I went to Klamath to stay with his aunt for about a week, and then they brought me back home because my garden was drying out and I had to get up here and take care of it. I went to the Jump Dance, or the High Mountain Dance, as it's sometimes called now. Long Gone was there dancing, and I had relatives in every camp at the dance. I usually stay in the camp that's closest to the dance ground so I don't have to walk too far. I feel that I can go to the High Mountain Dance and to the White Deerskin Dance, but because of Darrell's passing, not the Brush Dance, because it is largely a social dance. According to customs, some people go a year without going to a dance after someone they are close to passes. I went to the high dances because they are not social dances. They are dances to heal your spirit and to heal the world that you are living in, so I felt that I needed to go to the dances. But I will not go to a Brush Dance until after Darrell has been gone for a year.

I had a dream vision six months after Darrell passed away. First there was a woman and a child stacking glass vases on a counter. Then I saw a large billboard with large sheets of paper with red writing on the corners, and then I heard the sounds of a loudspeaker. I couldn't tell what was being said. Then, just past a group of men in 1940-style hats, Darrell was singing beautiful White Deerskin songs. He was standing by Albert Gray, a renowned Yurok singer, who was smiling but not singing. Darrell had on his fisherman-style basket hat with a scenic print on it and appeared to be very happy.

Notes

1. [Duane Allen was a Karuk man of about the same age as
   Mavis McCovey. This story comes from an interview with him.]
   Daisy Jones could pretty much see the future, like she did for
   my brother and me. The Korean War had just broke out, and
   before my brother Almie left for Korea, our dad talked to our
   mom and said we should take the soldiers up to Daisy and
   let her do her thing with them before they go to war. Daisy
   was like our grandmother. She took care of the cooking in
   my grandfather's mine, and he fell in love with her and lived
   with her—although he had his wife on this side of the river,
   he had Daisy on the other side. She was another grandmother
   to us, really. She had no children of her own, but she had the
   Henry boys, who were her nephews, so she treated us all like
   one family. In fact, we were lucky to have a lady like that, now
   that I look back at it. Those days, you didn't think too much
   about it.

   She didn't know where Korea was, she could just barely
   speak English, but she had a vision while she was making medicine for my brother, preparing him to go into the Army. She
   told him that what was going to happen to him in Korea was
   that he was going to get shot right through the leg, and "the
   bullet will kill the guy behind you." Then she explained the

terrain, and when it happened, it was exactly like she said—and she had probably never been out of the state of California. She explained to him how the mountain looked, the trees. She said, "There's going to be nobody to help you, and you will have a bad wound. So go down from where you're at on that mountain toward the west side. You go down the mountain and go to your left. Follow the stream down to the bottom of the ridge where you're at, and there is going to be another little stream coming into it. You go up that stream, just around the corner a ways, and on the right-hand side, you'll see blue mud coming out of the bank. You take that and pack it on your wound, and you'll be all right."

It happened like she said, and when he was shot there were no medics, nothing. The bullet passed through his leg and killed his sergeant behind him. There was nobody to give him medical attention, so he did what she had said and then rested for a long time. When he was feeling better he took some of the mud with him and walked back up to where he had been when he first started down to look for that mud. When he got back up on the mountain there was not a soul left. There was no Chinese. There was no Americans. There was nobody there. The Americans had been overrun and they were scattered all over to hell and breakfast, and he was one of the first ones to come back. The Chinese took all their dead and wounded and left. This mountain was sort of like Sheldon Butte, straight up and down, and it took a long time to reassemble on kind of a flat spot up on top. He was eighteen at the time. So with that happening, when they regrouped they had to take in other outfits to make up whatever they had left. There was quite a few people left after they got organized, but he became a platoon leader of the unit he was in. He got a battlefield commission and was made a first lieutenant. He thought he was probably the youngest to ever receive a battlefield commission. When they regrouped they were able to hold that position, and he went back into the fighting right away because he had healed himself.

Another time, when I was around nineteen, I was in Hoopa, swimming with my girlfriend, and this girl's mother told me that there was a lady that wanted to see me. This woman worked at the old Indian hospital in Hoopa, and she said that a patient at the hospital wanted to see me. When she told me the woman's name was Daisy Jones, I said, "What, she's over there?" So I jumped in my car and went over there to the hospital.

She said, "Something's wrong. Be careful. I can hear something roaring, *rrrrrrr*, like that. Then the wind is blowing something bad. You need to be awful careful. I don't know what it is."

I thought about it and kind of shrugged it off. Then, after I got in the Army, I jumped over at Fort Campbell, Kentucky. It didn't dawn on me until about a year or two ago, but what she heard was that airplane. That's what she didn't know nothing about. On the way down, after jumping out of the plane, the ground wind came up and I got right in the middle of it. After I hit the ground, my chute drug me for quite a ways. I had hit wrong because the wind was blowing so hard, and I went what we called ass-end-over-head and messed my back up. She was confused about the sound of the engine and the sound of the wind. She told me this about two years before it happened.

2. Bessie Tripp said that one of the few good things white men brought in their religion was the right to communicate directly with the Great Spirit. In Karuk religion, non–medicine people only communicated with the individual spirits, and only the Fatawanun communicated with the Great Spirit, and that was rare and occasional. But the white man's coming opened up the way for her to speak directly with the Great Spirit, which was a great liberation in her mind. [Bessie Tripp was a Karuk woman born around 1881 who was always looked up to as a person of the highest quality and rectitude and whose knowledge of early Karuk life and values could be relied on.]

3. [Mavis McCovey] Before white men came to the Klamath River, a Karuk medicine man named Rape-Chien had a vision of
   what was to come. The Great Spirit told him he had to warn
   the people and get them ready. His vision had warned him that
   they needed to build a village away from where they lived at
   that time, and to start preparing for an invasion that was coming to the river. They should get ready to move to some place
   that wasn't easy to get to but was near water, and to start stor-
   ing food there.

   He did not understand why the Creator had told him what
   was coming, but he called the people together and told them
   that new people were coming who were not like them. They
   looked like bears. They had brown hair all over their bodies
   and they were big, big like bears. To people whose men are
   around five feet, six inches, I guess the people who were coming would be very big. He said these people would bring sickness and terrible times, and that they were going to kill people
   over certain rocks. They were going to be crazy about these
   rocks and would do anything to get them.

   He said they were going to bring other people with them
   that would have black tails coming out of their head, and they
   would dig holes in the ground all over and tunnel around like
   Gopher. The Indian people just laughed at him and would not
   believe his prophecies.

   Rape-Chien left the village in shame and went to live at a
   place on the north fork of Red Cap Creek. He chose a place
   to build a camp like he had been directed in his vision. There
   were sheer cliffs coming into it and a nice bench above the
   flat. To get to the flat he had to go clear up over the top and
   drop down the cliff onto the flat. It was hard to get to, and
   the people who were coming would not just fall on this place,
   because you couldn't see it from where the main trails were.
   So that was the beginning of what would be the coming of
   white people.

   I don't know how many years passed, and then the white

people came, and they did have hair all over their bodies like bears, and they were six feet tall, so they were big and a lot heavier than the Indian men. And the Chinese came with them and started digging their trenches and tunnels through the ridges, to move the water they needed for mining. When the white people came to what is now Orleans, the Indians ran away so fast that they left their elders and babies home. The older children got away with their parents and hid in the caves in the hidden valley up by Somes Bar. They lived in the caves for quite some time before they came out, because they were afraid of what might happen, because they had been warned by Rape-Chien.

4. Duane Allen recalls Daisy Jones and the Red Cap warriors: I remember her telling me that once, as a young girl, she was in a big house down at Red Cap and all the Karuk men, Indian soldiers, came in and put their rifles in a corner as they entered the house. They had a meeting but she didn't tell me exactly what it was about. They wanted her there to let them know how the outcome of the war between the Red Cap warriors and the Army was going to be, because they were going to war with the soldiers from Fort Humboldt. She said they were all brand-new rifles, bright and shiny. Red Cap Tom was quite a warrior, quite a military strategist. He fought his war by way-laying pack trains, to where they had to have five pack trains to get one shipment of gold out of here. This way he raised the price of gold so high that they could hardly afford to mine it. They would fall trees across the trail and harass the packer, and there were times when they took the whole train.

There's a song we sing when we dance out here for the White Deerskin Dance that is the Old Captain's song. Old Captain had one leg, and I think he is the one that Red Cap Tom sent out to kill a packer. But Old Captain was pretty religious, a medicine man, so as he was going to shoot the packer, he drew off and shot his horse instead, and then the packer shot him and he lost his leg.

Going by what Daisy said about those rifles all being brand-new repeating rifles, I think it was tied to when my great-grandfather Almie Hiram Allen, a white guy, got out of the Army. He had been in the Civil War, and then he fought in the Indian wars in the Dakotas, and when he was discharged he was in the California volunteers. He was shipped back to California and got discharged at Sutter's Fort, but somehow, according to the way I heard the story, about that time when all of this was happening, a whole shipment of brand-new repeating rifles disappeared from down in San Francisco, at the military post down there. They were arming places like Fort Humboldt up here, so then the Red Cap warriors came up with a whole bunch of brand-new repeating rifles that put them out ahead of the Army. How the hell these rifles got to the Klamath River I don't know, but I do know that they did, and that my great-grandfather was the only white man allowed to mine over there in the Red Cap country, so it may have had something to do with him showing up with new rifles.

My grandfather said that Red Cap Tom was such a powerful leader that the Karuk would not go to war without his say-so. He got that name because when the first white people came they were traders, and because he had the power over the people, they gave him a red cap. He liked it so well that he wore it every place he went. That was the color that the Indians liked. The red color of all their beads represented the red race, and there were the white, yellow, and black beads representing the colors of all the races. Now, how they knew there are all those other races I don't know.

5. Bessie Tripp said that when she was young, Karuk girls had the choice of being basket weavers or gardeners. She chose to garden, since basket weavers did much of their work indoors and she preferred being outside. For many years she would get up when the mockingbirds started singing, sometime before daylight. At some point she got an alarm clock and, setting it

for what she thought was a reasonable hour, was outraged to look at the clock and realize that the mockingbird had been waking her at four-thirty a.m. [This information came from an interview of Bessie Tripp by John Salter circa 1977.]

6. Around 1890 or 1900 baskets were worth a lot of money as trade goods. When the average man made a dollar a day, a finely made basket could be traded for goods or services. In return for a basket, a whole family could stay for three days in the hotel in Orleans or trade for goods at the store which were priced at five to ten dollars.

7. [Beavi McCovey] They had a flush toilet in the school I went to in Pecwan and the teacher said, "I don't know what's the matter with these kids, they go in the restroom and flush the toilet, and they flush the toilet, and put things in the toilet and flush them down—I just don't know what is wrong with them."

She was from up at Oregon, and I told her, "You know, there's very few people around here that have flush toilets. We all have outhouses, and those kids go to school and that's the first flush toilet they've seen, and it's fascinating to flush and it goes down, flush and it goes down. When we go up to Orleans we have flush toilets and hot and cold running water there, but we don't have that around here."

This was a brand-new school and it had flush toilets. But we were terrified of that toilet because it made so much noise when it was flushed. It would say *whoosh,* and I just knew there was some kind of devil in it. That's why we were always stuffing that toilet up. We were trying to keep that devil down there. We were going to smother it or do something to plug it all up. We were forever plugging that toilet up, because most of us were scared of it. The girls who had braids were afraid it would grab them by the hair and pull them down into the toilet.

8. Traditionally, visitors to a Karuk home would be invited to eat. To refuse this offer of hospitality was an insult which required payment to satisfy. One story recalls a man who, having been invited to eat, said that he had been visiting with people all down the river that day and had already eaten so much he could eat no more and, having paid fines for not eating at several houses, had no more money to pay with, so he would just have to stay until he got hungry enough to eat again.

9. The dance dresses are constructed like aprons and made of leather, braided bear grass, pine nuts, cedar berries, and shells, and they are fringed. Abalone shells are used to make a distinctive sound, and you can hear the women dancers coming from their camp to dance.

10. Bessie Tripp, on making medicine and gaining a long life: I made medicine down across the river. That's about the hardest thing I ever done. I never eat, never drink water, [for] two days. And they tell me I have to sit there, look at one corner [of the river] all day. Not supposed to sleep, because I won't live long if I go to sleep. Oh, I was tired and sleepy and thirsty. You prayed for everything...fish...that's why I had to look at one corner across the river there. Wishing how the fish would stop there and not go up straight, and acorns, and how the kids gonna grow up—no sickness, old people, all that. It was just about the hardest thing I ever done. I didn't go to sleep because I wanted to live long time.

   Then I went to get wood on this side of the river. Just medicine men, two of them [were] there too. [They] were the first ones to eat the salmon. Before that nobody eat, till they eat. After that, then everybody eat. And I have to cut the wood for that [fire], have to cook the fish. I don't know how far up I went [up] the hill till I found a nice dry tree. I had, I don't know, some kind of horn, elk horn, and a rock where I could hold it, big end down here, small end up. I put wedge in crack (makes pounding motions) till it crack open, put it in somewhere else till the tree fell. And I had to pick up all the…oh, there was a man with me. He had ax, [to] chop it all up. I put it in my basket. I had to pick up all the little sticks. They tell me too, if I didn't, there would be all kinds of bugs (chuckles); you know, just everyplace, bugs.

So I had to pick up all them little sticks, limbs. And he told me to tie that up with a hazel bush, put it on top [of a pack basket]. So I did. "And don't you talk!" [said in a harsh, man's voice]. And that was his first words to me. [After that] he just talk all the way [back], say all kind of funny things. He want me to laugh but I won't laugh. I never even look back at him and I tote that wood down the hill by the river.

When I got back they told me I had to sit there in the hut. There was a sweathouse there with about thirty or forty of them in there, the men in it, and they told me, when I hear them singing that's when the medicine man go. You know, they [medicine men] walk like that…[places her hands in front of her to indicate long, straight, firm strides. On alternate steps the leg goes down, so that both knee and foot touch the ground.] Long steps. Pretty soon I hear *poom…poom;* that's when he's making medicine. I sit there all day. They told me that somebody will hit the house, "then you can look around." Then I can look around. So somebody hit the house. And pretty soon I hear them singing in the sweathouse. They're all singing the medicine.

Then the medicine man was coming back again and I hear that walking, [drumming] *poom…poom,* back there, and they quit singing when he got back to the sweathouse.

And the fifth day, I had to go get some more wood again, and the last thing they tell us [was] "Don't you talk" [said in a soft, counseling voice]. [There] used to be a lot of pigs and they [he] saw them, a pack of pigs down there. I know I heard him throw an axe down there. He chased them pigs, and I finally heard a pig squealing, way down the hill. I keep on walking; I never look back. I keep on walking [a note of mild outrage].

Pretty soon he caught up with me. He throw a pig in my basket [and] upset all my tools and everything [the wood].

I didn't look back; I keep on walking. He was gone for a long time. He caught up with me a ways up the hill. He said, "Here's your tools. You meant to throw them away" [said in a harsh, man's voice]. I never look back.

In the evening I told what he was [had been] doing, and his mother holler at him. I says, "You know, you ain't supposed to make fun of what they doing." He laughed and said, "She big shot." He says, "I bet you live long time." I says, "And you be dying soon, [for] making fun of that medicine." And he did, he died young.

The first day, they start down where the store is now. That's where they start. The next day, cross the river. The next day, on this side, here and there. They never eat till we come back from when we was shooting the arrows for our luck, shoot at a mark. There was a lot of people shooting arrows. And maybe a bunch of girls, maybe twenty of us; we all sitting there. We never eat, all during that before Pikiawish. When we come back we took a bath, then we eat. We was doing that for our own luck. Everybody, lots of girls and boys. We had that sometimes ten days, sometimes not ten days. That first night...was evening, Pikiawish started in the evening, but they had been hiding all day. Then they holler not to hide. We all look around. Oh, there are lots of people sitting around there, lots of people from up the river, down the river, even from Etna. Everyplace.

Well, then pretty soon they say, "Hurry, hurry the medicine man's gonna come up." Pretty soon we see the medicine man coming. Two ladies came up from down [at] the river. Then the medicine man he gets up there. Then he's taking long steps. They lots of people, and they say, "Hurry up, the medicine man's gonna come up," and they dance there. Like the Deerskin Dance, but they didn't have no skins, just brush.

And the medicine man took a long step. He was all painted

up, red and black [motions with her hands, indicating a wide black strip across the eyes]. Oh, and there be lots of girls, maybe twenty [or] thirty of them, boys and girls. They all marked up like that, black and white, red. And when they get to the end of that dance, the medicine man, he jump up and run just as fast as he could run. And all these girls and boys, up the hill they go, fast as they could run [chuckles]. And they go up there where the medicine house was. All night they keep that up. They got beads on the Indian dresses tinkling all night. And in the morning the two ladies have to pack in acorns, and they run with that [chuckles]. I don't know how they didn't spill it; I always wondered.

When they taking that long steps, that's when they making that medicine. Praying for everything. And he's [the medicine man] got to stay in for ten days after Pikiawish if it [was] the first time you been medicine man, but if you [had] done it before, it [was] maybe only eight, or seven. But I only seen that two [twice], the way they used to do [it]. After that they didn't do it right, not even the medicine man.

I used to hear old people talking, terrible people down where I was living. They said whenever they quit doing all that Pikiawish medicine down there everything's gonna cave off; there won't be any more luck for that place. Well, I see that has happened.

I'm walking yet, because I believed everything they told me. I was doing it for my own luck, and that's why I'm living yet [said emphatically]. I always believe everything they say. If you don't do it, you won't live long. They had lots of believing.

11. [Johnny Bennett, a Karuk man who lived on the Salmon River, was born in 1904 and was engaged to Mavis's mother for a time. These are his comments.] And I'd like to know what the fire's for. I'd just like to know, what was the fire for in lightning, why did it have to burn? It's for some cause, now. It could storm without that, y'know, but it had to burn. I

think about it many times. The old Indians say God made it that way to clean out the forest. In places where it hit there would be a burn-out, y'know. And they never put it out. They'd push it back up the mountain and it would burn, let it go. They wouldn't bother it, because they claim it was put there for some cause, and they said it was good because they could sneak up on their game, pick up their acorns, and it generally never damaged much, because you could go in a forest, great big old trees, like redwoods, been burnt once; the bark is black. One time there was fire there. And the same way in this country: when the lightning hit they never put it out—push them back, make a fire line, let them go back up the mountain. Take sticks out there, burn against it. But like the other day, that thunder, jeez, I liked it. I just thought, "Boy, it don't come often enough." It seems to me it cleans the air when it gets hot and sultry. Oh, it can get wild sometimes. They used to stop 'em [storms, by seeding clouds with iodine crystals], remember? When they'd do that, it'd cut all that [moisture] off. That's why I said...it's like going against something. Like a lot of times folks'll do something [and] I say, "Why don't you just let nature take care of it? It done it before, it'll do it again. It'll grow, what's gonna come there."

12. [Duane Allen] When I was working for the Yurok Tribe in Eureka and driving home one day, my wife and I stopped at Tish Tang to take a break. I looked at this domestic ivy on the ground around an old Forest Service guard station, and I could see that something had walked through it. I told my wife that somebody had walked through there. She said it was probably a bear, and I said a bear don't drag their toes like a human, so I started following this curiosity. I walked a few hundred yards up the hill, and looking down, there was a big tan oak forest below me with a few fir trees on it but mostly big tan oak, and kind of like a flat down there. I could feel something looking at me, kind of a scary feeling. In the military they had taught

me to never look at one place, keep your eyes moving. And I looked down, and when my eyes went right past him, I knew it, and I could feel it was looking right at me. This flat was covered with fallen tan oak that was off the ground. I could see his legs clear up to his waist.

So I just nonchalantly turned around and walked back the way I had come. When I got out of sight, I ran to the car, where I had a .357 Magnum in my trunk that I was bringing home to sight in—of course it was clear to the bottom—and I hollered at my wife hard to get in the car. She wanted to know why she had to get in the car, and I said, "Just shut up and get in the car, I don't have time to tell you." Then she saw me take that pistol out and load up, and by the time I ran back it was gone, of course. When I stood where he had stood, the log was up almost to my head, so his waist had been where my head was and he was two or three feet taller than me, and I'm about five feet, nine inches.

I thought at first it was a guy down there with black pants, and I almost hollered to him. That was my first thought. Then I looked at that tree, and I saw that it was a pretty good-sized tree. I work in the woods and I could tell that it was about a thirty-six-inch tree.

They have to be like humans, because they are smart. Most animals, when they are cornered...The one I saw stood still and wouldn't move while it knew I was watching it.

13. The following is from *Surviving Through the Days: Translations of Native California Stories and Songs*, edited by Herbert W. Luthin (©2002 Regents of the University of California. Published by University of California Press. Reprinted here with permission of publisher):

To understand the story, one needs to know what the Indians of northwestern California mean by a "devil" (Karuk *apurúvaan*). The term has nothing to do with demons from Hell, but rather refers to sorcerers: human beings, male or female, who practice malicious magic. (One could use the term "witch" except for the female connotation of the English word.) Devils get their power from magical objects called *ápu-roon* 'devil machines'; armed with these, they prowl around human dwellings at night, sometimes emitting *machnat,* or small flashes of light (will-o'-the-wisps?), spying on the inhabitants and choosing their victims.

In Mamie Offield's story, a pair of devils come to spy on a man and his wife, who are occupying a temporary house in an acorn-gathering area. But the devils get a surprise, and never have a chance to practice their sorcery. Stories in which devils are thwarted seem to be a recognized genre; Mrs. Offield told me three such stories on a summer afternoon in 1950 [see Bright, *The Karok Language,* University of California Publications in Linguistics 13, 1957]. The humor of such stories is perhaps enhanced by being at the expense of a hated and feared class of people; we might imagine a similar modern story in which the prowlers were tax collectors.

The Devil Who Died Laughing

A lot of people were gathering acorns,
    up in the mountains,
    in acorn season.

And then they had gone home,
    all those people.

Only one man was left,
    he and his wife.

And then he said,
    "I think I'll go spear some fish."

And then he caught a sucker.
And then the woman said,
    "I'm going to roast it."

And then she roasted it,
    that sucker.

And then she ripped out the guts.

Now then, there was a hole in their house-wall,
    at a certain place.

And then she flung them through that hole,
    those guts.

And there he was peeking through that hole,
    a certain devil!

And there she had flung them right smack in his eye!

And then that other devil burst out laughing.

And then he just laughed himself to death;
    the next day his friend saw him,
      he was lying there,
    he was still laughing
      even though he was dead.

So then the other one told what happened.

14. The G-O Road was proposed in the early 1960s by the Forest
Service as a means of transporting timber some fifty-five miles,
from Gasquet to Orleans. A six-mile section of this road was
to pass through the high country adjacent to Elk Valley and
sacred to the tribes of the area. Eventually plans for the road
were halted due to Congress's establishing the Smith River
Recreation Area.

15. One sunny afternoon in November 2007, Mavis and I walked

a short distance from her home in order for her to show me where the crossroads was located, and what it looked like. We came into a beautiful small meadow surrounded on three sides by fir trees and somewhat overgrown by bushes. Mavis was walking in front of me and remarked that the crossroads itself moved around from time to time to different places in the meadow. She continued her search as I took a few photographs, when suddenly I became lightheaded and with a feeling of acceleration seemed to rise up out of my body fifteen or twenty feet into the air. I looked down and could see the top of my head where my body still stood, with dense and foglike streamers rising up to where my consciousness was. I stayed that way for a few seconds and then could feel myself drop back down into my body. I was completely amazed by the experience and before I could say anything Mavis said, "Here it is, do you feel anything?"

I told her of my experience of rising out of my body and she responded, very calmly, "That's right. Remember, I told you that the first time I was taken up from here the powers took me all the way across the mountains."

16. [Duane Allen] I always knew that Upsancutta was there by listening to elders talk about it. But then my dad refused to believe it, or maybe he did believe it. Dad was a funny guy. He would never tell us, we would have to find out for ourselves, because I guess he didn't want us to go around talking about it, because other people might think it was pretty much a hoax. But yeah, I've seen that sucker! We were getting ready to high-water dip up around Jack Sanderson's, the last straightaway before Somes Bar, and down below there is where the Sanderson ranch is. We were getting out of the car and [we] look down and something was splashing around in the shallow water below us. I thought it was a bunch of otter chasing fish. My nephew and I were with Wilford and Zona Ferris. Then Zona came over and started hollering because she had seen its eyes. When she stopped hollering, that thing just went under

the water, and pretty soon its head popped up way out in the middle of the river, looking back at us. In the meantime my nephew Floyd and Peter, my stepson, ran down to the river bar and ran down the river watching it. We got a good view then. Just the head was sticking up and part of the body, then all of a sudden they had disappeared underwater, and the body ran for a long ways—behind it the tail flipped and went under, and the head popped up again. That thing might have been fifty feet long, and the head looked like it was about a foot and a half long or bigger. It looked like a big, oversized python.

My son and his friends saw it another time and they thought it had little legs like a lizard. Whatever it is, it don't come around people. You just have to accidentally see it.

17. *Kishwuf* is a sacred herb of the angelica family that is used in ceremonies to produce a sweetly pungent smoke.

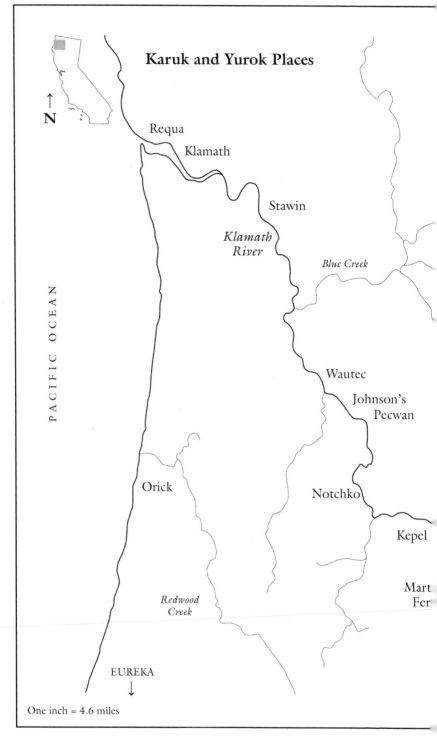

Karuk and Yurok Places

N

Requa

Klamath

Stawin

Klamath River

Blue Creek

PACIFIC OCEAN

Wautec

Johnson's
Pecwan

Orick

Notchko

Kepel

Mart
Fer

Redwood Creek

EUREKA

One inch = 4.6 miles

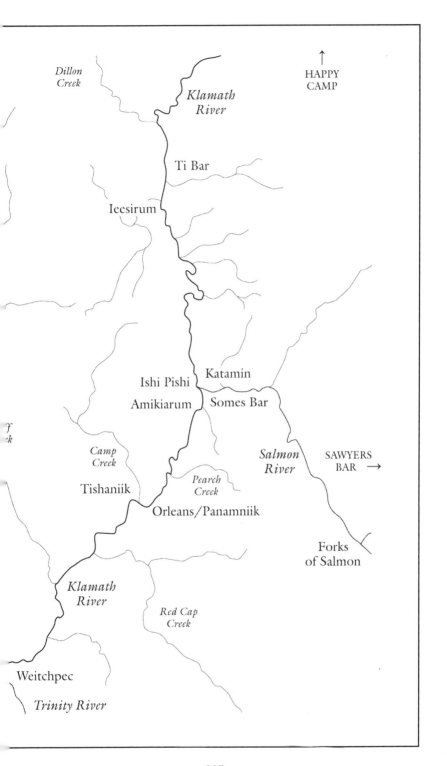

Mavis and Darrell McCovey
Family Tree

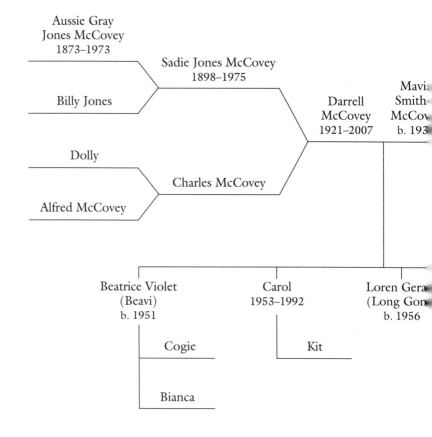

Aussie Gray
Jones McCovey
1873–1973

Billy Jones

Sadie Jones McCovey
1898–1975

Dolly

Alfred McCovey

Charles McCovey

Darrell
McCovey
1921–2007

Mavis
Smith
McCov
b. 193

Beatrice Violet
(Beavi)
b. 1951

Cogie

Bianca

Carol
1953–1992

Kit

Loren Gera
(Long Gon
b. 1956

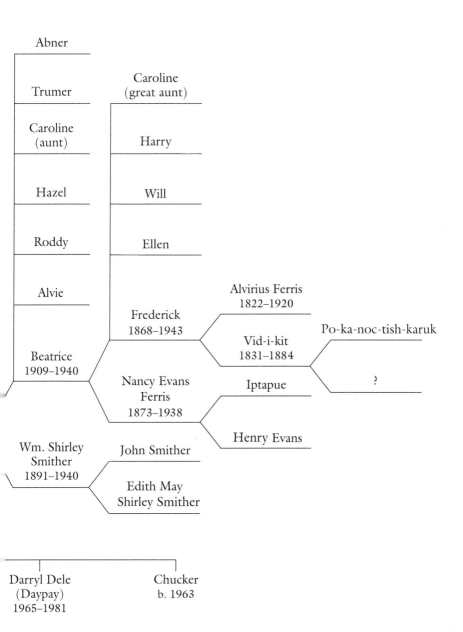

Abner

Trumer

Caroline
(aunt)

Hazel

Roddy

Alvie

Beatrice
1909–1940

Caroline
(great aunt)

Harry

Will

Ellen

Frederick
1868–1943

Nancy Evans
Ferris
1873–1938

Alvirius Ferris
1822–1920

Vid-i-kit
1831–1884

Iptapue

Henry Evans

Po-ka-noc-tish-karuk

?

Wm. Shirley
Smither
1891–1940

John Smither

Edith May
Shirley Smither

Darryl Dele
(Daypay)
1965–1981

Chucker
b. 1963

HEYDAY INSTITUTE

Since its founding in 1974, Heyday Books has occupied a unique niche in the publishing world, specializing in books that foster an understanding of the history, literature, art, environment, social issues, and culture of California and the West. We are a 501(c)(3) nonprofit organization based in Berkeley, California, serving a wide range of people and audiences.

We thank the following for their help in launching and supporting Heyday's California Indian Publishing Program:

Barona Band of Mission Indians; Fred & Jean Berensmeier; Joan Berman; Black Oak Casino; Buena Vista Rancheria; Joanne Campbell; Candelaria Fund; Columbia Foundation; Colusa Indian Community Council; Lawrence Crooks; Laura Cunningham; Elk Valley Rancheria; Federated Indians of Graton Rancheria; Fleishhacker Foundation; Ben Graber, in honor of Sandy Graber; Marion E. Greene; Walter & Elise Haas Fund; Cheryl Hinton; Hopland Band of Pomo Indians; LEF Foundation; Middletown Rancheria Tribal Council; Morongo Band of Mission Indians; National Endowment for the Arts; River Rock Casino; Robinson Rancheria Citizens Council; San Francisco Foundation; Deborah Sanchez; Sandy Cold Shapero; and Orin Starn.

For more information about Heyday Institute, our publications and programs, please visit our website at www.heydaybooks.com.

Photo by Hedy Salter.

ABOUT THE AUTHORS

Mavis McCovey has lived along the Klamath River in northwestern California all her life. Trained as a child to be a medicine
woman, she assists with the traditional ceremonies of her tribe,
the Karuk. The mother of five children, she has also worked
as a community health representative and a nurse, and she has
been an advocate on issues affecting the health and well-being
of the native people of her region.

John Salter is an anthropologist who has worked on a variety of
projects in the Klamath and Salmon River country, beginning
in 1968. He is a teacher, consultant, and lecturer whose work
has addressed issues of culture as well as political and environmental justice.